Noise Matters

Noise Matters

Towards an Ontology of Noise

GREG HAINGE

B L O O M S B U R Y

NEW YORK • LONDON • NEW DELHI • SYDNEY

Bloomsbury Academic
An imprint of Bloomsbury Publishing Plc

175 Fifth Avenue
New York
NY 10010
USA

50 Bedford Square
London
WC1B 3DP
UK

www.bloomsbury.com

First published 2013

Library of Congress Cataloging-in-Publication Data
Hainge, Greg, 1971-
Noise matters : towards an ontology of noise / by Greg Hainge.
p. cm.
Includes bibliographical references and index.
ISBN 978-1-4411-6046-1 (hardback : alk. paper)– ISBN 978-1-4411-1148-7 (pbk. : alk. paper) 1. Noise (Philosophy) 2. Noise–Psychological aspects. 3. Noise in art. 4. Noise music. I. Title.
B105.N64H35 2013
155.9'115–dc23
2012031990

ISBN: HB: 978-1-4411-6046-1
PB: 978-1-4411-1148-7

Typeset by Fakenham Prepress Solutions, Fakenham, Norfolk NR21 8NN
Printed and bound in the United States of America

CONTENTS

ACKNOWLEDGEMENTS

Without wanting to give my whole game away in advance, one of the major contentions of this book is that noise is medial, which is not only to say that it is related to a medium, but also that it arises in and as an artefact of the expression that takes place in the in-between of a communicative act passing between different poles, subjects or sites. In this respect, this book itself is excessively noisy, because it has arisen out of so many different conversations with so many different interlocutors. These conversations have often taken place through personal contact and been conducted both face to face and/or electronically, but not exclusively. For there are many interlocutors who have had a profound effect on this book *in absentia* thanks to their work, both creative and scholarly (which is not of course to say that these are mutually exclusive terms in either direction).

Over the past decade or so, there have been a large number of excellent scholarly works that have appeared on the subject of noise and related matters; many of these seemed at the time of their publication like the book I was trying to write, but they always made me realise that their authors had done a much better job than I could have done and thus forced me to think differently about what it was that I wished to say. Many of these books are discussed in the pages to come, but in some cases these works have been so important, that regardless of whether I know their authors personally or not, I feel their scribes deserve to be acknowledged here.

In addition to this, the ever-changing face of music production and distribution has provided a consistent source of inspiration and frustration simultaneously, more and more music that fired my neurones in increasingly challenging ways becoming more and more available with every passing year. In the end, this book has ended up being much less about music than I thought it would be,

x   ACKNOWLEDGEMENTS

but music has been my major inspiration for this whole project. Even if I have not been able to include discussion of all of those artists who could easily have provided rich source material for this book, therefore, I wish to thank those with whom I have had the privilege of exchanging ideas, as well as friends and colleagues who have provided all manner of help, advice and support throughout the life of this project. All of these people have helped to shape this project in important ways and I thank them all.

Masami Akita, Oren Ambarchi, Paul Attinello, Andrew Benjamin, Ronald Bogue, Ian Buchanan, Kim Cascone, Collin Chua, Marcel Cobussen, Nicolas Collins, Wayne Cristaudo, Jason Cullen, Lawrence English, Julian Enriques, Aden Evens, Kane X Faucher, Robin Fox, Michael Gendreau, Michael Goddard, Philippe Grandrieux, Haco, Vince Harrigan, Russell Haswell, CM von Hausswolff, Jason Jacobs, Philip Jeck, Douglas Kahn, Caleb Kelly, Thomas Köner, Brandon LaBelle, Francisco López, Kaffe Matthews, Akifumi Naikjima, Carsten Nicolai, KK Null, Peter Rehberg, Robin Rimbaud, Philip Samartzis, Torben Sangild, Larry Schehr (how I wish you were able to read this book), Davis Schneiderman, Robert Sinnerbrink, Nick Smith, Jonathan Sterne, Charles J Stivale, Marcel Swiboda, Clayton Thomas, Tony Thwaites, Graeme Turner, Darrin Verhagen, Mitchell Whitelaw.

To be singled out for special thanks is Paul Hegarty, whose career, strangely, has often followed a parallel trajectory to my own, albeit at a great distance, and whose work has for many many years now provided a source of inspiration. In addition, I want to thank Elizabeth Stephens who read drafts of the entire book and provided sometimes challenging but always incisive feedback and then gently insisted that I listen to good advice rather than drowning it out by sticking on another Merzbow CD, knowing that the end result would be better for it.

Without an approach from David Barker at Bloomsbury, I fear that this book may not ever have been completed and I am therefore grateful to him for being the necessary catalyst to finish something I started longer ago than I care to remember.

In addition, I must thank the Centre for Critical and Cultural Studies and the Faculty of Arts at the University of Queensland for making available to me periods of concentrated research time without which this project would never have reached completion, and William Fryer and Shigemi Kurahashi who worked as research assistants at various points during this project and helped me with things beyond my linguistic abilities.

I am also grateful to Roger Richards from Extreme Music (http://xtr.com), the publisher of the 50 CD Merzbow retrospective box set *Merzbox*, for permission to use substantial sections of Brett Woodward's descriptions of the set's CDs in the 'remix' that appears at the start of Chapter 8.

I acknowledge also that sections of chapter four have been previously published in two different articles and appear here substantially reworked. I am grateful to the publishers of these journals for permission to rework this material. The articles in question are: Greg Hainge, 'Of Glitch and Men: The Place of the Human in the Successful Integration of Failure and Noise in the Digital Realm', *Communication Theory*, 17 (2007): 26–42, reprinted by permission of the publisher (John Wiley & Sons, Inc, http://www.wiley.com); and Greg Hainge, 'No(i)stalgia: On the Impossibility of Recognising Noise in the Present', *Culture, Theory and Critique*, 46, no.1 (2005): 1–10, reprinted by permission of the publisher (Taylor & Francis Ltd, http://www.tandfonline.com).

Finally, I want to thank my two wonderful kids Elize and James for making me realise things that they could not even imagine, and my incredible wife Jo who is, in a sense, my noise, since without her nothing would be possible.

Introduction

Manifesto

The highest expression of the conflict of things, as a sponta-
neous eruption of possibilities, as movement, as a simultaneous
poem, as a symphony of cries, shots, commands, embodying an
attempted solution of the problem of life in motion ... Every
movement naturally produces noise.[1]

*So wrote Richard Huelsenbeck. But let us go further and write our
own manifesto. Let us think about the problem of life in motion
and movement to see, if we follow this line of thought, how far we
can go.*

*The material world is one in which mechanical vibration is an
unavoidable fact. Even at a subatomic level, matter moves around
a central point situated at the average co-ordinate of the trajectory
traced by the vibration of matter. When the material vibrating
does so in an elastic medium – such as air or water – the vibration
produced is termed acoustic, which is to say that it produces sound,
regardless of whether or not the human ear is capable of perceiving
the acoustic vibration as sound – as is the case with infrasounds
and ultrasounds that lay outside of the realm of the human
auditory sense. Since all matter naturally vibrates in an elastic
medium – a vacuum not being a natural earthly phenomenon –, all
matter produces sound, its vibrations propagating vibrations in the
medium surrounding it, creating sound waves. Sonically speaking,
then, there is no such thing as inanimate matter.*

*What is more, the interaction of any two material bodies will
create further vibrations not only in the very matter of those bodies,
but also in their surrounding medium, creating further sound waves.
Just as matter creates sound, then, so does any process in which two
or more material bodies come into contact with each other.*

But why stop here, why let matter have all the fun? Do ideas and concepts not also move and vibrate, resonate with and impact upon each other, vibrate in and beyond the time into which they are released?

Everything, then, is expressive, not only embodying a form but for ever forming an embodiment. Or rather, for this will be our contention, everything is in noise, and noise is in everything.

Let us then not attempt always to amputate that on which we depend, to struggle always and for ever to have done with noise, let us rather welcome it in and think through it. This will be a philopsophy.

* * *

Turn it up

The twentieth century is, among other things, the Age of Noise. Physical noise, mental noise and noise of desire – we hold history's record for all of them. And no wonder; for all the resources of our almost miraculous technology have been thrown into the current assault against silence.[2]

Noise is everywhere and on the rise. Since the advent of the post-Industrial society, the world has become louder and louder, and noise has invaded our lives more with every passing year. Its logic seems viral, the more noise there is, the more critics, philosophers, and (irony of ironies) anti-noise campaigners add to the hubbub, talking about noise incessantly as though the only response possible in the face of so much noise were to join forces with it. As if to prove the point and make it harder still to retreat from noise into the orderly harmony of music, for so long held to be the opposite of noise, the history of twentieth century Western music seems to have followed a similar trajectory, becoming noisier and noisier as time goes on. From Schoenberg to Stravinsky to Russolo to Cage to Hendrix to Merzbow, atonality, dissonance, explosions, coughs, splutters, feedback, distortion, glitch and various shades of noise have done their best to (dis)colour music and to make of it what we had thought it was not. Herein, however, lies a problem, for if noise can become what it is not, what exactly is it?

The question may seem absurd to many. After all, everyone knows what noise is. As Garret Keizer writes, 'Like Justice Potter Stewart, who famously said that although he could not define obscenity, he knew it when he saw it, most of us feel confident in our ability to identify noise. We know it when we hear it'.[3] Some, however, can be more categorical. For the physicist, noise can be defined as a non-periodic complex sound, in other words, a sound that can be decomposed into a large number of sound waves all of different frequencies that (according to Fourier's theorem) are not multiples of one basic frequency and which do not therefore enter into harmonic relations with each other.[4] This would not seem to be incompatible, and yet is significantly different from the very common and common sense definitions of noise outlined by Marie-Claire Botte and René Chocholle in their book *Le Bruit* and which itself draws on an officially sanctioned standard.[5] For them, noise is either 'an erratic acoustic vibration which is intermittent or statistically aleatory' or else (or hence?) 'any auditory sensation which is disagreeable or uncomfortable'.[6] To the physicist's mathematical definition, they therefore add a subjective measure, a combination found also in the definition of noise enshrined in Shannon and Weaver's *The Mathematical Theory of Communication*, the foundational work of traditional communications theory.

Defining communication 'in a very broad sense to include all of the procedures by which one mind may affect another [including] not only written and oral speech, but also music, the pictorial arts, the theatre, the ballet, and in fact all human behaviour',[7] Weaver, in his summary of Shannon's contributions to communications theory, notes that,

> In the process of being transmitted, it is unfortunately characteristic that certain things are added to the signal which were not intended by the information source. These unwanted additions may be distortions of sound (in telephony, for example) or static (in radio), or distortions in shape or shading of picture (television), or errors in transmission (telegraphy or facsimile), etc. All of these changes in the transmitted signal are called *noise*.[8]

Having ascertained that the transmission of all communicational signals contains noise, the problem becomes, for Shannon, to discover the general characteristics of noise and to understand how it affects the accuracy of the message finally received at the destination so as to ascertain how to minimise the undesirable effects of noise and to discover to what extent it is possible to eliminate it. It would be a mistake to extrapolate from this desire to minimise the 'undesirable' effects of noise, however, that noise harboured some desirable effects. For Shannon and Weaver, such a possibility is merely a semantic trap to be avoided. As Weaver explains:

> If noise is introduced, then the received message contains certain distortions, certain errors, certain extraneous material, that would certainly lead one to say that the received message exhibits, because of the effects of the noise, an increased uncertainty. But if the uncertainty is increased, the information is increased, and this sounds as though the noise were beneficial!
>
> It is generally true that when there is noise, the received signal exhibits greater information – or better, the received signal is selected out of a more varied set than is the transmitted signal. This is a situation which beautifully illustrates the semantic trap into which one can fall if he does not remember that 'information' is used here with a special meaning that measures freedom of choice and hence uncertainty as to what choice has been made. It is therefore possible for the word information to have either good or bad connotations. Uncertainty which arises by virtue of freedom of choice on the part of the sender is desirable uncertainty. Uncertainty which arises because of errors or because of the influence of noise, is undesirable uncertainty.
>
> It is thus clear where the joker is in saying that the received signal has more information. Some of this information is spurious and undesirable and has been introduced via the noise. To get the useful information in the received signal we must subtract out this spurious portion.[9]

The problem, of course, as Shannon knew well, is that from an engineering perspective one cannot in fact subtract out this spurious portion, that noise is the ineluctable travelling companion of information.

Noise, then, increased at an exponential rate throughout the twentieth century and became more than ever both ineluctable and undesirable. When filtered through noise in this way, the history of the twentieth century, from both a social, artistic and scientific perspective, can then sometimes look like the story of a dog who, having become aware of its tail, tries to run away from it.

This is not to say that noise is a uniquely twentieth century phenomenon, far from it, but it is to suggest that the increase in certain forms of noise has brought it to our attention in a more insistent way in the twentieth century and beyond than was the case previously – which in turn has led to the self-generative logic mentioned above as more noise leads to more noise. This capacity to insist upon us once noticed would indeed seem to be one of the peculiar properties of noise. Prochnik proposes a definition of noise 'as sound that you can't get a distance on – sound that gets inside your head and won't go away',[10] and this is the case even at relatively low decibel levels since once one notices a noise, it seems to preoccupy us disproportionately. Whilst this may then go some way towards explaining why it is that we might wish to attenuate or eradicate it, why the dog would wish to run away from its tail, the absurdity of that proposition in this allegory should be enough to indicate the folly of this course of action.

When one does turn one's attention to noise, however, giving into its insistence, another problem quickly becomes apparent that may, once again, push us away from it. For whilst noise may seem like an eminently unproblematic term, concept or phenomenon when one does not really attend to it – and, as claimed here, we spend most of our time attempting *not* to attend to it – as soon as one does stop to think about what noise actually *is*, one quickly realises that its meanings and definitions are highly subjective and unstable. Even in Shannon's mathematical theory of communication, whilst there may appear to be an objective certainty in the formulae that show how, given the ineradicability of noise, information can be transmitted reliably through a noisy channel, the decision as to what constitutes noise in the signal and what constitutes its information is a necessarily subjective matter that assumes the absolute intentionality of the originary emitter to be the only defining characteristic of the information that needs to be considered. And if noise then becomes nothing but a matter of personal choice, it is hard to say precisely what it is and to what it might be applied as a descriptor.

This somewhat bipolar aspect of noise is apparent in many of the recent studies of noise, whether these are interested in noise itself as an object of study or else as something to be eradicated. Bart Kosko puts it most succinctly when he writes, 'Noise has two parts. The first has to do with the head and the second with the heart'.[11] Garret Keizer, for his part, forms a title out of noise's impossible contradictions and double binds, calling his book *The Unwanted Sound of Everything We Want*. What is more, in his chapter of that same name, he titles his subsections, respectively: 'Noise is Easy to Define' and 'Noise is Not so Easy to Define'; 'Noise is Objective and 'Noise is Subjective'; 'Noise is New' and 'Noise is Old'; and finally, 'Noise is Meaningless' and 'Noise is Seldom without Meaning'.[12]

Adopting the different strategy of all-inclusiveness, the sheer scale of Hillel Schwartz's recent magnum opus *Making Noise: From Babel to the Big Bang and Beyond* is in itself testament to the vast range of meanings that have been attributed to noise and the number of sites that it has inhabited or that have produced it. His survey ultimately can bring no consensus as to what noise is in a definitive sense, however, and on the penultimate page of his book he writes:

> Timeless and untimely, noise is the noisiest of concepts, abundantly self-contradictory. Profligate. It compels us at every stage to reorganize, take our lives up a notch; or it does us in, deafening us to our relations, obligations. Noise must be what we were waiting for all along, an encounter with the chaotic that loosens the lug-nuts of routine. Or, grating and incessant, it sends us over the edge. Sound and unsound, something or *other*.
>
> Bound up with bone and tissue, with solids, liquids, gases, and plasmas, with the tactile and cortical, with the chthonic and the cosmic, all those vibrations that are soundmusicnoise have been historically re-cognized from era to era, within a cultural logic as nonlinear as the coils of the hairs of our inner ears. Distinctions between sound and noise, or noise and music, or music and sound, can only be provisional – not because they are matters of taste but because they are matters of history and histrionics: of what becomes audible through time and how the acoustics are staged, in auditoria or bedrooms, in laboratories or courtrooms.[13]

Whilst all of this might appear to be incontrovertible, and whilst it would seem that noise must for ever remain only ever a kind of *portmanteau* word on which we can hang the referent of our choice depending on temporal, geographical, cultural or disciplinary context, there nonetheless remains the possibility of finding across all of these contradictions and shifting meanings some consistency, of asserting, like Justice Potter Stewart on obscenity, that we recognise noise when we hear or (or, indeed, see it) but find it hard to say precisely what it is. This book is an attempt to do precisely that and to understand why it matters.

Noise matters

One might of course ask why it matters, not noise itself (at least not yet), but why we would want to find this consistency, why, if the term noise can be used in many different ways that are mutually incompatible, we cannot allow that inconsistency to be maintained. The first reason is that, given the recent interest in noise as a phenomenon to be studied and not simply an annoyance to be eradicated, a form of pollution, it is important to investigate the possibility of arriving at any such consensus or, perhaps better, to see if there is a way to bring the various definitions that have been given of noise together in such a way as to lend them some consistency – which is not necessarily to say coherence. If this is not done, in spite of the amount of ink that has been spilled on the subject in recent years, it is hard to know how noise will be able to coalesce into a field of study whose individual parts reaffirm, build upon or differ from each other as opposed to merely offering yet another subjective point of view on the topic that can be seriously contested by every other such work. And whilst one might of course pretend that this stands in fact as a metadiscursive move that makes the field of noise studies itself a noisy discourse, nothing but a tale full of sound and fury, the danger of this approach is that the tale ends up signifying nothing.[14] This is to say that if the unstated definitions of noise implicitly accepted are highly dependent on subjective variation and the perception of the individual, then those definitions are not in actuality definitions at all because the subjective variation in operation prohibits those definitions from being able to do as is their wont and point us towards a discrete object, phenomenon or concept, from signifying.

The result of this is similar to Deleuze and Guattari's observation that 'it's nice to talk like everybody else, to say the sun rises, when everybody knows it's only a manner of speaking',[15] because, just as here, no matter how commonplace it might be to use a term or phrase as shorthand in full knowledge of its falsity or insufficiency, the statement will always remain problematic and the enunciator guilty of a certain bad faith. This, however, is just how noise has been treated, as it has been used to apply to everything and nothing at the same time, subject to a whole host of mutually contradictory definitions and usages, its apparently ineffable nature the result of divergent agendas rather than something proper to noise itself.

This is not to say that I wish to tie noise down to an overly simplistic definition; as Kelly points out, 'Noise [...] eludes simple definition'.[16] Indeed, it would be absurd to pretend that noise is an object towards which a signifier can point, in the way that the word giraffe signifies a spotty animal with an oversized neck and long spindly legs – although it should be noted here, as should be clear already from the book's opening salvo, that it will be suggested that all objects, both animate and supposedly inanimate, are somehow noisy. Nor do I believe, however, that it is sufficient to state, as does Frances Dyson, that noise unites many different phenomena 'in a single but ineffable term that is shared by all fields, and surfaces as a *prima causa*',[17] for to do so would be somewhat incongruous in a book that seeks precisely to talk about noise.[18] Nor is it to say that I wish to survey the various definitions that have been given of noise and discount some in favour of others. Rather, my intention here is to see what commonality or consistency there may be across the various commonly accepted and common-sense definitions of noise so as to draw up what might be termed an operational taxonomy of noise. To put it more simply, since I will contend as have others before me that all ontology is necessarily relational, I will attempt to map an ontology of noise.[19]

What noise has been

In order to suggest what noise is by identifying the commonality of what it has been, it will, in the first instance, be necessary to enumerate some of these common sense definitions of noise. As commonsensical as these definitions might seem and as commonly accepted as they might be, I would like to contend that such definitions are problematic in large part because, precisely, they are often mutually incompatible and, in themselves, subject to high degrees of subjective variation that can turn noise into its opposite (in the way, for instance, that one parent's noise is another teenager's music).

Firstly, and perhaps most obviously, noise is mostly, although by no means exclusively, considered to be an auditory phenomenon, something that we humans can hear. More specifically, as we have seen already, noise is often considered (by both the physicist and anti-noise lobby alike) to be 'an erratic acoustic vibration which is intermittent or statistically aleatory' – which is to say that it is random, unpredictable and unordered.

Many others, especially those belonging to the anti-noise lobby, qualify it as 'any auditory sensation which is disagreeable or uncomfortable – and none hold this position more vehemently than Garret Keizer who documents the decibel levels at which noise actually causes physical harm and hearing loss but more generally suggests that noise is a question of power and domination and thus invokes an ethical problem since 'anything amplified to a deafening volume or imposed on me against my will is noise no matter how "pure" its tone or "classic" its pedigree'.[20] And yet, as if to prove the point that noise is in the ear of the beholder, another scholar fighting on the same side as Keizer, George Prochnik, tracing a lineage through Nietzsche and Theodor Lessing, suggests that the increase in noise in the modern world is in part the result of the subjugated masses refusing to be silenced, of the oppressed ' "making a noise" about unjust power relationships'.[21]

Linked to its disagreeable and hence undesirable characteristics, noise is also often considered to be a by-product of an event or process, which is to say that it is produced by certain actions that are effected to achieve an outcome unrelated to the production of noise from the point of view of intentionality. (In other words, the primary function of a hammer – outside of the avant-garde practices of an Industrial group such as Einsturzende Neubäten, of course – is not to produce noise even though when it is put to use (or even, at the subatomic level, when it is not) it will do precisely this.) This definition of noise is linked, what is more, to the definition of noise in information theory already touched upon, since here noise is considered to be a part of the signal that is not contained in the information emitted at the information source. In Shannon's simplified diagram, this noise source seems always to come from outside or to the side of the communications channel, but there is no reason why it could not in fact originate also in the communications channel itself, akin to what Kittler would term the communication system's mediality.[22] These undesirable qualities of noise in communications systems often seem to arise at moments when the system is considered to fail and not transmit its information as it should. As Kosko writes:

> Noise is a nuisance. Noise is the hiss and pop of the static we hear when we listen to a radio station or a walkie-talkie or an old vinyl record album. It is the flickering snow that mars a cable TV image when someone bumps the cable or when the cable company scrambles the pay-per-view boxing match. It is the grainy streaks that flash across the screen when we watch an old print of a film. Noise is the background chatter of people in a restaurant when we ask the server to tell us about the dinner special. Noise is the Internet or telephone signal that interferes with our own.[23]

In a slightly different take on the term, noise is also credited with a politically resistant charge, serving to disrupt the status quo and thus bring about some kind of change in the system. This is the case particularly in the influential work of Jacques Attali who links changes in music that come about through some kind of noisy interference to changes in the mode of production in which that music is created. In this analysis, noise is considered in large part, if not exclusively, to be (oftentimes a politically charged) content, a message transmitted by musical content that is fundamentally contestatory and resistant to the status quo, a force that has the potential to bring about a change in the system into which it is released as that system attempts to negate its subversive power and make of what was previously considered to be noise merely another acceptable form – as though noise were like the force in Kojève's reading of Hegel that renders change and thus history possible.[24] For Attali, indeed, social progress comes about via an 'aggression against the dominant code by noise destined to become a new dominant code'.[25] This, then, is noise placed firmly on the side of content even if that content performs a catalytic function for a process of change, and the opposition between noise and music here is merely one of degree or aesthetics as opposed to a fundamental formal difference.

Attali's work on noise has in turn been very important for theorists of the (often musical) avant-garde such as Russo and Warner[26] and Paul Hegarty who writes:

> What is of interest is the continual process opened up by [Attali's perspective on noise], where music becomes an avant-garde, and in so doing is always, initially at least, identified as noise. Only later does the old noise come to be seen as legitimate music.[27]

Hegarty's comments here once again point up the inconsistency of noise that has been noted previously. If before it has been said to be both new and old, subjective and objective, in Hegarty's analysis, and indeed Attali's, noise can be recuperated and brought into order as time progresses, made not-noise, and thus to fail as noise as Hegarty points out.[28] In a similar manner to Schwartz, Hegarty writes: 'Noise is not an objective fact. It occurs in relation to perception – both direct (sensory) and according to presumptions made by an individual. These are going to vary according to historical, geographical and cultural location'.[29]

Noise, then, has been and will no doubt continue to be many different things to many different people, and given the range of meanings and definitions it has generated, it is perhaps hard to see precisely how these parallel or divergent paths might be made to converge. That is precisely what I will attempt to do here, however, in part by making of the multiplicity of noise and its ability constantly to move across various categorical distinctions its virtue.

What noise might be: Towards an ontology of noise

> Where better [than in noise] to imagine ontological riches in the raw?[30]

It is undoubtedly not insignificant that noise is imbued with a particular propensity for transgressing and destabilising fixed boundaries and that it is, more often than not, associated with the auditory sense. For much recent critical literature has been concerned with an attempt to overthrow the dominant position of sight in our critical vocabularies (a move Janus terms the 'anti-ocular turn'[31]), in part because, by its very nature, sound makes us entertain a very different, far less Cartesian (and hence controllable) phenomenological relationship with the world around us. As Michael Bull and Les Back write,

> by listening we may be able to perceive the relationship between subject and object, inside and outside, and the public and private altogether differently. In its engulfing multi-directionality sound blurs the above distinctions and enables us to re-think our relationship to them.[32]

This is precisely the intention of Jean-Luc Nancy's *Listening* [*À l'écoute*], which encourages listening (*écouter*) over understanding (*entendre*, which has the double meaning in French of both to understand and to hear) because of the more open relationship with the world around us that it brings into the fray. He writes: 'If "to hear" is to understand the sense […], to listen is to be straining toward a possible meaning, and consequently one that is not immediately accessible'.[33]

In a similar vein, Frances Dyson explains how sound is an immersive medium that transcends metaphysical boundaries and troubles Western epistemologies, 'the phenomenal characteristics of sound and listening […] describing a flow or process rather than a thing, a mode of being in a constant state of flux, and a polymorphous subjectivity'.[34] This is undoubtedly true of sound generally and of auditory noise particularly in some definitions of what such a phenomenon actually is. Indeed, Michel Serres writes that noise

> settles in subjects as well as in objects, in hearing as well as in space, in the observers as well as in the observed, it moves through the means and the tools of observation, whether material or logical, hardware or software, constructed channels or languages; it is part of the in-itself, part of the for-itself; it cuts across the oldest and surest philosophical divisions.[35]

I wish to contend, however, that this is in fact true of noise more generally in an expanded definition, once the borders of this phenomenon or concept (for ultimately it is both) have themselves been destabilised in such a way as to bring them all together. This approach thus has much in common with Dyson's ideas on sound which take their lead from Chion. Dyson, indeed, notes how Chion thought of sound:

> as an event rather than an object, and in doing so [incorporated] a sense of organic process, of a multiple, mutating form found in a figure closely tied to sound – the figure of vibration. Vibration, figuratively and literally, fluctuates between particle and wave, object and event, being and becoming. Defying representation, it also gestures toward the immersive, undifferentiated, multiplicitous associations that aurality provokes, without committing to the (massive) representational and ontological ambiguities that aurality raises.[36]

Whilst the concept of vibration is of the utmost importance in the present study (as should be evident from its very first pages), noise, as it will be figured here, is not simply coterminous with vibration as it seems to be in much media theory, according to Dyson. She continues:

> Used to reconcile the sound/object event dichotomy in sound studies, vibration appears again in new media theory – often in the guise of flux, or noise – as a unifying force, one that dissolves the distinction between the body and technology, nature, and culture and resolves the problem of representation and mediation.[37]

Noise, rather, will be figured here as the trace and index of a relation that itself speaks of ontology. If noise is then immersive, this is not because it is all-pervasive and seeps through walls as the anti-noise lobby would claim, nor because we cannot shut our ears as we can our eyes. Rather, noise is immersive because there is nothing outside of it and because it is in everything. Indeed, noise is not only multi-medial, arising in many different kinds of forms and media, engaging many different senses, sensations, responses and affects, it is medial insofar as it is always in-between, produced in the passing into actuality of everything, both animate and inanimate – a false dichotomy in any case as has been suggested. Noise, this is to say, is the trace of the virtual out of which all expressive forms come to be, the mark of an ontology which is necessarily relational. In order to conceptualise noise in this way and attempt to draw up a taxonomic description of the ontology of noise, it is necessary to reconfigure the way in which ontology is often thought about and to conceive of the world and everything in it as expressive, arising out of the movement or force of differentiation through which all being expresses itself in existence. In this, of course, we follow in the footsteps of Spinoza and particularly Deleuze's reading of Spinoza.[38] Having said that, just as one might contend that Deleuze's reading of Spinoza is itself a noisy reading in which what is expressed is not so much the essence of Spinoza's thought as the noise created by the channel instigated between Deleuze and Spinoza, so our reading here will never pretend to employ this notion of expression in the precise way it was intended by either of these philosophers. Rather, this work will generate a new expression which is drawn from and faithful only to the noise of the channel that it sets up with all of its various interlocutors.[39]

In essence, then, for it is indeed a question of essence, noise will be seen to constitute the nature or essence of the relation that is inimical to all expression when everything is conceived of as an expression.[40] It is then through noise, I will suggest, that we are able to intuit the serial relations that link the heterogenetic modes through which everything comes to be in an ontology that does not believe in fixed identities, beings and transcendent essence, but only difference, becomings and relations. If noise inhabits everything because everything is in actuality formed out of noise, then what noise ultimately points us to is the relational ontology according to which the world comes to pass, the way in which there is nothing that falls outside of the event, of the realm of process, of an existence formed only through the heterogeneous assemblages of different forms of expression which inescapably and incessantly contract the virtual into the actual.

The point being made here is somewhat similar to something that Prochnik says, albeit from a very different ideological standpoint. Prochnik notes that 'Every structure, organic and nonorganic, has a special frequency at which it naturally vibrates when energized into motion [and thus] there are specific speeds at which every structure is predestined to vibrate'.[41] Every object then has its own fundamental frequency determined by its mass and tension. Therefore, he continues, the core physical truth of every structure determines the way it dances and shimmies off sound waves into the universe. An object's fundamental frequency is a kind of naked snapshot of identity. By definition, this snapshot also reveals the other structures that the object is most likely to mutually resonate with.[42]

For Prochnik, then, every object is necessarily acoustic or, in our terms, expressive of not only its own fundamental frequency but also what we might call its resonant frequency, the specificity that it brings to all of the relations instigated between it and the universe as it is contracted into existence – the dichotomy erected here between objects and the outside into which they are contracted into being in the context of a relational ontology is of course a false one, yet necessary to make my point. This resonant frequency, then, is similar to what is here termed noise, and it is this that we will listen out for. And it is here, of course, that we find the ideological difference between Prochnik's study and this one, since he is interested, as his title indicates, in pursuing silence, not noise, a position that leads him to suppose something that, according to the present study, is not only untrue but fundamentally impossible, namely that 'everything likes to be still – to be silent – as much as possible'.[43] If, as Prochnik seems to claim, the universe is necessarily expressive, this 'perfect state of rest'[44] can only ever be an idyll that will never be achieved, for noise is produced by the very expression of being.

Noise, then, in and of itself is nothing, for it arises only in the relational process through which the world and its objects express themselves in an infinite number of possible relations, assemblages or expressive forms. This position is close to Hegarty's when he writes,

[noise] does not exist independently, as it exists only in relation to what it is not. In turn, it helps structure and defines its opposite (the world of meaning, law, regulation, goodness, beauty, and so on). Noise is something like a process, and whether it creates a result (positive in the form of avant-garde transformation, negative in the form of social restrictions) or remains process is one of the major issues in how music and noise relate.[45]

However, if Hegarty's distinction here between result (form/content) and process is crucial, it is because it describes the difference between our two approaches. I wish here to analyse noise as a process, and thus need to modify Hegarty's formulation slightly in order to generate the terms of my position: for me, noise does not exist independently either, for it arises only in an event or expression. Noise exists only in relation to what it is not, then, only to the extent that it is in and of itself nothing. This, of course, can be said of everything if all ontology is relational; the particularity of noise is its propensity to stress this relation. For noise is the artefact of the relation in which being expresses itself in its actualisation. It is the mark of an assemblage which pulls us away from the apparent fixity and transcendence of an expression's identity (its manifest content) and reveals even the apparently inanimate to be an event. As such, of course, it cannot petrify into a result, a pseudo-object with a stable identity or program. Rather, as Brandon LaBelle suggests, discussing the work of Yasunao Tone, noise is

> a meta-operation: it directs a certain understanding onto the field of the symbolic, onto the territory of code, without putting into practice that very code. It directs the ear not to escape routes or alternatives, to "complaints or suggestions", but to the mechanics at work in the system. Here, a theory of noise is defined by its ability to remain an operation rather than a sign, to always remain a pure drive away from heralding anything.[46]

Noise is then indeed oppositional, but the opposition that it presents is irrecuperable (*contra* Hegarty and Attali). It does indeed resist, but the resistance that it proffers is better conceived of not merely as political, as a 'resistance toward the dominant ideals of music, and consequently, of the larger society',[47] but, rather, as the kind of resistance found in electrical circuits. An electrical circuit (read text) set up for the purposes of the transmission of current (read content) will itself necessarily resist the passage of that current due to its own material properties at the same time as that material system is crucial for the transmission of that current since without it no current could be transmitted (read expressed) in the first place. In a metal conductor, for instance, the outer electrons of the lattice of atoms are able to dissociate from their parent atoms and float in such a way that they form a fluid environment that makes of the metal a conductor since when a voltage is applied to the circuit the electrons in this fluid field travel from one end of the conductor to the other. What electrical resistance illustrates beautifully, then, is the way in which any expression, which is to say any material entering into expressive relations (which is to say, of course, everything) necessarily enters into a systemic process with its own material ontology (read medium). This medium *resists* the transmission of the expression at the same time as the expression is entirely dependent on the system at the most fundamental level of base materiality, for its expressive potential can only be actualised in a material assemblage formed between the system and the expression that reconfigures both of them.[48]

Noise, then, expresses the nature of the relation and deconstructs the binary oppositions that generally channel our attention towards a discrete and isolated aspect of an expression: form or content, for instance, or medium or message. This is not to say that I am merely proffering an alternative formulation of McLuhan's famous dictum 'the medium is the message',[49] for my point is quite different. For whilst it is undoubtedly the case, as McLuhan has suggested, that 'it is only too typical that the "content" of any medium blinds us to the character of the medium',[50] I wish neither to concentrate solely on the content of expression, nor on its medium, for, as should be becoming clear, there can be no absolute separation between content and form in a relational ontology and it is precisely the deconstruction of such binaries to which noise points. If noise is often imagined to arise when the medium encroaches upon and disturbs the message – when we hear the vinyl hiss and pop or see the TV image break up, as we have seen Kosko suggest –, to be then simply an artefact of the media, this is only half of the story.[51] For whilst noise will indeed become most apparent at times such as this, it is nonetheless not reducible to this; rather, what the incursion of the medium points us to is the necessarily mediated nature of all ontology, the fact that everything necessarily comes to be *in media*, in the in-between of the components of a communications system or expressive assemblage.

Lest this all seem a little abstract, let us filter the argument through noise itself, the 'pure or ideal noise' that is white noise.[52] As Kosko explains:

> White noise is noisy because it has a wide and flat band of frequencies if one looks at its spectrum. This reflects the

common working definition of noise as a so-called wideband signal. Good signals or wanted signals concentrate their energy on a comparatively narrow band of the frequency spectrum. Hence good signals tend to be so-called narrowband signals at least relative to the wide band of white noise. White noise is so noisy because its spectrum is as wide as possible – it runs the whole infinite length of the frequency spectrum itself. So pure or ideal white noise exists only as a mathematical abstraction. It cannot exist physically because it would require infinite energy.[53]

Let me put this another way. White noise is a plane (that does not exist in actuality) composed of the sum total of all possible sonic frequencies emitted simultaneously. Any sonic expression is then necessarily the contraction into actuality of a zone of this plane or the conjugation of different points on this plane. Every expression is therefore born out of noise and carries noise within it. As expression passes into actuality, however, it is all too easy to forget this and to imagine that that expression is a discrete and autonomous object that exists independently of a greater whole, to concentrate on its content or identity as opposed to the process by which that content or identity comes to be expressed. It is, however, impossible for the content of expression to separate itself from the immanent plane out of which it is formed and the differential process through which it comes to be – 'meaningful' expression becoming such only by contracting noise into a form that no longer seems noisy. When we attend to the noise of expression, such delusions are dispelled and the apparent matter of factness of existence fades away, matter itself being unveiled as expressive.[54] This is how and why noise matters.[55]

Something similar is suggested by Michel Serres, for whom noise is also primordial and foundational. Indeed, Serres suggests that noise forms the cosmological and – we can infer from the title of his book *Genesis* – genetic background of our world and universe. As he writes:

> Background noise is the background of the world, and the world began, it is said, with a big bang. A founding blow in which the universe is embryonic, it precedes the expansion in the universal, space has already received this before receiving the things themselves, it has already formed the space where the things are

going to be lodged. I am assuming that there was no big bang, that original cosmological preconcept; I am assuming that there was and still is an inaccessible number of different noises.[56]

Serres does not then attribute the originary noise of the cosmos to a single, unitary event which would henceforth act as the catalyst for all life on our planet and the existence of the astral bodies that surround us, which would be to interpret the originary noise of the universe in a far too literal and somewhat simplistic manner. Rather, the name noise is reserved for the condition of infinite multiplicity that precedes even this event and that subsists in all of its products. Thus, for Serres:

> The cosmos is not a structure, it is a pure multiplicity of ordered multiplicities and pure multiplicities. It is the global basis of all structures, it is the background noise of all form and information, it is the milky noise of the whole of our messages gathered together.[57]

For Serres, noise might thus also be said to be fundamentally philosophically oppositional insofar as it constantly undermines the possibility of a complete knowledge of any system, message or object. Indeed, by suggesting that all matter, meaning and messages are drawn from a ground of infinite multiplicity, Serres strips every aspect of or object in the world of fixity, transmogrifying all apparent stability into a state of flux and process and denying the possibility of any kind of taxonomic order. For Serres, however, noise seems always to remain only ever a potentiality, a kind of pre-ontology which would necessarily fade away in the act of expression. Indeed for Serres noise is:

> a set of possible things, it may be *the* set of possible things. It is not potential, it is the very reverse of power, rather it is capaciousness. This noise is the opening.[58]

Serres thus draws a distinction between ontology and phenomenology and suggests that noise belongs only to the former (although this may be because of the distinction he makes in another work between the plenitude of white noise which would be 'the heart [*fond*] of being' and the parasite or 'parasitism [which] is the heart of relation').[59] He writes:

Background noise may well be the ground of our being. It may be that our being is not at rest, it may be that it is not motion, it may be that our being is disturbed. [...] *As soon as a phenomenon appears, it leaves the noise; as soon as a form looms up or pokes through, it reveals itself by veiling noise.* So noise is not a matter of phenomenology, so it is a matter of being itself.[60]

Conceived of in this way, noise bears a striking resemblance to Deleuze and Guattari's concept of the abstract machine – even though in their transcendental empiricism, there is obviously no such rejection of the phenomenological – and one might even go so far as to say that Serres is effectively describing here, through the figure of noise, the abstract machine of the world or cosmos. For Deleuze and Guattari's abstract machine is that which has no form or fixed substance, only function and which is, as such, as Brian Massumi describes it, 'a continually changing, turbulent pool of matter-energy'.[61] The abstract machine is then pure virtuality and as such, as Massumi goes on to point out, is 'outside our space of relatively stable matter and quantifiable energy', it is 'a pure outside, an outside so far out that it would have no "itself" of any kind to be "in"'.[62] And this in turn means that,

If the virtual is a space of pure exteriority, then every point is adjacent to every other point in the actual world, regardless of whether those points are adjacent to each other (otherwise some actual points would separate the virtual from other actual points, and the virtual would be outside their outside – in other words, relative to it and mediated by it).[63]

Deleuze and Guattari never related the abstract machine or plane of immanence to the concept of noise, nor did they ever really address noise in depth in any of their single or joint-authored works.[64] They were occasionally interested in music, and especially in the section of *A Thousand Plateaus* called '1837: Of the Refrain', but whilst they praise Varèse's creation of what they term 'a *sound machine*' and the very idea of the synthesiser which 'makes audible the sound process itself' and supplies them with a model for a new form of philosophy which functions in such a way as 'to make thought travel, make it mobile, make it a force of the Cosmos (in the same way as one makes sound travel)',[65] this has nothing to do with something they would term noise. Indeed, if the synthesiser that they praise works by synthesising disparate elements, there lies in this process the danger of going too far, of producing noise – the term here being, of course, negatively inflected. They write:

> This synthesis of disparate elements is not without ambiguity. It has the same ambiguity, perhaps, as the modern valorization of children's drawings, texts by the mad, and concerts of noise. Sometimes one overdoes it, puts too much in, works with a jumble of lines and sounds; then instead of producing a cosmic machine capable of 'rendering sonorous', one lapses back to a machine of reproduction that ends up reproducing nothing but a scribble effacing all lines, a scramble effacing all sounds. The claim is that one is opening music to all events, all irruptions, but one ends up reproducing a scrambling that prevents any event from happening. All one has left is a resonance chamber well on the way to forming a black hole. A material that is too rich remains too 'territorialized': on noise sources, on the nature of the objects ... (this applies even to Cage's prepared piano).[66]

Here, Deleuze and Guattari perhaps fall prey to a similar kind of misprision of noise to those already seen, however, or rather they limit noise to one of its common sense definitions. For in their reading noise arises out of cacophony, the result of the coexistence of too many disparate elements or an excessive materiality. Whilst perhaps unsurprising, this is nonetheless somewhat of a shame since the links to be made between their abstract machine and noise or, perhaps, between their pure outside and pure noise (or white noise) are striking – if, of course, one leaves behind common-sense definitions. For the abstract machine is a synthesiser, that which operationalises expression, traversing the plane of immanence and contracting the virtual into events, assemblages, flows, expressions and affects through differentiation, intensification and the infolding of various zones – expressions which are themselves perceived as objects, meanings, bodies or identities only in the mistaken apprehension of the secondary effects of these processes.

The plane of virtuality (or immanence) thus constantly deploys the powers of the unknown that are proper to heterogenetic creation, the articulations and conjugations between various zones, partial objects or machinic-becomings taking place upon and within its surface only ever able to produce the new – even if force of habit may lead us to believe that this is not the case. As such, the plane of virtuality does indeed seem to share many characteristics with white Gaussian noise which, as J. R. Pierce notes, contains all frequencies and is thus, mathematically, 'the epitome of the various and unexpected. It is the least predictable, the most original of sounds'.[67] White noise, in other words, is the sound of the virtual: it is a continually changing pool of matter-energy, it is the pure outside of sound in which every point is adjacent to every other, it is the aleatory exterior from which any sonic expression is drawn from an infolding, intensification or differentiation of any point, zone or frequency of the limitless possible sonic spectrum.

And yet, perhaps it does not matter too much if Deleuze and Guattari did not turn their attention to noise, for in spite of the obvious points of contact and affinities here, there is nonetheless an important difference. True white noise, as we have seen, is bound always to remain only ever a mathematical abstraction, just as Deleuze and Guattari's pure outside is condemned to remain for ever virtual. In order to pass from the virtual to the actual, to expression, however, Deleuze and Guattari need to mobilise a separate figure, that of the abstract machine. Whilst this machine, being merely an operational catalyst for an infinite number of possible expressions, is called abstract precisely because it is never able to take on a fixed form, this term's etymology runs the risks of leading us to believe that the abstract machine is somehow drawn away from the plane in the process, taking place on top of it as opposed to from within it, as it were. The problem is undoubtedly less acute than with some of Serres' formulations which make it hard to see how noise would ever be able to pass into expression, to be anything other than pre-evental, and yet I cannot help but feel that there is nonetheless a break in their thought. There is no such break if we think through this move via noise, precisely because white noise is simply modulated into different colours of noise as the virtual is contracted into the actual via expression.

In effect, what I want to suggest here, then, is that there need not be a split between the operations of noise as a philosophical concept and its manifestations in expression, that it is not necessary to separate out the ontological from the phenomenological. I want to suggest that noise is more than just a concept, a figure of pure potentiality, that it is produced in the actualisation of expression whilst never leaving behind the outside from which expression is drawn and thus reminding us of it. To put it crudely, noise is not only of the future (*à-venir*) but omnipresent. Noise straddles both the actual and the virtual, the realms of concept and matter, multiplicity and singularity; it is the by-product of the event taking place in the becomings situated across these poles, the very precondition for expressivity that is born only as an unintended yet inexorable consequence of expression itself.

Noise, then, makes us attend to how things come to *exist*, how they come to stand or be (*sistere*) outside of themselves (*ex-*). Noise, then, is fundamentally about ontology, and in order to sketch an operational taxonomy of noise, it is only fitting that each of the categories to be used should also address how things come to exist (*-sistere*). Let me then suggest the following:

1 Noise *resists* – not (necessarily) politically but materially because it reconfigures matter in expression, conduction and conjugation.

2 Noise *subsists* – insofar as it relates the event to the field from which expression is drawn and thus subtends all being.[68]

3 Noise *coexists* – as its ontology is only relational and does not come into being by itself but only as the by-product of expression.

4 Noise *persists* – because it cannot be reconfigured or recontained, cannot become thetic as it passes into expression, but remains indelibly noise.

5 Noise *obsists* – since it is fundamentally anathema to stasis and thus opposes all illusions of fixity, pulling form beyond itself through expression and bringing about the collapse of meaning.

Where noise will (and will not) be found

There is, of course, an alternative cultural history of (predominantly Western) civilisation that documents those moments when noise has burst through the veil of respectability, bulldozed idle complacency, bawled in the face of tradition and blasted the status quo. This is a tale that has been told many times in the recent past, be it in an all-encompassing survey or in relation to specific instances of noise or arenas into which noise has been released. It is then resolutely not my intention here to add yet another voice to this this cacophony. Rather, in what follows I will expand upon this taxonomy directly through theoretical reflection as well as indirectly through analyses of the noise accompanying and/or constituting various expressions at those points when it becomes perceptible. For whilst it is my contention that noise necessarily inhabits all expression and therefore all cultural forms, this is not to say that noise is always easily identified or perceived. I will then seek out cultural forms where noise of some kind is foregrounded, entering the text or expression through that noise to see what it might tell us about that expression – and accordingly each of my chapters, like this introduction, will begin with a noisy prelude of some kind. Given that I am interested in cultural forms in which noise is brought to the fore, even though it is not my intention to double up on existing work in the field, my investigation may occasionally lead me, of course, to the same places as those scholars who have charted these territories before me. In these instances, however, it is hoped that the definition of noise used here will always produce a different reading when this occurs and that, true to the operations of noise, these readings will arise in an in-between that will speak to both my understanding of noise and those sites where it is found.

More often than not, however, I will not venture into those sites and texts that crop up with alarming frequency in studies that set out to examine the history or culture of noise. The methodology that results from this choice, as well as the decision resolutely not to restrict noise to the auditory realm, makes this an extremely diverse work that wanders across many disciplinary boundaries; in concert with the hypotheses formulated on the ontology of noise herein, it is hoped that each of the different chapters will display both a certain consistency yet, at the same time, something of the nature of the various objects under examination in each part. Nonetheless, it should not be thought that this diversity is the result merely of a polemical impulse or an idiosyncratic stylistic quirk. If I choose most of the time to examine noise through a different set of sites and texts to those that have provided such fertile ground for many studies of noise in the recent past, this is because, oftentimes, according to the understanding of noise outlined here, many of those sites and texts may not be all that noisy after all.

Consistent with the operations of noise itself that is deployed only through the workings of difference, I will thus begin to define noise by looking at what it is not – even if what it is not is oftentimes what it has previously been said to be. Chapter One will examine some such figures and forms that have generally been considered paragons of noise. In particular, I will suggest that the Futurists, and particularly Luigi Russolo, widely proclaimed to have integrated noise into the realm of art, were in actuality not noisy at all. I will then turn my attention to the holy grail of noise studies, John Cage, whose 'silent' piece, 4'33", is similarly talked of in elegiac terms as the work which more than any other brings noise into the realm of music/art. I will suggest, however, that whilst there is undoubtedly noise in Cage's piece (just as there is in everything), the true noise to be found there has nothing to do with incidental sound, nor indeed with music.

Chapter Two will examine Jean-Paul Sartre's novel *Nausea* which is linked to noise not only by etymology but also because the noise of a phonograph record plays an important role in the novel. More than this, however, I will suggest that we can find in the novel's philosophical reflections (that are generated out of the main protagonist Roquentin's nausea) many similarities to the philosophical insights that are produced by noise. Ultimately, however, I will suggest that the importance of his insights is not fully apprehended by Roquentin, neither in regards to the importance of the phonograph's noise, nor in relation to the ramifications of his nauseous breakdown for an existential project. In this novel, in other words, noise will ultimately be elided and eradicated.

Following on from Roquentin's rejection of the operations of noise, I will show that noise has often been explicitly figured as something that is threatening, a danger to the autonomy and integrity of the organism, and thus a site of horror. Examining three horror films where a form of noise acts as a threat to life and thus the autonomy of individual identity, and touching on the phenomenon of Electronic Voice Phenomenon, I will examine how, in the popular imagination, noise has once again been figured at times as a disruptive or, in these instances, evil force that must be attenuated.

In these three chapters, the focus will thus be on cultural forms where there would seem to be a form of noise foregrounded yet where the operations of noise as understood here are either not present or else rejected. In the second Part of the book, I will move to an examination of some sites where noise would seem to be present or, conversely, entirely absent and suggest that, in actuality, noise is, respectively, absent and present. The chapters in this section will then suggest, through a number of case studies, why it is that noise is often so hard to identify or difficult to attend to.

Chapter Four begins with an examination of a series of 'noisy' computer fonts that simulate the print of early typewriters. I do this in order to instigate a reflection on the constant recoding that noise is subject to through time and technological change and suggest that noise is, perhaps understandably, very hard to recognise in its own time due to the dominant logic of technological progress. Turning explicitly to this logic by examining discourses of high-fidelity audio reproduction across time, I will suggest, however, that the difficulty of recognising noise in its own time is not ultimately an indication that the technological ideal of high-fidelity is brought ever closer by each successive technological advancement and new recording format. On the contrary, I will show that the CD is full of noise and do so via an in-depth analysis of a specific musical form, namely glitch. Glitch music is widely accepted as being music crafted from the failures of the hardware system used for the reproduction of sound. Examining closely critiques of glitch music, however, I contend that whilst glitch does indeed open up a site in which we are able to find noise defined according to the ontological taxonomy drawn up here, most existing commentaries on glitch fail to apprehend how the noise of glitch operates.

Recognising that the noise of digital media may well only reveal itself to us under the kind of abnormal operating procedures that glitch forces upon its technological medium, in Chapter Five I will turn to the analogue realm and ask why it is that the kind of noise figured here seems to be so hard to hear. I will suggest that the problem is similar to that faced by Roland Barthes when he seeks to uncover the ontology of photography (in *Camera Lucida*) and to talk about grain in music (in 'The Grain of the Voice') and fails in both cases to make a necessary modal distinction. For noise, I will suggest, changes its nature depending on the specific assemblage out of which it arises and we must then be very careful about the kinds of claims that we make at an ontological level. The temptation to make grand sweeping claims for noise that do not take account of this differential deployment of noise, I will suggest, has often led to inconsistent and self-contradictory statements about noise that, in turn, leave critics unsure of what precisely they are looking for. I then attempt to listen to noise without falling into this trap by turning my attention to Alvin Lucier's piece 'I am Sitting in a Room' and *musique concrète*, but find that some more work needs to be done to prepare the ground for this analysis since it is so hard to release music and sound from existing common sense definitions of what noise is in relation to them.

In the final part of the book, I thus turn my attention to various cultural expressions where we can find explicit, foregrounded instances of the kind of noise that I have set out to categorise. In the first two instances, sensitive to the difficulties of decoding noise in the auditory realm, I turn my attention away from the sonic to see what results are produced by an analysis of film and photography that explicitly sets out to examine noise in those realms.

Noise is oftentimes figured as an interference, as a glitch in the clean transmission of information, a point at which something is not quite right. Bearing this in mind, Chapter Six looks at cinematic noise in two works by maverick American filmmaker David Lynch. Through a close analysis of his first and (to date) last feature films, *Eraserhead* and *INLAND EMPIRE*, I suggest that something is indeed not right here and that his films are extremely noisy, but that this has nothing (or little) to do with their 'noise'-filled soundtracks. Whilst this kind of literal or common sense 'noise' may indeed point us towards the importance of noise as a fundamental principle for the construction and subsequent analysis of any Lynch film, I propose that a better understanding of the place of noise in his films forces us not only to reconsider many preconceptions about the meaning of his films, but also to rethink our critical strategies in the face of them. This is to say, then, that his films require us to attend to their noise and thus adopt a non-hermeneutic stance.

In Chapter Seven, meanwhile, I turn to photography and, specifically, the photographs of Thomas Ruff. Starting from an analysis of the series of photos that he has created in which the artefacts of the jpeg format are massively exaggerated, creating an indisputably noisy image, I will suggest that all of his photographic work is in fact inhabited by this kind of noise. When we attend to this noise, however, what it reveals to us is not merely something about the artefacts of the technological medium of photography, its mediality, but something about the very ontology of photography that has nothing to do with the analogue/digital divide.

Having suggested how noise might operate in some other, non-musical realms, in chapter eight I finally turn my attention back to music in order to probe the eternally fraught relation between music and noise. Examining some of the most common assumptions made about the ontology of music, I suggest that certain 'noisy' works render the assumptions of many such philosophical investigations deeply problematic. Through an analysis of *musique concrète* and Merzbow, indeed, I propose a new ontological taxonomy of music that is related to the ontological definition of music provided by Deleuze and Guattari yet which rejects outright the privilege that they accord to the refrain.

It may seem somewhat ironic or contradictory that a book claiming to move towards the ontology of noise ends up positing a new ontology of music. It is not, however, for the simple reason that noise, as it is figured here, always and necessarily points us towards the ontology of other things. Noise, arising as the artefact of the specific relation instigated between partial objects in a relational ontology, is, as I have suggested, nothing in and of itself. So whilst in what follows I will always be talking about noise, in order to do this I will necessarily have to talk about many other things, listening to noise awry.

Notes

1 Richard Huelsenbeck, 'En Avant Dada: A History of Dadaism', in *The Dada Painters and Poets: An Anthology*, ed. Robert Motherwell (orig. German 1920; New York: Wittenborn, 1951; reprint, New York: G. K. Hall, 1981), 26. For a discussion of avant-garde noise in relation to Huelsenbeck, *bruitism* and the Cabaret Voltaire, see Douglas Kahn, *Noise, Water, Meat: A History of Sound in the Arts* (Cambridge, MA: MIT Press, 1999), 44–53.

2 Aldous Huxley, *The Perennial Philosophy* (New York: Harper and Row Perennial Library, 1970), 218.

3 Garret Keizer, *The Unwanted Sound of Everything We Want: A Book About Noise* (New York: Public Affairs, 2010), 24.

4 For an excellent and accessible account of the use of noise in many scientific disciplines and particularly of its importance in Einstein's theories on Brownian motion, see Leon Cohen, 'The History of Noise (On the 100th Anniversary of its Birth)', *Signal Processing Magazine, IEEE*, 22, no. 6 (2005).

5 They quote from documents issuing from l'AFNOR (l'Association Française de Normalisation).

6 Marie-Claire Botte and René Chocholle, *Le Bruit*, 4th edn (Paris: PUF, 1984), 14; my translation. See also William Burns, *Noise and Man* (London: John Murray, 1968).

7 Warren Weaver, 'Recent Contributions to the Mathematical Theory of Communication', in Claude Shannon and Warren Weaver, *The Mathematical Theory of Communication* (Urbana: The University of Illinois Press, 1949), 95.

8 Weaver, 'Recent Contributions to the Mathematical Theory of Communication', 99.

9 Weaver, 'Recent Contributions to the Mathematical Theory of Communication', 109.

10 George Prochnik, *In Pursuit of Silence: Listening for Meaning in a World of Noise* (New York and London: Doubleday, 2010), 112.

11 Bart Kosko, *Noise* (London: Viking Penguin, 2006), 3.

12 Keizer, *The Unwanted Sound of Everything We Want*, 21–46.

13 Hillel Schwartz, *Making Noise: From Babel to the Big Bang and Beyond* (New York: Zone Books, 2011), 858.

14 It would of course be improper and unfair to go so far as to apply the epithet Macbeth uses to the authors of those already published studies on noise that fall into this category, for in spite of my frustrations with their refusal to probe seriously what it is that they are talking about, there are nonetheless some excellent scholarly works in the field already, many of which have explicitly informed the present study.

15 Gilles Deleuze and Félix Guattari, *A Thousand Plateaus: Capitalism and Schizophrenia* 2, trans. Brian Massumi (orig. French, 1980; Minneapolis: University of Minnesota Press, 1987), 3.

16 Caleb Kelly, *Cracked Media: The Sound of Malfunction* (Cambridge, MA: MIT Press, 2009), 61.

17 Frances Dyson, *Sounding New Media: Immersion and Embodiment in the Arts and Culture* (Berkeley: University of California Press, 2009), 189.

18 This should not be read as an outright dismissal of Dyson, whose study is an excellent and important work of scholarship in the field of noise studies. However, where we differ is in my suggestion that it is precisely the relational aspect of noise that enables us to talk of it as a quasi-material object/singular object, whilst for her it is precisely this aspect of it that makes of it an impossible and ineffable subject.

19 This is said in the full knowledge to many that it may seem somewhat counterintuitive or patently absurd to assert that there could be any such thing as an ontology of noise. Indeed, Keith Moliné closes his review of Paul Hegarty's book *Noise/Music: A History* by suggesting that 'the central question of course, must remain unanswered: just what is noise?', and he goes on to assure readers of *The Wire*, the magazine in which his review is published, that 'in the unlikely event that someone comes up with an answer', they will be the first to know (*The Wire: Adventures in Modern Music*, 285 (November 2007), 74.

20 Keizer, *The Unwanted Sound of Everything We Want*, 120. For a more objective survey of the power struggles occasioned by noise, see Karin Bijsterveld, 'The Diabolical Symphony of the Mechanical Age: Technology and Symbolism of Sound in European and North American Noise Abatement Campaigns, 1900–40', in *The Auditory Culture Reader*, ed. Michael Bull and Les Back (Oxford and New York: Berg, 2003), 165–89 [abridged from original published in *Social Studies of Science* 31, no. 1: 37–70].

21 Prochnik, *In Pursuit of Silence*, 128.

22 See Friedrich A. Kittler, *Gramophone, Film, Typewriter*, trans. Geoffrey Winthrop-Young and Michael Wutz (orig. German, 1986; Palo Aldo, CA: Stanford University Press, 1999).

23 Kosko, *Noise*, 3.

24 See Alexandre Kojève, *Introduction to the Reading of Hegel: Lectures on the Phenomenology of Spirit*, ed. Allan Bloom, trans. James Nichols (orig. French, 1947; Ithaca, NY: Cornell University Press, 1980).

25 Jacques Attali, *Noise: The Political Economy of Music*, trans. Brian Massumi (Minneapolis: University of Minnesota Press, 1985), 34.

26 Mary Russo and Daniel Warner, 'Rough Music, Futurism, and Postpunk Industrial Noise Bands', in *Audio Culture: Readings in Modern Music*, ed. Christoph Cox and Daniel Warner (New York and London: Continuum, 2004).

27 Paul Hegarty, *Noise/Music: A History* (New York and London: Continuum, 2007), 10; see also 138.

28 Hegarty, *Noise/Music*, ix.

29 Hegarty, *Noise/Music*, 3. In a separate article, Hegarty suggests something far closer to the line that will be adopted here and writes: 'Is noise subjective? Could we not instead say that noise has to do with the subject: that which occurs as/at the limit of the subject; that which signals an immanence outside of the subject/object divide, however reclothed in phenomenology?' (Paul Hegarty, 'Full With Noise: Theory and Japanese Noise Music', *ctheory*, a097 (2001), http://www.ctheory.net/articles.aspx?id=314 [accessed 15 May 2012]).

30 Kahn, *Noise, Water, Meat*, 21.

31 Adrienne Janus, 'Listening: Jean-Luc Nancy and the "Anti-Ocular" Turn in Continental Philosophy and Critical Theory', *Comparative Literature*, 63, no. 2 (2011).

32 Michael Bull and Les Back, 'Introduction: Into Sound', in *The Auditory Culture Reader*, ed. Michael Bull and Les Back (Oxford and New York: Berg, 2003), 5.

33 Jean-Luc Nancy, *Listening*, trans. Charlotte Mandell (orig. French, 2002; Bronx, NY: Fordham University Press, 2007), 6.

34 Dyson, *Sounding New Media*, 4–5.

35 Michel Serres, *Genesis* (orig. French, 1982; Ann Arbor: University of Michigan Press, 1995), 13.

36 Dyson, *Sounding New Media*, 10–11; see also 188 where noise becomes, 'like flux, vibration, pulse or signal […,] a good metaphor, its ceaseless movement between signal, music, rumor, and language unhing[ing] any dialectic with which it is engaged, or to which it is applied'.

37 Dyson, *Sounding New Media*, 11.

38 See Gilles Deleuze, *Expressionism in Philosophy: Spinoza*, trans. Martin Joughin (orig. French, 1968; New York: Zone Books, 1990).

39 Similarly, much of the vocabulary to be used throughout this study will sound somewhat Deleuzean, which might lead one to ask why a Deleuzean term could not have been found to replace noise, so as not to have to struggle with a term anchored in a long, complex and contested history and in little need, one would have thought, of further complication. The reason is quite simply because noise as figured here, the kind of noise which can be talked of in terms of ontology, is not equivalent to any single term in Deleuze's work, even if many of his concepts are conceptually sympathetic to what

is referred to here by the term noise – concepts such as, for instance, the Spinozist vocabulary of univocity, substance, attributes and modes, or, indeed, Deleuze's own terms such as the plane of desire/ immanence/consistency and becoming. Another reason, of course, is quite simply because whilst the findings of this study will differ radically from what has been said of noise in the past, its reflections will always arise out of a consideration of various kinds of noise that have been termed precisely this. So whilst noise is figured here in philosophical terms as the (potentially) perceptible aspect and by-product of the events that constitute both phenomenal and noumenal reality, this formulation is arrived at only through contact with many different kind of works where noise seems to arise at first under a somewhat different guise.

40 Whilst it may seem somewhat heretical to talk of essence in this way, I take my lead from Deleuze who writes: 'No doubt, if one insists, the word "essence" might be preserved, but only on condition of saying that the essence is precisely the accident, the event, the sense; not simply the contrary of what is ordinarily called the essence but the contrary of the contrary: multiplicity is no more appearance than essence, no more multiple than one' (Gilles Deleuze, *Difference and Repetition*, trans. Paul Patton (orig. French, 1968; London: The Athlone Press, 1994; New York: Columbia University Press, 1994), 191).

41 Prochnik, *In Pursuit of Silence*, 80–1.

42 Prochnik, *In Pursuit of Silence*, 81.

43 Prochnik, *In Pursuit of Silence*, 81.

44 Prochnik, *In Pursuit of Silence*, 81.

45 Hegarty, *Noise/Music*, 5.

46 Brandon LaBelle, *Background Noise: Perspectives on Sound Art* (New York and London: Continuum, 2006), 224–5.

47 Paul R. Kohl, 'Reading Between the Lines: Music and Noise in Hegemony and Resistance', *Popular Music and Society*, 21, no. 3 (1997), 9.

48 It should be noted that the notion of *resistance* also plays a role in Michel Serres' work on noise, particularly in *The Parasite*, trans. Lawrence R. Schehr (orig. French, 1980; Minneapolis: University of Minnesota Press, 2007). However, there is here a major difference insofar as in Serres' work, the parasite that introduces noise into the system is always a third term (as in Shannon and Weaver's communication theory) rather than the result of the operations of the system itself. He writes, for instance, 'The parasite, nesting on

the flow of the relation, is in third position' (53). It must be noted, nonetheless, that this line is not always consistent in this work, since he takes a line with more in common with his writings in *Genesis* elsewhere in *The Parasite*. Indeed, well before the parasite is aligned with thirdness, he suggests that '[the rats] are, as the saying goes, always already there. Part of the building. Mistakes, wavy lines, confusion, obscurity are part of knowledge; noise is part of communication, part of the house' (12), and that 'The difference is part of the thing itself, and perhaps it even produces the thing. Maybe the radical origin of things is really that difference, even though classical rationalism damned it to hell. In the beginning was the noise' (13). The seeming inconsistency of this line may well be due to the fact, as Cary Wolfe suggests in his introduction to this work, that this is an experimental work in many respects, designed to figure the changing and unstable operations of noise in its very style. As he writes, 'it is noise that Serres's writing doesn't just talk about but generates' (Cary Wolfe, 'Introduction to the New Edition', in Michael Serres, *The Parasite*, xiii).

49 Marshall McLuhan, *Understanding Media: The Extensions of Man*, 2nd edn. (New York: McGraw Hill, 1964; New York: New American Library, 1964), 23–35.

50 McLuhan, *Understanding Media*, 24.

51 Frances Dyson suggests why this particular story has been complex and misleading when she writes 'Establishing a credible, though unobtrusive, interface between reality and artifice, the real and the reproduced, has been a constant preoccupation of media technology. Like the speaking tube of deific transmission, it has been necessary to construct and then deny a mechanism that channels, delimits, transduces, and sanitizes the materiality it transports' (*Sounding New Media*, 47).

52 Kosko, *Noise*, 66.

53 Kosko, *Noise*, 66.

54 Note that one would be perfectly able in formulating this idea to take a detour through Henri Bergson's *Matter and Memory*, trans. N. M. Paul and W. S. Palmer (orig. French, 1896; New York: Zone Books, 1994), in which matter is always imbricated in a process of becoming and vibrating (208).

55 In the light of these assertions, it is my hope that this study might be considered an instantiation of what Karen Barad terms a 'posthumanist performativity'. See Karen Barad, 'Posthumanist Performativity: Toward an Understanding of How Matter Comes

to Matter', in *Belief, Bodies, and Being: Feminist Reflections on Embodiment*, ed. Deborah Orr, Linda Lopez McAlister, Eileen Kahl and Kathleen Earle (Lanham, MD: Rowman and Littlefield, 2006).

56 Serres, *Genesis*, 61.

57 Serres, *Genesis*, 111.

58 Serres, *Genesis*, 22.

59 Serres, *The Parasite*, 52.

60 Serres, *Genesis*, 13.

61 Brian Massumi, *A User's Guide to* Capitalism and Schizophrenia: *Deviations from Deleuze and Guattari* (Cambridge, MA: MIT Press, 1992), 170.

62 Massumi, *A User's Guide*, 170.

63 Massumi, *A User's Guide*, 170.

64 It should be noted that noise plays a somewhat important role in Deleuze's *The Logic of Sense*, but in this work it is generally figured as being opposed to meaning and language and is for the most part left behind in the passage from noise to its others, especially the passage from noise to voice. See, for instance, Gilles Deleuze, *The Logic of Sense*, trans. Mark Lester with Charles Stivale (orig. French, 1969; New York: Columbia University Press, 1990), 194.

65 Deleuze and Guattari, *A Thousand Plateaus*, 343.

66 Deleuze and Guattari, *A Thousand Plateaus*, 343–4.

67 J. R. Pierce, *Symbols, Signals and Noise: The Nature and Process of Communication* (London: Hutchinson, 1962), 251.

68 It is interesting to note there is here a lexical affinity with Deleuze's work *The Logic of Sense* in which great emphasis is placed on the *effects* of bodies in a relational ontology. He writes: 'The *effects* are not bodies but, properly speaking, "incorporeal" entities. They are not physical qualities and properties, but rather logical or dialectical attributes. They are not things or facts but events. We cannot say that they exist, but rather that they subsist or inhere (having this minimum of being which is appropriate to that which is not a thing, a nonexisting entity)' (Deleuze, *The Logic of Sense*, 4–5).

PART 1

CHAPTER ONE

The (Not So) Noisy Elephants in the Room

Sound

The most obvious starting point for noise in music is Luigi Russolo's manifesto The Art of Noises *written in 1913. In it Russolo, in an overtly futurist fashion, hails the modern noise of the industrialized urban environment, calling for these noises to enter music [...].*

Russolo's manifesto and his book published in 1916 were highly influential on a number of composers of the time, including Claude Debussy, Igor Stravinsky, Darius Milhaud, Arthur Honegger, Edgard Varèse and Henry Cowell. He is also now recognized as a key precursor to much of the 'noisy' experimental music produced in the second half of the twentieth century.[1]

The most important single achievement in the early history of avant-garde noise was the Italian Futurist Luigi Russolo's The Art of Noises. *Included under this term were his manifesto of 1913, a book of 1916, the music he developed through the design of his new noise-intoning instruments, the intonarumori, and a new form of notation.*[2]

Futurist Luigi Russolo was one of the first in the early twentieth century to put the institutionalized division between music (Russolo mostly uses the term 'sounds' instead of 'music') and noises on the agenda.[3]

C'est surtout Luigi Russolo (1855–1947), qui vécut en Italie et en France, qui conçoit le «bruitisme». En 1913, il abandonne la peinture et se consacre à la construction et au perfectionnement de bruiteurs. Il pense qu'il faut écouter les bruits du monde et ceux des machines en marche pour faire une musique «concrète».[4]

There was also the case of Luigi Russolo, who dreamt the dream of noise-music.[5]

The first intimations of a new attitude towards noise occurred well into the age of the phonograph but were strangely independent of it. The immediate inspiration for Russolo's noise instruments, which he presented at concerts in Milan, Paris and London in 1913, came from fellow Italian Futurists like Marinetti, for whom noise signalled the ascendancy of the modern age. Sound is defined (wrote Russolo) as the result of a succession of regular and periodic vibrations, while noise is caused by irregular motion.[6]

In 1913, Pratella introduced his music at a concert at the Teatro Costanzi in Rome. He conducted his piece called Musica Futurista *for orchestra, much to the delight of his Futurist compatriots. One painter, Luigi Russolo (1855–1947), was so inspired that he quickly wrote his own manifesto,* The Art of Noise *(1913). Russolo's ideas were more extreme than Pratella's. Pratella's objective was to develop new pitch and rhythm systems to expand the potential of existing instruments. Russolo envisioned entirely new ways of making music through the use of noise. He not only put his ideas on paper but immediately abandoned painting and devoted himself full-time to the design and invention of new mechanical noise-makers to produce his music.*[7]

Disappointed by Pratella's dependence on traditional musical instruments to create untraditional music, Russolo began immediately to theorize, and then to build, new kinds of instruments that he called 'noise-intoners' (intonarumori). [...] Machines, having sapped all vitality from the old music, would now become the basis for a vital new music.[8]

In Italy, where the Futurists were promoting an art of speed, struggle, aggression, and destruction, Luigi Russolo issued a manifesto for a 'MUSIC OF NOISE' and began to construct noise-instruments with which to produce the roaring, whistling, whispering, screeching, banging, and groaning sounds that he had predicted in his pamphlet.[9]

Russolo invented an orchestra of noise makers, consisting of buzzers, howlers and other gadgets calculated to advance his philosophy. The 'pastorale' and the 'nocturne' give way before machine-music like Honegger's Pacific 231 *(1924), an imitation of a locomotive, Antheil's* Ballet mécanique *(1926), which employed a number of airplane propellers, Prokofioev's* Pas d'acier *(Dance of Steel), Mossolov's* Iron Foundry *and Carlos Chavez's* HP *(Horse-power) all dating from 1928. This blurring of the edges between music and environmental sounds is the most striking feature of twentieth-century music. Finally in the practices of* musique concrète *it became possible to insert any sound from the environment into a composition via tape; while in electronic music the hard-edge sound of the tone generator may be indistinguishable from the police siren or the electric tooth-brush.*[10]

Fury

A notion of sonic warfare lies at the heart of modern experimental music and takes us back to the apex of the sonic avant-garde, to Luigi Russolo's Futurist manifesto for music, The Art of Noises, *which glorified explosions, rifle fire, and the dissonance of industrial machinery as an assault on the deadened sensorium of classical music and bourgeois aesthetics. The futurist* art of war in the art of noise *framed cultural innovation in the field of music as a sensory war in which the stakes were no less than the distribution and hierarchical stratification of the nervous system. A crystallization of the belligerent libidinal field of the early twentieth century, futurism processed the schizzed and shell-shocked psyche of the battlefield, seeking a new synthesis – one claiming to break with the organic wholeness of the past in favor of a technical enhancement [...], a rewiring of the body and its sonic sensations.*[11]

Luigi Russolo, one of the early and most enthusiastic young followers of Marinetti, was a signatory of many of the most audacious and interesting futurist manifestos. Russolo seems to have endorsed all the major principles of Marinetti's futurist program: radical and innovative interventions into the art forms; the glorification of the machine and the virile qualities of speed, volume, and power associated with it; the spectacularity of war; and the eternal exuberance of youth and cultural revolution. The old, the traditional, and the feminine were relegated to the 'silence of the ancient world'; modernity in Futurist terms was noisy. The futurist project included not only the much-quoted manifestos (many of which were declaimed from theatre stages), but their

enactment in and intrusion into various political scenarios, trans-
forming and aestheticizing the tumultuous activities of modern
life.[12]

A year later Russolo gave a concert in Milan featuring specially
made and named instruments of his own invention, including a
'howler', a 'gurgler', a 'croaker', and a 'roarer'. Unimpressed, his
audience began making some noise of its own. One might suppose
this would have pleased the Futurists – why not a 'cat-caller' and
a 'boo-maker' to add to the mix? – but instead Russolo's artistic
cronies jumped into the seats and began punching people, eleven of
whom wound up in the hospital.[13]

The Intonarumori *caused a sensation and were presented in*
salons, concert halls and theatres to riotous acclaim. The usual
form of presentation was the Serata Futurista *or Futurist Evening.*
This was a chaotic mixture of theatre, concert and political rally.
The events were announced well in advance and the venues were
always packed with an audience high on wild anticipation. The
Futurists' reputation went before them, thanks to Marinetti's
publicity skills, so the outcome of the evening was inevitable.
Insults were hurled back and forth between the performers and
the audience, fights broke out and riots ensued pouring out into
the streets, bars and cafes. There were always indignant outcries
in the following day's press thus fuelling the publicity machine
and ensuring maximum capacity audiences wherever the Futurists
went. Violence, chaos and noise spoke of the irreversible changes
in society's hierarchical structures that would occur as a result of
the cataclysm that would shortly engulf Europe.[14]

The first public performance of the noise orchestra took place
on 21 April 1914 at the Teatro del Verme in Milan. [...] As soon as
the orchestra began to play, the crowd broke into a violent uproar.
The musicians continued undaunted while fellow Futurists hurled
themselves into the audience and defended the Art of Noises with
their fists. In the end, eleven people were sent to the hospital, none
of them Futurists, as belligerence was a central component of the
Futurist approach to art and life, and many were talented boxers.[15]

Marinetti and a contingent of his rat-tat-tat *pack climbed*
to the top of the clock tower in Venice's Piazza San Marco. It
was no accident that they'd chosen to launch their movement in
one of the world's most famously quiet cities. Leaning over the
tower's balcony, Marinetti's disciples proceeded to dump 800,000

pamphlets titled 'Against Past-loving Venice' down onto the heads of the bewildered public below, while he howled through a megaphone: 'Enough! Stop whispering obscene invitations to every mortal passerby, O Venice, old procuress!'[16]

* * *

The story of noise in the twentieth century has many different sides and they rarely align. As we have seen in our introduction, noise elicits impassioned responses from those who are fond of it and find in it all kinds of revolutionary or creative potential and, conversely, those who despise it and wish to have done with it in many or all of its various forms and guises. Whilst we find this divide in many of the disciplinary fields where noise is of concern, be this communications theory or electrical engineering, the debate seems to become most heated when noise is talked of as either a cultural expression – where it is oftentimes held in opposition to music – or else a by-product of our increasingly mechanised societies in a post-Industrial age. What is more, these two distinct understandings of noise are often conflated together, these two essentially distinct narratives converging often, it would seem, because of a sense that the increased noise of the world resulting from its increased mechanisation could but lead to works of art that integrated noise into their palette in order better to reflect the world in which they were born.[17] Such a move, of course, is condemned or lamented by some and praised by others. And yet, regardless of which side of the fence such commentators find themselves on, authors on both sides of this ideological divide seem to find some common ground in relation to the figures that they posit as foundational in the histories that they recount, even if, of course, these figures are mobilised for very different ends in each case. As the cacophony of quotations that opens this chapter should hopefully indicate all by itself, the figure invoked more than any other in these conflicting histories is without doubt Luigi Russolo, closely followed by John Cage.

R. Murray Schafer's *The Soundscape: Our Sonic Environment and the Tuning of the World* might be considered the ur-work of the anti-noise lobby. For Schafer, our soundscape, which is to say the sonic environment in which we unavoidably bathe at every moment, has become populated with more and more unpleasant noises, in greater numbers and emitted at greater volume as the technological advances of post-Industrial society have frogmarched us ever onwards in the name of progress. For Schafer, however, as with any environmental pollution, what this represents for us as humans is not so much an ameliorated condition but, rather, an impoverished one, and he calls for us to retune our ears, to elevate ourselves out of noise in order to bring about a renewed recognition of the diversity of sounds, an appreciation of the beauty of certain sounds lost in the amplified maelstrom of the modern world. Only then, for Schafer, will we be able to distinguish between certain sounds and appreciate the 'good' ones whilst attenuating the others (read 'noise'). Keen to construct such a hierarchical and value-laden taxonomy, Schafer is understandably resistant to the integration of all sounds into the realm of music that takes place in the twentieth century, and blames the noise pollution problems of our era largely on the shoulders of music educators who 'have failed to give the public a total schooling in soundscape awareness'.[18] Schafer, however, reserves special ire for John Cage for having 'opened the doors of the concert hall to let the traffic noise mix with his own',[19] and Russolo, about whom he writes the following:

> Russolo's experiments mark a flash-point in the history of aural perception, a reversal of figure and ground, a substitution of garbage for beauty.[20]

For Schafer, it is Russolo and the year 1913 that mark the tipping point, the moment of no return that led us to the mess we find ourselves and our soundscape in now. As he writes:

> By 1913 Luigi Russolo was able to point out that the new sensibility of man depended on his appetite for noise. Today, as the machines whirl in the hearts of our cities day and night, destroying, erecting, destroying, the significant battleground of the modern world has become the neighbourhood Blitzkrieg. It is another reminder of the truth of Constantin Doxiadis's statement that for the first time in history we are less safe inside the city gates than outside them.[21]

Whilst many other volumes have continued the spirit of Schafer's work since 1977 (which is perhaps my own watershed, as 1913 is for Schafer) and railed against noise on purely aesthetic or subjective grounds, in recent times some more sober and considered responses to the intersection of urban/industrial and avant-garde artistic practices have appeared in which the authors chart how the increasing noise of post-industrial urban society has been integrated into art in a productive manner. Notable among such studies is Emily Thompson's *The Soundscape of Modernity: Architectural Acoustics and the Culture of Listening in America, 1900–1933*.[22] In this work, Thompson charts the ways in which 'the constant sonic background that has always accompanied human civilization'[23] was intensified through urbanisation, then transformed in early twentieth century America by the onset of industrialisation which introduced a whole new array of noises into the urban soundscape. Thompson not only provides a history of various noise abatement movements and the effects that the unprecedented levels of noise have had on architectural practice and on the development of building materials, however, but also tells the story of those inventors and artists who were excited by the noise of this new world and welcomed its din into their work.

Russolo is an important figure in Thompson's study also (although, interestingly, she does not mention Cage), and she provides an excellent and much more nuanced account of Russolo's attempts to create 'music out of the noise of the modern world' than does Schafer, placing his experiments in the broader context of the Futurists' integration of noise into other kinds of artistic endeavours.[24] More than this, however, she conducts a broad survey of the history of noise in modern music, from the integration of the sounds of the city in jazz, to Henry Cowell's invocation to rethink the barrier between music and noise, to Charles Ives' representations of city noises into his compositions, to Ferruccio Busoni's desire to access every possible gradation of the octave and not merely those tones situated on the tempered system, to Edgar Varèse and George Antheil's determination to transform noise into music, to Lev Termen's (aka Leon Theremin) invention of a new instrument, the Etherophone, Theremin Vox or simply Theremin, via a creative reappropriation of the feedback squeal produced when an early radio listener's hand approached the tuning dial, thereby entering the locally generated electromagnetic field surrounding the receiver.[25]

Whilst it would be churlish to claim that the artists that Thompson refers to and who explicitly invoke noise are not, in fact,

talking about noise at all, it is possible to suggest that the definition
of noise in operation in the examples Thompson provides is what
we have termed a common sense definition of noise and thus very
different to that used here. What I would like to suggest, then,
is that if we put into operation the definition of noise proposed
herein that enables us to talk about noise from an ontological point
of view, it may be the case that the apparent integration of noise
into these various artistic palettes in fact performs an erasure or
abnegation of the kind of noise posited in this study. In jazz and
the work of Ives, for instance, the imitation of sounds of the city by
conventional instruments merely enforces a rigid representational
hierarchy in which there is a strict equivalence between original
and copy, as music attempts to become a mimetic reproduction of
an external reality. There is here no sense, then, in which noise is
anything other than a sound that can be repeated or imitated in
order to paint a quasi-faithful representation of an external reality,
no sense in which noise resists the transmission of content because
it is here merely content, a mode of signification. What is more, not
only does such a conception of noise take it to be something that
is fundamentally different to what noise actually *is* or might be,
such uses of noise oftentimes result in another kind of abnegation
of noise since, integrated into a 'musical' or organised structure
in this way, noise itself becomes more acceptable, losing much of
its oppositional nature and becoming then something else entirely.
This is a movement that can be found again and again in the work
of Jacques Attali and Paul Hegarty, but it is present in Thompson's
book also. Indeed, she notes how William Carlos Williams and
Paul Rosenfeld were able, after listening to Antheil's *Ballet pour
Instruments Mécaniques et Percussion* and the music of Varèse,
respectively, 'to conquer noise, to transcend its offensive character,
by hearing it in a new way' and thus transform their own creative
practice.[26] And we might say something similar of Leon Theremin
who effectively tamed noise, converting it into an ordered, controllable musical expression, since although the instrument to which
he gave his name operated on the same principles as the radio
feedback that had inspired its creation, the noise which had previously been a by-product became instead the primary product of the
instrument. Whereas the feedback howl of the radio might then be
considered properly noisy insofar as it is a parasitic element that
interrupts the transmission of the message (the radio program

listened to), in (or rather near) Theremin's hands it became the thing to be listened to and not an index of the relation by which that content came to be expressed or transmitted.

In brief, if we wish to talk of noise in such a way that it is no longer a purely arbitrary and subjective qualifier but, rather, something that expresses a consistency in and of itself, it may be that the history of noise in the twentieth century needs to be rewritten, for it may be that many of the last century's most infamous noisemongers may not in actuality be all that noisy. I have (too) briefly suggested how this might be so in relation to some of the examples proffered by Thompson, and it would no doubt be possible to do this in more depth for all of her examples and many more besides. This is, however, not my primary concern in this book and I wish first and foremost to understand how works other than those that reappear so obsessively might be figured as noisy in this other way. Nonetheless, in what remains of this chapter I do want to show how it is possible to say that some of the most (apparently) indisputably noisy sites of cultural production are perhaps not all that noisy in an absolute sense. In order to do this, I will turn my attention to the two figures mobilised again and again in studies of noise, the paragons of noise in the histories written by noiseniks and Schaferians alike. I am talking, of course, about Luigi Russolo and John Cage.

Signifying

Luigi Russolo, futurist painter and later composer, created a series of noisemakers or *intonarumori*, instruments intended to introduce into music sounds and timbres which more faithfully represented the contemporary reality of the Futurists' post-industrial machine age. This is not to say that his noisemakers were intended solely to mimic the sounds of industrial society and its machinery (although many thought they did, an accusation which rankled with Russolo and Marinetti so much because, no doubt, of its justness),[27] for Russolo also wanted them to reflect the increasing complexity of the age and to express that complexity through other means than mere polyphony and harmonic dissonance – as had been the case increasingly in late nineteenth and early twentieth century music.[28]

In Marinetti's account of the foundational moments of the Futurist movement, it is the noise of public transport and automobiles that provides the originary moment of inspiration and drive. He writes:

> Suddenly we jumped, hearing the mighty noise of the huge double-decker trams that rumbled by outside, ablaze with colored lights, like villages on holiday suddenly struck and uprooted by the flooding Po and dragged over falls and through gorges to the sea.
> Then the silence deepened. But, as we listened to the old canal muttering its feeble prayers and the creaking bones of sickly palaces above their damp green beards, under the windows we suddenly heard the famished roar of automobiles.
> 'Let's go!' I said. 'Friends, away! Let's go! Mythology and the Mystic Ideal are defeated at last. We're about to see the Centaur's birth and, soon after, the first flight of Angels!' ...[29]

For Russolo also, noise was unmistakably associated with the new technological condition of his time, and was as such opposed to nature. As he writes:

> Ancient life was all silence. In the 19th Century, with the invention of machines, Noise was born. Today, Noise is triumphant and reigns sovereign over the sensibility of men. Through many centuries life unfolded silently, or at least quietly. The loudest of noises that interrupted this silence was neither intense, nor prolonged nor varied. After all, if we overlook the exceptional movements of the earth's crust, hurricanes, storms, avalanches, and waterfalls, nature is silent.[30]

For Russolo to posit such a mutually exclusive binary between music and nature may, of course, seem somewhat strange given his later pronouncement that 'Every manifestation of life is accompanied by noise. Noise is thus familiar to our ear and has the power of immediately recalling life itself',[31] but this inconsistency ultimately matters little. For what mattered most about noise, and indeed what mattered most for the Futurists in general, was that noise could be theorised as oppositional in relation to the established order and thus capable of producing shock, outrage and henceforth change. If Russolo then writes that 'we delight much more in combining in our thoughts the noises of trams, of automobile engines, of carriages and brawling crowds, than in hearing again the "Eroica" or the "Pastorale"',[32] this is quite simply because the former noises were so anathema to the traditions that created the latter pieces, were considered to be incommensurable with artistic expression. Noise was, this is to say, eminently capable of attacking the petrified, passéist attitudes of complacent bourgeois society that the Futurist Manifesto was explicitly formulated to combat, expose, struggle against or at least ridicule. Thus, the Futurist movement set out to 'destroy the museums, libraries, academies of every kind, [...] fight moralism, feminism, every opportunistic or utilitarian cowardice'.[33]

Yet its most oppositional and confrontational declaration of intent was even more extreme, stating in point seven of the manifesto:

Except in struggle, there is no more beauty. No work without an aggressive character can be a masterpiece. Poetry must be conceived as a violent attack on unknown forces, to reduce and prostrate them before man.[34]

Whilst statements such as this undoubtedly spring from the Futurists' desire to provoke violent reactions and their apparent love of a good fight – both Russolo, Marinetti and the local press of the cities where Futurist events took place delighted in detailing the commotion, brouhaha and fisticuffs that often accompanied their performances – there is, perhaps especially in regards to noise, more than just a lively anarchism here. For Marinetti, noise was itself produced in violence, in a percussive act as different elements entered into conflict with each other. As he writes, 'noise is the result of rubbing or striking rapidly moving solids, liquids, or gases'[35]; and elsewhere, 'noise [is] the result of the rubbing together or the collision of solids, liquids, or gases in fast motion'.[36] Whilst this account of the ontology of noise leaves much to be desired, it is nonetheless significant for an understanding of the significance of noise for the Futurists. For even though Marinetti does not make the link himself, conceived of as here, noise becomes that element best able to express the synaesthetic experience of tactilism since, produced through a physical, percussive action, it is able (like sound more generally as Marinetti states) to express 'the dynamism of objects'.[37] Indeed, breaking through the rigid hierarchy of the senses when classified and separated in a rigid taxonomy ('The distinction between the five senses is arbitrary', writes Marinetti[38]), noise becomes that element, so desired by the Futurists, that would be capable of liberating the fixed form of matter itself in our perceptive field, of expressing the process inherent in all material essences before perception or usage petrifies them in a structure signalling death. As Marinetti writes of architecture:

> The frame of a house in construction symbolizes our burning passion for the coming-into-being of things.
> Things already built and finished, bivouacs of cowardice and sleep, disgust us!
> We love only the immense, mobile, and impassioned framework that we can consolidate, always differently, at every moment, according to the ever-changing moods of the winds, with the red concrete of our bodies set firm by our wills.[39]

Whilst inextricably linked to matter, in Russolo's conception of it, noise was able to resist this kind of petrification because of its inherent complexity. Indeed, drawing a clear distinction between sound and noise that once again highlights the oppositional, disruptive nature of the latter, Russolo writes:

> Sound, estranged from life, always musical, something in itself, an occasional not a necessary element, has become for our ear what for the eye is a too familiar sight. Noise instead, arriving confused and irregular from the irregular confusion of life, is never revealed to us entirely and always holds innumerable surprises.[40]

As should be clear from this, in many of the Futurists' writings, noise thus takes on many of the qualities that I wish to impute to it also. In Marinetti and Russolo's view, indeed, noise appears to signal the irreducible expressivity of everything and the incommensurability of identity, the fundamental internal oppositionality that, as argued here, is one of its (non-) defining characteristics. The sentiment expressed here, indeed, resonates deeply with Roquentin's nauseous vision of the true nature of existence that we will go on to examine in the next chapter. Just like Roquentin, however, as we will see, the Futurists did not follow through on the full implications of their insight. Indeed, noise for the Futurists is always ultimately recontained and limited, bounded by the will to dominate that was so prevalent in the extremely masculinist, virile, proto-Fascist Futurist mentality. Thus, Marinetti's advocacy of a flowing, freeform architecture (a beautiful, fictional description of which can be found in his novel *The Untamables*) is ultimately cemented in place by 'the red concrete of our bodies, set firm by our wills',[41] whilst Russolo, in spite of his adulation in praise of the uncontainable complexity of noise, ultimately desires only to control and contain noise completely, to harness it for musical (or aesthetic) ends with a strict taxonomic categorisation and his *intonarumori*, each of which would correspond to one of these categories.[42] We thus find many contradictions in his proclamations and he states, for instance:

> Stir the senses and you will also stir the brain! Stir the senses with the unexpected, the mysterious, the unknown, and you will truly move the soul, intensely and profoundly! Here lies the destined and absolute necessity of borrowing the timbres of sounds directly from the timbres of the noises of life.[43]

And yet he goes on to assert that 'the ear must hear these noises mastered, servile, completely controlled conquered and constrained to become elements of art'.[44]

The very oppositional potential of noise that attracted the Futurists to it was, then, ultimately that which prevented them from retaining the noisiness of noise in their use of it. So while, as Russolo states, 'Noise must become a prime element to mould into the work of art', in order to do this it was necessary for it 'to lose its accidental character in order to become an element sufficiently abstract to achieve the necessary transformation of any prime element into [sic] abstract element of art'.[45] In other words, it was necessary for noise no longer to be noise. It is surely for this reason also that noise in Russolo's art always ultimately ended up being merely imitative of the industrial and mechanical sounds that spawned it in spite of his constant declamation that '*The Art of Noises* would certainly not limit itself to an impressionistic and fragmentary reproduction of the noises of life'.[46]

Indeed, as he states just before this, '*As it comes to us from life*, in fact, noise immediately reminds us of life itself, making us think of the things that produce the noises that we are hearing',[47] and noise thus always maintains a strictly referential or indexical relation to the matter or content of the world that it has the potential to destabilise.

The Futurists' inability fully to exploit the potential of noise (or, we might say, to integrate noise into their aesthetic at all) can be easily explained by their progressivist and triumphalist mindset which abhorred 'grotesque funeral of passéist Beauty (romantic, symbolist, and decadent)' and praised instead 'Geometric and Mechanical Splendor',[48] or even by their elaboration and embrace of the fundamental tenets of modernism critiqued by Bois and Krauss.[49] What is more important for the purpose of the present study, however, is what the implications of this failure fully to integrate noise into the Futurist aesthetic means for a history of noise in the arts. For Russolo's *The Art of Noises* is, in very many accounts of either noise in music or electronic music more generally, posited as the direct precursor for many different and diverse musical movements or individual composers throughout the twentieth century from *musique concrète* to Cage, Ruttman to industrial, Messiaen to minimalism, as though all of these disparate centres of expression were somehow situated on a continuum which was not merely historical. This is indeed what seems to be suggested by the inclusion of Luigi and Antonio Russolo's *Corale* (1921) as the first track on the first disk of the first volume of the now five-volume set, *An Anthology of Noise and Electronic Music*. (And let me add that whilst not surprising in and of itself, since for Schafer and many others Russolo's work is the watershed moment,[50] it is a little surprising that this should be intimated by this compilation which is published on the sub rosa label which professes a Deleuzean heritage[51] and thus rejects the very possibility of considering history to be a closed and stable field – each volume is subtitled an *a*-chronology –, preferring to talk of plateaus and strata and maintaining that the line drawn between movements and composers is curved and not straight.[52]) What is perhaps slightly odd about this is that the privileged position Russolo is accorded here might be seen to imply that he constitutes not only the first point in a lineage of 'noise' music, but also in a history of electronic music, even though Russolo's instruments were primarily not electronic but mechanical. I would suggest, however, that it is slightly odd not only for this reason but also because of the unproblematic acceptance of Russolo's work as noise.

To suggest that *The Art of Noises* in both its written and musical forms is not actually all that noisy is not to deny that it would have been considered extremely noisy and oppositional by its first audience, nor indeed that it would still be considered relatively noisy and confrontational by many audiences today. It is rather to suggest that, in spite of Russolo and Marinetti's intuitions regarding the disruptive power of noise and its ability to evoke or bring into being the mysterious and unknown, their subsequent theorisations and deployments of noise within the masculinist, progressivist rhetoric and discourse of the triumphalist modernism that was Futurism do not allow this potential fully to come to fruition and its disruption then remains purely contextual, an affront to existing discourses and paradigms. Indeed, given the industrial, technological and mechanical objects which served as the primary inspiration for Futurism's whole aesthetic project, and which themselves marked a radical material historical break and subsequent paradigm shift in many areas of late nineteenth and early twentieth-century post-industrial society, it is entirely feasible that the Futurists' ultimate desire and attempts to harness and control noise are indicative not only of their proto-Fascist tendencies, but of a more general *malaise* which, underneath the bravado, expresses an underlying insecurity or fear in front of such radical breaks, changes and new modes of production. Indeed, one could argue that the intuition of the Futurists regarding the incommensurability and thus ultimate meaninglessness that noise potentially augured was simply too much to bear or, more literally, that the massive proliferation of new technologies and the exponential increase in the *speed* of society that is commented on so frequently by Marinetti signalled an unknowable and thus threatening future. Given this possibility, is it not in fact possible that *The Art of Noises* might be in the final analysis not a radical confrontational, aggressive work but, rather, a defensive, reactionary move which wishes to contain phenomena perceived to be threatening within the strictly delimited and apprehensible bounds of representation and a coherent aesthetic? If this is indeed the case, then Russolo's *Art of Noises* is far from the radical break that it is often assumed to be.[53]

Nothing

If Russolo constitutes the earliest and seemingly obligatory case study for any scholarly work dealing with the conjunction of noise and art, the other unavoidable figure who must be attended to in all work of this kind is, of course, John Cage, and especially his now infamous piece *4'33"*. Indeed, to write a book on noise and not confront Cage would be once again to tiptoe around the elephant in the room or, perhaps, to pretend it wasn't there because it was so quiet. Let me explain.

The story hardly needs telling again, for it has been re-recounted so many times. Cage, in an anechoic chamber, expects to hear silence but is instead assaulted by the sounds of his own body. Realising that there is then no such thing as silence, he writes *4'33"*, a piece which instructs the performer merely to mark off time in three movements during a period of four minutes and 33 seconds, and otherwise to sit motionless at his/her instrument, thereby allowing the ambient sounds of the performance space and its surroundings to invade the aural consciousness of the audience and become the musical text. In spite of its obvious radicality, however, the result of Cage's attempts to erase entirely the boundary between music and sound, silence and noise is arguably no different from that of Russolo, which is to say that Cage might ultimately be said to eradicate noise entirely through this gesture. For, by sculpting his musical text from the incidental sounds and noises of the concert venue, it was Cage's desire, as has been stated by many, to render all sound musical, converting noise into the primary, desired content of his piece and therefore leaving noise behind in the process. This point has been made very well by Douglas Kahn who, what is more, establishes the same link between Cage and Russolo as that made here. Kahn writes:

> Even this century's most noted radical attacks upon music – conducted, as they were, under the sign of noise and sound – ultimately returned to music. Luigi Russolo's 'art of noises' was recuperated immediately into the goal of 'a great renovation of music'; Edgar Varèse's 'liberation of sound' was a motto of retreat when compared to Russolo's position; and at the core of John Cage's emancipatory project was a will to impose musical

precepts upon all sounds. The main avant-garde strategy in music from Russolo through Cage quite evidently relied upon notions of noise and worldly sound as 'extra-musical'; what was outside musical materiality was then progressively brought back into the fold in order to rejuvenate musical practice.[54]

This, of course, is a movement that we have already observed often, noise becoming music and serving a political function in the process, its recuperation bringing about a necessary shift in a clearly demarcated field. I have suggested that this is problematic for an analysis of noise that wishes to speak of it ontologically because, whilst ontology may be conceptualised relationally, the transmogrification of noise observed here is closer to a transubstantiation. Kahn suggests another reason why such a move is problematic, however, arguing that the ground on which this transformation takes place brings about a necessary separation between the musical text and the *realpolitik* which others claim this strategy engages. He suggests:

for a sound to be 'musicalized' in this strategy, it had to conform materially to ideas of sonicity, that is, ideas of a sound stripped of its associative attributes, a minimally coded sound existing in close proximity to 'pure' perception and distant from the contaminating effects of the world. This discursive block, bountiful in writings on Western art music, has inhibited the fusion of artistic ideas and activities with sociopolitical realities, with trenchant critiques and rapturous moments culled from aurality in general, with operations of the body and psyche, technological im/machinations, institutional workings – all that might be encountered beyond musical materiality.[55]

There are then good reasons why we should be cautious about accepting Cage's *4'33"* as an important work for thinking about noise. What is more, when we start to unpack these, we find even more reasons why it is problematic to construct noise as a figure with no consistency, as something that can, miraculously, be converted into something else entirely. In doing this, however, we are of course remaining within common sense definitions of noise that posit it as both auditory and either incidental, random, undesirable or opposed to music. If *4'33"* effectively annuls all noises of this kind in its very conceptualisation, this does not actually tell us whether it can be considered noisy according to the ontological taxonomy posited herein according to which noise is the artefact of expression itself, that which arises in the in-between of an expression passing between different poles and points us not towards the content (semiotic or otherwise) of that expression but, rather, its very expressivity and relationality. The problem when we pose this question of *4'33"* is that it becomes incredibly difficult to ascertain what it is that would constitute the piece's expression, what it is that would constitute the expressive assemblage.

According to nearly all accounts of the piece, *4'33"* is of course a work about sound that admits into the musical work the sounds of the performance venue and its surrounds. Indeed, for Kyle Gann, the piece is resolutely not a joke or hoax as some have claimed but, rather, 'a "thought experiment", a kind of "meta-music" that makes a statement about music itself'.[56] As he goes on to note in his book which is about *4'33"* and nothing else,

> Through the conventional and well-understood acts of placing the title of a composition on a program and arranging the audience in chairs facing a pianist, Cage was *framing* the sounds that the audience heard in an experimental attempt to make people perceive as art sounds that were not usually so perceived. One of the most common effects of *4'33"* – possibly the most important and widespread effect – was to seduce people into considering as art phenomena that were normally not associated with art. Perhaps even more, its effect was to drive home the point that the difference between 'art' and 'non-art' is merely one of perception, and that we can control how we organize our perceptions.[57]

In a view such as this, the art in question, of course, is music, a sonic art, since the framing conventions used are those of the musical performance as Gann notes. And it is at this point that we begin to see the problem. For if *4'33"* is a sonic expression, that expression, sonically speaking, comes from a centre which is not so much indeterminate as entirely absent. This is to say, then, that the sounds Cage's piece foregrounds are not noises that are instrumental to the musical assemblage but, rather, the noises of passing automobiles and creaking chairs and the splutterings of the audience, which is to say the sounds of the context into which musical content would normally be emitted, noises, that is to say, that are outside of music. Whilst this statement would seem to accord perfectly with Cage's stated aims, what it ultimately suggests is that he not only eradicates noise by bringing it within the fold of music, but that he concomitantly eradicates music by making of it anything at all and, therefore, nothing, there being no possible fundamental or resonant frequency. This is to say, in effect, that music is not merely a question of context, that it is born of expression, and for this reason I cannot accept Andrew Bowie's position even if I am delighted that he espouses a more sympathetic stance towards noise than most of his fellow philosophers of music. Commenting on Ramberg's comments on Donald Davidson's notion of 'radical interpretation', Bowie writes,

> The relevance of this view of language to music is apparent in the question of whether a series of acoustic phenomena is mere noise or is music: if it is the latter, it possesses a kind of 'meaning' that noise does not. This is in part because we may inferentially relate it to other things which we have interpreted as music. Our understanding of music depends on correlations between hearing the production of noises and an awareness that what is produced is not merely arbitrary and so is susceptible to and worthy of interpretation and evaluation in the widest senses, which can, for example, include dancing to the noises. Any noise can become music if it occurs in the appropriate contexts, rather in the way that non-literary language can change its status when incorporated into a literary context, or an object becomes a work of art if put into the right context.[58]

Whilst Bowie is not actually talking about *4'33"* here, his comments could no doubt be used to mount an argument that this work is indeed music. For reasons that will become clearer in Chapter Eight, however, I would contend that whilst music's centre is necessarily indeterminate, it is nonetheless necessarily more determinate than this. Indeed, the point I will make is somewhat similar to something Bowie says elsewhere in this same work, in a comment that seems somewhat to contradict his previous comment. Bowie writes: 'Music is [...] not simply a piece of an objectively characterisable world, because it involves communicative intentions, of a kind related to those present in language, by the very fact of its being music rather than noise'.[59] Whilst I shy away a little from the notion of intentionality here and believe that intention is never absolute and, indeed, only one aspect of the resistant operation by which any expression comes into being via an assemblage, I agree with the general principle here that music emerges out of a singular communicative act that displays a relative degree of consistency. And, for this reason, I would also suggest that it is not the case, as Frances Dyson argues, that a piece such as *4'33"* which aims to disrupt conventional modes of aesthetic appreciation through a reversal of figure and ground, can be considered 'as much about systems of representation as about the nature of sound and music', the rupturing of the very meaning of the concepts *music, silence, sound* and *performance* which are revealed 'as metaphors *only*',[60] since the systems of representation are here elided completely.

To put it another way, the supposed disruption of the representational system apparently taking place here is actualised outside of or, better, in the absence of that representational system, the piece unfolding through the intensification of an originary lack, this being the very antithesis of noise which can only assert itself as a primordial yet never fully present *presence* (or potentiality). It is then not the case, as Chua suggests, that *4'33"* is a piece in which the sound content is undetermined, meaning that 'the work begins to decompose into its "outside", into noise',[61] for the outside (or noise) of a musical assemblage is never enfolded in the first place. This perhaps is somewhat similar to Attali's comment (although obviously not applicable in the same way to the Rolling Stones as it seems to be for him) when he writes (in a comment intended as a positive critique and valorisation of these musical strategies): 'Both Cage and the Rolling Stones, *Silence* and "Satisfaction", announce a rupture in the process of musical creation, the end of music as an autonomous activity, due to an intensification of lack in the spectacle. They are not the new mode of musical production, but the liquidation of the old'.[62]

Noise, though, as I have already said repeatedly, need not be thought of only in musical/sonic/auditory terms, so if there is ultimately none of this kind of noise in *4'33"*, the question still remains as to whether there is any other kind of noise in it. In order to think about this, I want to jump off Attali's statement here somewhat obliquely and suggest that no matter what the conditions of its birth and statements made by its creator, *4'33"* is not about sound, music or noise at all, but that it *is* about time.

Indeed, what provides this piece with any kind of expressive centre is not, in fact, sound, music or noise at all but, rather, spatiotemporal situation. The only constants that might provide us with the necessary tools to talk of an assemblage here are, for any given performance of the piece, space and time. This, on one count at least, may seem unsurprising given the piece's title, yet given the proclamations that are frequently made about it, this is patently not so.

The difference of opinion here may well stem from a fundamental philosophical disagreement. Gann, for instance, does a wonderful job of tracing the many different *dramatis personae* that were important to the very conceptualisation of *4'33"* and makes a convincing link to Cage's lecture 'Defense of Satie'. In this lecture, as Gann notes, 'Cage elaborated the fourfold division of music into structure, form, method, and materials, and credited Satie, along with Anton Webern (1933–45), with producing the only new idea of structure in modern music'.[63] This was done, he argues, by placing the emphasis firmly on the structural element of time lengths, and Gann quotes Cage in order to explain the point fully:

> It is very simple. If you consider that sound is characterized by its pitch, its loudness, its timbre, and its duration, and that silence, which is the opposite and, therefore, the necessary partner of sound, is characterized only by its duration, you will be drawn to the conclusion that of the four characteristics of the material of music, duration, that is, time length, is the most fundamental. Silence cannot be heard in terms of pitch or harmony: It is heard in terms of time length. It took a Satie and a Webern to rediscover this musical truth, which, by means of musicology, we learn was evident to some musicians in our Middle Ages, and to all musicians at all times ... in the Orient.
> There can be no right making of music that does not structure itself from the very roots of sound and silence – lengths of time.[64]

For Cage, then, *4'33"* qualifies as music precisely because silence is the necessary partner of sound, but there is in fact no reason to suggest that this *is* actually the case (even if it is normally so) since it is perfectly possible for a piece of music to have no silence within it (think, for instance, of the drone music of Niblock or La Monte Young's Theatre of Eternal Music).[65] This is not to say that Cage was wrong in placing such emphasis on the structural element of time lengths, but, rather, to claim that duration internal to the work of art can be conceptualised from within as a flow that can be modulated by relations between sound and silence but, equally, by relations between, for instance, tones or timbre. This is to say that when conceptualised as expressive, music does not require silence, even though silence may form part of its expressive assemblage. What it does require, however, is an expressive assemblage that would display some structural consistency. In saying this I am not falling into the old trap of claiming that music is always reducible to a score, but suggesting, rather, that music is the result of an expressive centre (a formulation which does not necessarily predicate a single composer) which puts various sonic bodies into relations with each other *as an expression*. So whilst it may be the case that for the audience the sounds inside and outside of the venue enter into relations with each other, the relations between them are entirely aleatory and can only be interpreted as otherwise in the perception of the individual listener. As with conflicting definitions of noise, then, it is hard to claim that *4'33"* is musical from an ontological point of view, for it can only be interpreted as music at an individual level with absolutely no guarantees that it will be by all individuals – and *4'33"* exemplifies this last point perhaps better than any other piece in the history of music.

Whilst *4'33"* can thus be said to be 'noisy' in a common sense manner since it is nothing more than a random set of (perhaps) bangs, coughs, creaks, sneezes, distant car horns and the patter of rain on the venue roof, none of these sounds can be objectively qualified as noises in the sense given to this term here. This is not to say that there is *no* noise in *4'33"*, since, as I have suggested, there is noise in everything. It is to suggest, however, that if we attend to the noise of *4'33"*, to the specificity of the expressive assemblage that this piece deploys, this noise will tell us that on an ontological level, *4'33"* has very little to do with music and sound and everything to do with space and time – a suggestion in line with yet no doubt exceeding the intent of Kim-Cohen's comment that 'the perceived sound of a performance of *4'33"* is secondary to the "noise" it creates in the circuits of music as a category'.[66] To put this another way, *4'33"* may well be a noisy piece but not for the reasons generally given. Cage's piece does not in fact sound the noise of music via silence; rather, true to its title, the noise it generates is that of time, for ultimately the piece has far more to tell us about the deployment of existence in time than it does about music.

It would be unfair, however, to judge Cage on the basis of this piece alone, for his career is so vast and took so many different turns that it could not possibly be summed up by four minutes and 33 seconds. Yet the same problem for thinking about noise in Cage persists even when we move into the latter stages of Cage's trajectory when he developed the concept of *panaurality*. This concept would seem to resonate strongly with the present study, for it is born of the recognition, invoked herein, that all matter is acoustic since vibrating at a submolecular level. As Douglas Kahn notes, in this stage of Cage's career, sound 'was no longer tied to events but existed as a continuous state as it resonated from each and every atom [...]. Everything always made a sound, and everything could be heard; *all sound* and *always sound* paralleled *panaurality*'.[67] Having abolished the barrier between sound and silence, asserting that silence was merely 'all of the sound we don't intend' and, as such, could include loud sounds, the concept of panaurality provided Cage with his next step. This concept, indeed, would allow Cage, as Kahn explains, to

> interpolate sound (and thereby music) back onto a seemingly intransigent silence of objects. If silence was actually sound, then all matter too must be audible, given the proper technology to detect the soundful activities at the level of subatomic vibrations. Matter is dissolved as technology denies inaudibility and forbids silence.[68]

Implicit in Cage's incorporation of all matter within the realm of sound, then, is the recuperation of all sound into the realm of music, a manoeuvre which once more, as was the case with Russolo, effectively eliminates noise by rendering all sound, even at the subatomic level, discursive, meaningful in such a way that noise passes fully into the level of content, entertaining a transcendent relation to the medial plane on which and from which the discursive event or expression is drawn.[69] We can then only agree wholeheartedly with Kahn when he suggests that 'during the twentieth-century Age of Noise, the most noted promulgator of musical noise was involved in the business of noise abatement',[70] for the recuperation of noise by music necessarily annuls noise. This is not to say that Cage is a noise-free zone, however, but, rather, that all of those who have spilled so much ink writing about

Cage and noise have been duped by common sense, believing that
noise necessarily exists in a relation with music. So whilst I felt a
compulsion to tackle head on the elephant in the room that Cage
represents in the field of noise studies, it turns out that many others
have been tiptocing around him.

Notes

1 Caleb Kelly, *Cracked Media: The Sound of Malfunction* (Cambridge,
   MA: MIT Press, 2009), 66–7.

2 Douglas Kahn, *Noise, Water, Meat: A History of Sound in the Arts*
   (Cambridge, MA: MIT Press, 1999), 56.

3 Marcel Cobussen, 'Noise as Undifferentiated Sound', http://
   deconstruction-in-music.com/proefschrift/300_john_cage/313_noise_
   undifferentiated/noise_undifferentiated.html [accessed April 18, 2012].

4 Jean-Pierre Gutton, *Bruits et sons dans notre histoire: essai sur la
   reconstitution du paysage sonore* (Paris: Presses Universitaires de
   France, 2000), 139–40.

5 Michael Chanan, *Musica Practica: The Social Practice of Western
   Music From Gregorian Chant to Postmodernism* (London: Verso,
   1994), 243.

6 Michael Chanan, *Repeated Takes: A Short History of Recording and
   its Effects on Music* (London: Verso, 1995), 140.

7 Thom Holmes, *Electronic and Experimental Music: Pioneers in
   Technology and Composition* (New York and London: Routledge,
   2002), 38.

8 Emily Thompson, *The Soundscape of Modernity: Architectural
   Acoustics and the Culture of Listening in America, 1900–1933*
   (Cambridge, MA: MIT Press, 2002), 136.

9 Alex Ross, *The Rest is Noise: Listening to the Twentieth Century*
   (London: Harper Perennial, 2009), 63.

10 R. Murray Schafer, *The Soundscape: Our Sonic Environment and the
   Tuning of the World* (New York: Knopf, 1977; rep. Rochester, VT:
   Destiny Books, 2009), 34.

11 Steve Goodman, *Sonic Warfare: Sound, Affect, and the Ecology of
   Fear* (Cambridge, MA: MIT Press, 2010), 6.

12 Mary Russo and Daniel Warner, 'Rough Music, Futurism, and
   Postpunk Industrial Noise Bands', in *Audio Culture: Readings in*

Modern Music, ed. Christoph Cox and Daniel Warner (New York and London: Continuum, 2004), 50.

13 Garret Keizer, *The Unwanted Sound of Everything We Want: A Book About Noise* (New York: Public Affairs, 2010), 119.

14 Robert Worby, 'Cacophony', in *Music, Electronic Media and Culture*, ed. Simon Emmerson (Aldershot: Ashgate, 2000), 147–8.

15 Emily Thompson, *The Soundscape of Modernity*, 137.

16 George Prochnik, *In Pursuit of Silence: Listening for Meaning in a World of Noise* (New York and London: Doubleday, 2010), 127.

17 This is of course not surprising because, as we will see, such is explicitly stated by many artists and is one of the fundamental aims of the Futurist manifesto.

18 Schafer, *The Soundscape*, 111.

19 Schafer, *The Soundscape*, 111.

20 Schafer, *The Soundscape*, 111.

21 Schafer, *The Soundscape*, 185.

22 See also Kahn, *Noise, Water, Meat*, especially Chapter 2, 'Noises of the Avant-Garde', 45–67.

23 Thompson, *The Soundscape of Modernity*, 116–17.

24 See Thompson, *The Soundscape of Modernity*, 134–6.

25 See Thompson, *The Soundscape of Modernity*, 130–44, 152–4.

26 Thompson, *The Soundscape of Modernity*, 143.

27 Benjamin Thorn quotes Russolo in *The Art of Noises* saying 'Despite the fact that it is characteristic of sound to remind us brutally of life, the Art of Noises must not limit itself to reproductive imitation' but goes on to suggest that 'It was perhaps unfortunate that the practice could not match the theory. Russolo's own works seem to have been somewhat clumsily constructed and too overtly imitative' (Benjamin Thorn, 'Luigi Russolo (1885–1947)', in *Music of the Twentieth-Century Avant-Garde: A Biocritical Sourcebook*, ed. Larry Sitsky (Westport, CT: Greenwood Press, 2002), 417–18).

28 Russolo's analysis of the physical properties of noise as opposed to sound is based on precisely this premise that noise is constituted of a greater number and thus complexity of harmonies. See Luigi Russolo, *The Art of Noises*, trans. Barclay Brown (orig. Italian, 1913; New York: Pendragon Press, 1986), 37–40.

29 Filippo Tommaso Marinetti, 'The Founding and Manifesto of Futurism', originally published in *Le Figaro*, 20 February 1909,

reprinted in *Marinetti: Selected Writings*, ed. and trans. R. W. Flint and Arthur A. Coppotelli (London: Secker & Warburg, 1972), 39–40.

30 Russolo, *The Art of Noises*, 23.

31 Russolo, *The Art of Noises*, 27.

32 Russolo, *The Art of Noises*, 25.

33 Marinetti, 'The Founding and Manifesto of Futurism', 42.

34 Marinetti, 'The Founding and Manifesto of Futurism', 41.

35 Filippo Tommaso Marinetti, 'Geometric and Mechanical Splendor and the Numerical Sensibility', original 1914, reprinted in *Marinetti: Selected Writings*, 101.

36 Filippo Tommaso Marinetti, 'Manifesto of the Futurist Dance', original 1917, reprinted in *Marinetti: Selected Writings*, 138.

37 Filippo Tommaso Marinetti, 'Technical Manifesto of Futurist Literature', original 1912, reprinted in *Marinetti: Selected Writings*, 88.

38 Filippo Tommaso Marinetti, 'Tactilism', original 1924, reprinted in *Marinetti: Selected Writings*, 111.

39 Filippo Tommaso Marinetti, 'The Birth of a Futurist Aesthetic', from *War, the World's Only Hygiene*, original 1915, reprinted in *Marinetti: Selected Writings*, 82.

40 Russolo, *The Art of Noises*, 27.

41 Marinetti, 'The Birth of a Futurist Aesthetic', 82.

42 This is not necessarily to impute a concrete political agenda to Russolo, for, as Thorn suggests, Russolo demonstrated a lack of sympathy for fascism ('Luigi Russolo', 416).

43 Russolo, *The Art of Noises*, 86.

44 Russolo, *The Art of Noises*, 87.

45 Russolo, *The Art of Noises*, 87.

46 Russolo, *The Art of Noises*, 86–87.

47 Russolo, *The Art of Noises*, 86.

48 Marinetti, 'Geometric and Mechanical Splendor and the Numerical Sensibility', 97.

49 In Bois and Krauss' analysis, traditional analyses of modern art (such as Greenberg's) require it 'to justify its existence as the search for its own essence [...,] to address itself uniquely to the sense of sight [..., to exclude] temporality within the visual and on the body of the perceiving subject [..., to be] addressed to the subject as an erect

being, far from the horizontal axis that governs the life of animals
[... and] to have a beginning and an end [so that] all apparent
disorder is necessarily reabsorbed in the very fact of being bounded'.
Yve-Alain Bois and Rosalind Krauss, *Formless: A User's Guide*
(Cambridge, MA: MIT Press, 1997), 25.

50 See, for instance, all of the commentators quoted in the prologue to
this chapter as well as: Julian Henriques, 'Sonic Dominance and the
Reggae Sound System Session', in *The Auditory Culture Reader*, ed.
M. Bull and Les Back (Oxford: Berg, 2003), 457; Wikipedia entry
on noise music; Jacques Attali, *Noise: The Political Economy of
Music*, trans. Brian Massumi (Minneapolis: University of Minnesota
Press, 1985), 26; Theo Van Leeuwen, *Speech, Music, Sound* (London:
Macmillan, 1999), 166; Phil Brophy, 'Collapsing Image Into Noise
Part 2: Noise, Noise, Noise', *The Wire: Adventures in Modern
Music*, 165 (November 1997); Doug Van Nort, 'Noise/Music and
Representation Systems', *Organised Sound*, 11, no. 2 (2006).

51 In the booklet to the first collection released by the label, explicitly
articulated to Deleuze and Guattari's philosophy, *Folds and
Rhizomes for Gilles Deleuze* (sub rosa, 1995), one of the label's
founders, Guy Marc Hinant, explains that it was on the basis of the
first sentence from *Mille Plateaux* that they conceived of sub rosa.

52 Guy Marc Hinant in the booklet accompanying *An Anthology of
Noise & Electronic Music/First a-chronology 1921–2001* (sub rosa,
2004).

53 We should note that whilst this is not the commonly accepted line
on Russolo, we are not entirely alone in suggesting this. For instance,
talking of the new works of composers such as Satie, Russolo and
Schoenberg, whilst admitting that they had caused a considerable
and unprecedented shake up of the foundations of music theory,
David Keane nonetheless contends that these early pioneers of
electroacoustic instrumentation did not challenge the traditional
concept of music as much as some later composers such as Schaeffer
and Stockhausen and, indeed, that they ultimately relied on fairly
classical notions of music (David Keane, 'At the Threshold of an
Aesthetic', in *The Language of Electroacoustic Music*, ed. Simon
Emmerson (New York: Harwood Academic Publishers, 1986)).
Schaeffer also notes how, after his disavowal of *musique concrète*,
many looked for other heroes and often turned to Russolo whose
conception of music was still very traditional in essence, relying
on score and interpretation (Pierre Schaeffer quoted in Michel
Chion, *L'Art des sons fixés ou La Musique Concrètement* (Fontaine:
Éditions Metamkine/Nota-Bene/Sono-Concept, 1991), 75–77). We

will see Douglas Kahn suggest something similar very shortly in relation to both Russolo and Cage, although he does not impute the same kind of intentional agency to Russolo himself (see Douglas Kahn, 'Introduction', in *Wireless Imagination: Sound, Radio, and the Avant-Garde*, ed. Douglas Kahn and Gregory Whitehead (Cambridge, MA: MIT Press, 1992), 3).

54 Kahn, 'Introduction', 3.

55 Kahn, 'Introduction', 3–4.

56 Kyle Gann, *No Such Thing as Silence: John Cage's 4'33"* (New Haven, CT: Yale University Press, 2010), 20.

57 Gann, *No Such Thing as Silence*, 20.

58 Andrew Bowie, *Music, Philosophy and Modernity* (Cambridge: Cambridge University Press, 2007), 6.

59 Bowie, *Music, Philosophy and Modernity*, 110.

60 Frances Dyson, 'The Ear That Would Hear Sounds in Themselves: John Cage 1935-1965', in *Wireless Imagination: Sound, Radio, and the Avant-Garde*, ed. Douglas Kahn and Gregory Whitehead (Cambridge, MA: MIT Press, 1992), 391.

61 Eu Jin Chua, 'The Film-Work Recomposed into Nature: From Art to Noise in Four Minutes and Thirty-Three Seconds', *Moving Image Review & Art Journal*, 1, no. 1 (2012), 91.

62 Attali, *Noise*, 136–7.

63 Gann, *No Such Thing as Silence*, 79.

64 John Cage, quoted in Gann, *No Such Thing as Silence*, 80.

65 Some might object that even with these examples, the pieces begin and end and are thus surrounded by silence, but this silence then serves as the framing mechanism, as that which signals the piece of music itself to be, precisely, no longer present. And some might object to this also that the challenge of Cage's work is to make us think about the border between what is art and what is not art, and this is undoubtedly true as it is in a similar manner with Marcel Duchamp's ready-mades. To believe, however, that everything becomes art following this questioning of the boundaries of art would be to claim that a urinal in a bar's toilets is automatically art, whereas Duchamp's point (and, indeed, Cage's) had to do with the framing of objects within specific kinds of spaces such that they could be considered as art.

66 Seth Kim-Cohen, *In the Blink of an Ear: Toward a Non-Cochlear Sonic Art* (New York and London: Continuum, 2009), 140.

67 Kahn, *Noise, Water, Meat*, 159.

68 Kahn, *Noise, Water, Meat*, 164.

69 In spite of their seemingly divergent projects, the link drawn between Cage and Russolo here is not in fact all that surprising given that, as Gann notes, Cage mentioned *The Art of Noises* in a lecture and listed it as one of the ten books that influenced him the most (see Gann, *No Such Thing as Silence*, 82) – this being then very much an acknowledged debt and not an unacknowledged one as Schafer suggests (see *The Soundscape*, 111).

70 Kahn, *Noise, Water, Meat*, 183.

CHAPTER TWO

Noisea

Haiku

When I see the root,
Existence unveils itself.
All is noisea.

* * *

Nausea and noise

The universe is noisy in all scales even if the universe itself is not noise. The fading noise of the ancient big bang explosion fills the cosmos. It still gently hisses and crackles all around us in the form of junk microwave radiation. Measurement and device noise attaches to all our measurements and devices. Our warm brains give off thermal noise while such thermal and other noise types infest the fine electrical circuitry of the neural networks that make up our brains. And peering down into the quantum world reveals noise fluctuations in the ultimate substrates of matter.[1]

From an etymological point of view, noise in both French and English is intimately related to nausea. Even though this may not be evident to the speaker of modern-day French, noise has its roots in the Old French '*noise*', meaning uproar or brawl and found in modern-day French only in the phrase '*chercher noise*' – to pick a quarrel.[2] 'Noise' itself can be traced back to the Latin *nausea* which evokes disgust, annoyance or discomfort and in vernacular Latin there exists a meaning of this word more directly linked to our own concerns here, namely, 'unpleasant situation, noise or quarrel'.

Michel Serres makes much of the link between these two terms in his book *Genesis* [*Genèse*] where he employs the Old French '*noise*' in preference to its modern-day French equivalent '*bruit*' in order to highlight the link to nausea and, indeed, the confrontational and contestatory nature of '*noise*'. As he writes, 'In Old French it used to mean: noise, uproar and wrangling; English borrowed the sound from us; we keep only the fury'.[3] And, as he continues in a section entitled 'Sea Noise', 'There, precisely is the origin. *Noise* and nausea, *noise* and the nautical, *noise* and navy belong to the same family'.[4]

I have suggested in the introduction that noise is the artefact of an expressive ontology, signalling the necessary movement that subsists in all being, whether this be at a subatomic, existential, philosophical, quantum or individual level. Noise, then, is that which unmoors the world from the illusory fixity to which we tie it down in an attempt to keep it in place, to separate its elements out from each other and elevate ourselves above the 'natural world', subjecting it to our will and mastery as though we were somehow separated from nature. Noise makes the world pitch, roll, heave and swell, like a ship in rough seas whose movement is never entirely its own but only ever the result of a relation between it and its environment. Noise makes the world bleed, ooze and seep, turning it into an undifferentiated (because hyperdifferentiated) mass. Noise, from many points of view, is then intimately related to nausea.

Nobody perhaps knows this better than Antoine Roquentin, the diarist-narrator of Jean-Paul Sartre's first novel *Nausea*.[5] Indeed, I will suggest in this chapter that the conceptualisation of existence that unveils itself to Roquentin during his existential breakdown and ensuing nauseous episodes could almost be considered a philosophical corollary of the scientific view of the universe as quantum noise espoused by Kosko in this chapter's opening quotation. The philosophical insights into the mobile and expressive nature of existence that Roquentin's nausea brings to him, however, are not fully followed through. Rather, somewhat strangely, explicit instances of noise in the novel actually serve to recontain and ground existence again, noise, when figured as noise, thus being elided as a means to reinstate an established and seemingly necessary order in the world.

Where *Nausea's* noise is not

Given the etymological origins of *noise* traced by Serres, one might imagine that the noise to be found in Sartre's *Nausea* would reside in the contestatory and combative nature of many of Roquentin's diatribes against the bourgeois '*salauds*' [bastards] in his hometown of Bouville. The '*salauds*', of course, are those members of society who live in a constant state of bad faith, their behaviour regulated and dictated at all times not by any kind of authenticity, spontaneity or relation to events around them taking place in real time, but only in accordance with long-established protocols, axiomatics and social mores that determine how people of a certain standing should act, dress, walk and talk. Roquentin's fulminations, however, do nothing to disturb the established order, to disabuse the '*salauds*' of their mistaken belief in their own self-importance that elevates them above not only the natural world that feeds their factories but also the lower classes who work in them. On the contrary, Roquentin's decision at the end of the novel to write a novel that would justify his own existence places him in a somewhat analogous position to those against whom he previously riled, muting any possible noise that his words might previously have contained.

Given that *Nausea* opens with an inscription lifted from a work by Louis-Ferdinand Céline, an author famous at the time of this novel's publication for having revolutionised the French literary landscape via a desecration that introduced both the smells (in his novels' content) and sounds (in their spoken style) of the street into the sacred realm of *les belles lettres*,[6] one might also perhaps imagine that *Nausea's* noise might come from its style. For Serres claims that the sound and fury of the old French *noise* was lost from its modern-day usage because of a desire to make the French language 'a prim and proper language of precise communication, a fair and measured pair of scales for jurists and diplomats, exact, draftsmanlike, unshaky, slightly frozen, a clear arterial unobstructed by embolus, through having chased away a great many *belles noiseuses*?'[7] The *noise*-less French described here is precisely the kind of respectable language favoured by the '*salauds*', and one would therefore have thought that Sartre/Roquentin would vehemently resist any such linguistic forms or corresponding literary style. For Denis Hollier, this is indeed the case since, for him, the key to an understanding of this novel lies in grasping its total transgression of genre.[8] This transgression, however, relies on what Arnold calls 'a sophisticated irony' that enables the reader to understand the intention behind Sartre's use of 'the most hackneyed conventions' of the epistolary/journal form and thus relies on that irony being apprehended as intended.[9] Ultimately, however, all of this matters little, for what is certain is that the über-conformity to generic literary conventions and deliberate inscription of the novel in a predominantly nineteenth-century literary lineage is nowhere near as contestatory as the extreme individualism talked of in the Céline-penned inscription that this latter author embodied in his very style and language.

If there is then a link to be found between *Nausea* and noise that runs deeper than the etymological roots of Sartre's eventual chosen title (which emerged out of a philosophical series of reflections referred to as a *Factum sur la contingence* and which was originally to be entitled *Melancholia*) this is not to be found, contrary to what one might be tempted to believe with the benefit of hindsight looking back over Sartre's career, in the kind of politically or aesthetically resistant ends for which noise is often deployed. I will suggest, rather, that in the course of the novel, Roquentin's whole world takes on a noisy aspect at those times when his nauseous existential breakdowns reveal a different facet of existence to him. This noisy/nauseous conception of the world colours the spatialities of the novel and opens up the possibility for Roquentin to entertain a very different kind of relation with the world around him. Ultimately, however, he rejects the extreme contingency of this noisy/nauseous existence and retreats back into order and necessity, very often by means of, significantly and ironically, various noises that are figured explicitly in the novel. Once again, therefore, in spite of his noisy/nauseous insights, the full potential and operations of noise are ultimately abnegated and recontained; noise is once more co-opted by a coherent aesthetic project that attenuates or eradicates entirely the ontological qualities particular to noise.

Black noise

Roquentin's existential crisis comes, as is well known and hardly needs repeating here, as the apparently immutable contours of the objects around him become porous and seem to float and meld before his eyes in a nauseating movement that mirrors his realisation of the absolute contingency of his own existence as any shred of Cartesian certainty fades away. This unmooring of existence from fixed forms and identities is prepared gradually throughout the first half of the novel. At first, for instance, Roquentin seems unable to recognise the face of the Autodidact whom he seems almost daily in the library.[10] Language seems suddenly insufficient for his needs, his thoughts remaining 'misty and nebulous' as words fail to fix them in place.[11] Gradually he is unsettled by the uncanny feeling that the objects around him are capable of touching him, refusing to remain in their place of subordinate, passive objecthood and utilitarianism, becoming instead like 'living animals',[12] his shirt, for instance, suddenly imbued with a troubling form of agency as it rubs his nipples.[13] Faced with sensations such as this, the entire world around him takes on a nebulous, mobile quality as all of the metaphysical certainty that had previously enabled him to effect a separation between his own identity and that of the things in the world outside him fades away in such a manner that the world seems able to enter into him. He writes:

> I was surrounded, seized by a slow, coloured whirlpool, a whirlpool of fog, of lights in the smoke, in the mirrors, with the benches shining at the back, and I couldn't see why it was there or why it was like that. I was on the doorstep, I was hesitating, and then there was a sudden eddy, a shadow passed across the ceiling, and I felt myself being pushed forward. I floated along, dazed by the luminous mists which were entering me from all directions at once.[14]

As Roquentin's ability to keep the world around him in its place is further eroded, his perception of everything is washed out in tones of grey, distinct forms – himself included – bleeding into each other due to a lack of chromatic contrast. He writes:

The grey thing has just appeared in the mirror. I go over and
look at it, I can no longer move away.
    It is the reflection of my face.[15]

Grey, of course, occupies a privileged place in the work of Walter
Benjamin's writings on Naples because of this colour's relation to
porosity and thus, as Andrew Benjamin notes, the way in which
normally discrete objects or categories are defined 'in terms of an
already present sense of "interpenetration" (*Durchdringung*)'.[16]
Whilst this kind of interpenetration of everything does indeed
capture well the diaphanous, oozing and undifferentiated nature of
existence as it appears to Roquentin during his nauseous episodes,
what is important (as becomes clear during his most extreme
episode) is not so much any specific colour, however, as a lack
of chromatic contrast between an object and its environs, such
as when, for instance, he beholds a black tree root in low light,
which appears to him as a 'black, knotty mass' that scares him.[17]
It is when faced with this spectacle that what Roquentin considers
to be the true nature of existence is revealed to him. Already, in
the days prior to this he tells us, words had lost their power for
him, their ability to hold things in place and to indicate how to
navigate the things around him.[18] Already he has suggested that
the normal order of the world is inverted such that he no longer
occupies a privileged position in the hierarchy of existence and
ordered distribution of objects in space, saying that 'The Nausea
isn't inside me [...]. It is one with the café, it is I who am inside *it*'.[19]
Now, however, the interpenetration or common expressive nature
of all existence is revealed to him in an almost hallucinatory and
terrifying illumination:

> Never, until these last few days, had I suspected what it meant
> to 'exist'. I was like the others, like those who walk along the
> sea-shore in their spring clothes. I used to say like them: 'The
> sea *is* green; that white speck up there *is* a seagull', but I didn't
> feel that it existed, that the seagull was an 'existing seagull';
> usually existence hides itself. It is there, around us, in us, it is
> *us*, you can't say a couple of words without speaking of it, but
> finally you can't touch it. [...] Even when I looked at things, I
> was miles from thinking that they existed: they looked like stage
> scenery to me. I picked them up in my hands, they served me

as tools, I foresaw their resistance. But all that happened on the surface. If anybody had asked me what existence was, I should have replied in good faith that it was nothing, just an empty form which added itself to external things, without changing anything in their nature. And then, all of a sudden, there it was, as clear as day: existence had suddenly unveiled itself. It had lost its harmless appearance as an abstract category: it was the very stuff of things, that root was steeped in existence. Or rather the root, the park gates, the bench, the sparse grass on the lawn, all that had vanished; the diversity of things, their individuality, was only an appearance, a veneer. This veneer had melted, leaving soft, monstrous masses, in disorder – naked, with a frightening, obscene nakedness.[20]

This, then, is a vision in which the noise of the world is revealed to Roquentin, in which he is able to glimpse the in-between of existence, to attend to the expressivity of being which comes to be always outside of itself. This, then, is a vision in which nausea is coterminous with noise.

And yet it is very much a *vision*, the descriptions here and throughout the novel of these foggy, misty, nauseous, diaphanous spaces being rendered in almost exclusively visual terms – as seen already with the lack of chromatic contrast and predominance of the colour grey in these moments. Far from increasing this sense of a fully immersive relation with the world, the auditory sense for Roquentin – and noise in particular, even more strangely – seem to serve as a means to orient himself, as a fixed point of localisation that attenuates his sense of visual disorientation. Noise, as it is more commonly understood, this is to say, serves not to disrupt but, rather, to provide a sense of fixity and stability that counters the contingency of the protagonist's visual and tactile space, to furnish what appear to serve as anchoring points of reference – even if these auditory expressions are ultimately just as non-localisable. Roquentin can thus write,

The fog was so thick … a wet light and it was impossible to know where the pavement finished. There were people around me; I could hear the noise of their footsteps or, occasionally, the slight hum of their words: but I couldn't see anybody.[21]

Or, even more significantly,

I wanted to hear the noise of his footsteps. The most I could hear was that of a little coal falling inside the stove. The fog had invaded the room: not a real fog, which had gone a long time before, but the other fog, the one the streets were still full of, which was coming out of the walls and pavements. A sort of inconsistency of things.[22]

That this is contrary to what one might expect can be seen in the following quotation from Serres' *Genèse* where he writes, having noted that 'the multiple is the object of this book [*Genesis*]':

These are objects I seem to live through more than view. I think I pick up noises from them more than I see them, touch them, or conceive them. I hear without clear frontiers, without divining an isolated source, hearing is better at integrating than analyzing, the ear knows how to lose track.[23]

For Serres, then, hearing, much more readily than sight or touch, allows us access to the contingent, the aleatory, the multiple or, rather, the loss of the unitary that lies at the heart of Roquentin's nausea.[24] This, however, is resolutely not the case in *Nausea* where time and again the destabilising or, rather, operative relationality of noise is perceived only in the visual and tactile realms, whilst noise experienced via the auditory sense inspires no such troubling insights. Thus, when talking of the noise his fellow clients at the Café Mably make, even though he describes it as an 'inconsistent noise', it is nonetheless (in striking contrast to the troubling 'inconsistency of things' seen above) 'an inconsistent noise *which doesn't bother me*', as he says.[25] What is more, this (what is to my mind) misprision of noise is not simply confined to odd asides such as these but occupies an important place in the novel's finale that leads to Roquentin's formulation of a possible salvation in the face of the crushing contingency of existence.

Vinyl noise

Throughout the novel, Roquentin listens to a particular jazz song, 'Some of these days', and is struck by its internal coherence and necessity. As he explains whilst listening to the song for the first time in the novel,

> The refrain will be coming soon: that's the part I like best and the abrupt way in which it flings itself forward, like a cliff against the sea. For the moment it's the jazz that's playing; there's no melody, only notes, a host of little jolts. They know no rest, an unchanging order gives birth to them and destroys them, without ever giving them time to recover, to exist for themselves. They run, they hurry, they strike me with a sharp blow in passing and are obliterated. I should quite like to hold them back, but I know that if I managed to stop one, nothing would remain between my fingers but a vulgar, doleful sound. I must accept their death; I must even *will* it; I know few harsher or stronger impressions.[26]

Roquentin hears this song again towards the end of the novel, which is to say after his nauseous visions and illumination and before his decision to try and write a book which might justify his existence a little, 'The sort of story, for example, which could never happen, an adventure [...,] beautiful and hard as steel'.[27] This time, however, he notes that the record has been scratched, which is to say that the song is accompanied by noise. Whilst we might expect Roquentin to be bothered by this noise, to be pulled out of his reverie as he loses himself in the melodic content of the song and made to attend to the mediated and thus contingent nature of the tune he loves so much, this is not the case in the slightest and he is able completely to elide this noise, to hear it, ultimately, as entirely separate from the recorded (and thus intentional) content of the disk. He writes:

> Somebody must have scratched the record at that spot, because it makes a peculiar noise. And there is something that wrings the heart: it is that the melody is absolutely untouched by this little stuttering of the needle on the record. It is so far away – so far behind. I understand that too: the record is getting scratched and worn, the singer may be dead; I myself am going to leave, I am going to catch my train. But behind the existence which falls from one present to the next, without a past, without a future, behind these sounds which decompose from day to day, peels

away and slips towards death, the melody stays the same, young and firm, like a pitiless witness.[28]

We might think of this elision of noise as simply an instance of a quite common and unconscious form of cognitive noise reduction (and I will examine this in more depth in Chapter Four in relation to a different context). Indeed, it may well seem that Roquentin is here simply deploying a mechanism well known to anyone who has listened to a scratched record. For the hiss, pops and scratches of old vinyl, whilst in a sense undeniably present, are often, and as far as possible, ignored by the listener who wishes to attend to the recorded content of the disk as part of a willed yet ultimately instinctive process of auditory filtration. This is to say that, like the gallery visitor looking at a picture presented behind glass and who makes a conscious effort not to see the glass in order to contemplate the painting, the melody of a song on a scratched record is necessarily affected by the scratch and only appears not to be because of a tactic one adopts in order to achieve the result desired.

For Sartre (via Roquentin), however, something more significant is in play, for the split effected here between musical or aesthetic expression and the material support on which that expression is recorded is entirely in accordance with Sartre's aesthetic theory as expounded in *The Imaginary* and in which the aesthetic object is ontologically separate from the rest of existence. His theory is formulated, once again, whilst listening to music, albeit Beethoven's Seventh Symphony and not jazz. Sartre writes:

> I am therefore confronted by the Seventh Symphony but on the express condition that I hear it *nowhere*, that I cease to think of the event as current and dated, and on the condition that I interpret the succession of themes as an absolute succession and not as a real succession that is unfurling while Pierre is, simultaneously, visiting one of his friends. To the extent that I grasp it, the symphony *is not there*, between those walls, at the tip of the violin bows. Nor is it 'past' as if I thought: this is the work that took shape on such a date in the mind of Beethoven. It is entirely outside the real. It has its own time, which is to say it possesses an internal time, which flows from the first note of the allegro to the last note of the finale, but this time does not follow another time that it continues and that happened 'before' the beginning

of the allegro, nor is it followed by a time that would come 'after' the finale. The Seventh Symphony is in no way *in time*. It therefore entirely escapes the real. It is given *in person*, but as absent, as being out of reach. It would be impossible for me to act on it, to change a single note of it, or to slow its movement.[29]

Whilst Sartre's theory as expounded here may seem to make perfect sense in relation to music, if we resituate it in the context of Roquentin's nauseous revelations about the true (noisy) nature of existence, it becomes problematic. Indeed, what nausea/noise reveals to Roquentin is precisely that, in effect, *nothing is* in actuality, nothing is fully present to itself, everything is only ever a relation that exists through the deployment of an expressive act. Whilst it may then seem that the melody of the Seventh Symphony or 'Some of these days' is ontologically far removed from the ontology of a tree root, let us say, a 'real object' in the world, Roquentin's nauseous episodes reveal to us that this is resolutely not the case. Indeed, one can suggest that just like the Seventh Symphony which does not actually exist in time but only as an 'absolute succession' that can lead to an expressive event in which one recognises a familiar line, so the tree root appears to Roquentin as the expression of a transcendental principle that enfolds existence into that particular pseudo-form in time.

Grey noise

To put this in slightly different terms, borrowed once again from Deleuze and Guattari, we might suggest that the nauseous, noisy ontology discovered by Roquentin is one in which existence is conceived of in terms of haecceities. This is indeed perhaps unsurprising, for the exemplars used by Deleuze and Guattari to talk of haecceities are oftentimes phenomena found also throughout Roquentin's nauseous descriptions of the world: fog, mist, smoke. More than this, however, as Deleuze and Guattari explain, a haecceity is a becoming that deploys a certain kind of affect at differing degrees of intensity, not a *thing* or *substance* or *subject* but a mode of individuation that has 'a perfect individuality lacking nothing' and that consists 'entirely of relations of movement and rest between molecules or particles, capacities to affect and be affected'.[30] It is no accident, of course, that this idea resonates strongly with Sartre's comment on Beethoven's Seventh Symphony in *L'Imaginaire*, for music also according to Deleuze and Guattari is a haecceity and it is so primarily because of the double movement of deterritorialisation and reterritorialisation (which is to say, in Sartrean terms, existence both corporeal and incorporeal, the in-itself and the for-itself) that comes from the refrain which, for them, is the very content of music.[31] Indeed, the refrain for them is 'a creative, active operation that consists in deterritorializing the refrain', which is to say, as they elaborate, 'whereas the refrain is essentially territorial, territorializing, or reterritorializing, music makes it a deterritorialized content for a deterritorializing form of expression'.[32] In other words, whilst music's blocks of expression are dependent on the creation of forms, on a territory defined by the refrain, music only becomes music(al) by undoing these forms, by pushing them to their limit, submitting them to the diagonal or transversal as music reterritorialises upon itself *qua* music.[33]

The implication of this for Roquentin is of course devastating, for what it suggests is that there is no ontological separation between the mode of expression that inheres in the form of existence he intuits during his nauseous illumination and the mode of expression by which music comes to be. Music, then, is also subject to the same crushing sense of contingency, the same lack of necessity, the same absurdity as material existence. This is to say that the refrain cannot provide an escape from contingency, that it does not allow the *pour-soi* to justify its existence through an aesthetic creation that would not be subject to the extreme indifference of the universe.

For Roquentin, however, and indeed for Sartre since, as we have seen, the same idea is formulated not only in his fictional work but his philosophical work also, the admission of this fact, of the idea that the nausea (or noise) of existence cannot be countered by music, by an expression that would arise from a necessary internal order, is impossible to bear. And so, rather than despair, Roquentin – and once again, of course, Sartre, as we find out from the autobiography he wrote at the end of his life in which he proclaimed 'J'étais Roquentin'[34] – chooses a different path and resolves to write 'The sort of story, for example, which could never happen, an adventure [...,] beautiful and hard as steel and [that would] make people ashamed of their existence'.[35] This project is explicitly formulated as a means to counter the absurdity of his existence and thus to dissipate his nausea, to make of him a necessary and justified part of the universe, to absolve him of the 'sin of existing'.[36] What should hopefully be clear by now, however, is that the very idea that there could exist such a story or, indeed, such a song is itself indicative of a certain bad faith, not because Roquentin has fundamentally mistaken the way in which music comes to be but because, just as throughout the novel he performs a misprision of noise, so here he chooses entirely to ignore his nausea as though it were a scratch on a record and to forget the insights gained during his illumination, namely, that even steel is not in fact solid and hard in an absolute sense, but also expressive.

As much as Roquentin may then claim to have become his nausea,[37] ultimately he does not attend to it, or mishears it, as he does with noise throughout the novel. That he cannot ultimately accept the full ramifications of his nausea and chooses instead to write as a means to justify his existence and thus attain a form of immortality is perhaps not surprising, for, as Simon Critchley suggests, throughout almost its entire history philosophy has been obsessed with meaning and 'the desire to master death and find fulfilment for human finitude'.[38] Critchley argues, however, that it need not, indeed perhaps should not be this way since 'Writing interrupts the dialectical labour of the negative, introducing into the Subject a certain impotence and passivity that escapes the movement of comprehension'.[39] Citing the examples of Schlegel and Blanchot, Critchley suggests that it is possible to write 'outside of philosophy [...,] ceasing to be fascinated with the circular figure of the Book, the en-*cyclo*-paedia of philosophical science, itself dominated by the figures of unity and totality, which would attempt to master death and complete meaning by letting nothing fall outside of its closure'. In doing this and concentrating on writing, on the act of expression rather than the objects that are the end result of that event, 'one is no longer attracted by the Book, but rather by *the energy of exteriority* that cannot be reduced to either the exteriority of Law – even the written Torah – or to the *Aufhebung* of the exteriority of Law in Christianity or dialectics: neither the Book of God nor the Book of Man'.[40]

Drawn towards the Book as a coherent artefact that would justify his existence, Roquentin ultimately turns away from this energy of exteriority, abnegating his nausea as he does noise. For just as nausea reveals the greyness or porosity of the world to him, stripping him of the illusion of sovereign subjectivity, so noise is this very energy of exteriority at those moments when it becomes perceptible. To attend to noise is then to admit to the finitude of the contents of expression, which is to say to admit death or, after Blanchot, the absence of life. For noise pulls the contents of life and expression back to the plane from which they are enfolded and thus brings us to the edge of the abyss that would engulf all forms. It is for this reason that noise has the power to bring about in those who cling to a belief in sovereign individuality a feeling of nausea or, perhaps, abjection. Little wonder, then, that Roquentin ultimately turns away from nausea/noise. Not that Roquentin is alone, of course, for noise has often figured as a site of horror and a gateway to the absence of life.

Notes

1 Bart Kosko, *Noise* (London: Viking Penguin, 2006), 65.

2 A variant is found also, of course, in the nickname given to Balzac's Catherine Lescault, 'la Belle Noiseuse', familiar to French ears nowadays mostly because of the Jacques Rivette film of this name that is loosely based on Balzac's text *Le Chef d'œuvre inconnu*.

3 Michel Serres, *Genesis* (orig. French, 1982; Ann Arbor: University of Michigan Press, 1995), 12.

4 Serres, *Genesis*, 13.

5 Jean-Paul Sartre, *Nausea*, trans. Robert Baldick (London: Penguin Books, 1965). Originally published in French as *La Nausée* (Paris: Gallimard, 1938).

6 Later in his career, Céline of course became famous for entirely different reasons, even if his stylistic innovations only increased as his career progressed. Indeed, if Céline is remembered for anything these days, it is mostly for the pseudo-fascist anti-Semitic pamphlets that he wrote. The inscription to Sartre's novel comes from Céline's play *The Church* [*L'Église*], written in 1933, which is to say before such controversies were to plague this author. It reads: 'He is a fellow without any collective significance, barely an individual'.

7 Serres, *Genesis*, 12.

8 Denis Hollier, 'La Nausée, en attendant', in La Naissance du phénomène Sartre, raisons d'un success 1938–1945, ed. I Galster (Paris, Seuil, 2001), 95.

9 James Arnold, 'La Nausée Revisited', The French Review, 39, no. 2 (1965), 209.

10 See Sartre, Nausea, 14.

11 Sartre, Nausea, 17.

12 Sartre, Nausea, 22.

13 Sartre, Nausea, 33.

14 Sartre, Nausea, 33.

15 Sartre, Nausea, 30. There are many instances of this grey colour palette. See also, for instance, 41, 179, 180. The use of colour and different kinds of light has been commented on by Woods who contends that the split between scenes in which there is a chiaroscuro effect and those in which there is a diffused, grey light corresponds to 'the difference between perceived phenomena and images summoned in the mind', mental images being 'conceived and understood instantly, as if light were evenly diffused throughout the landscape [… whilst] in the perceptive process, the gaze functions as the limited light source which allows only one or another aspect or profile of an object to be perceived – or illuminated – at one time' (George Woods, '"Sounds, Smells, Degrees of Light": Art and Illumination in Nausea', in Sartre's Nausea: Text, Context, Intertext, ed. Alistair Rolls and Elizabeth Rechniewski (Amsterdam and New York: Rodopi, 2006), 54). I reject this view since the difference between these different light effects to my mind corresponds to different mental states when nausea/noise is either admitted into Roquentin's perception of the world (both sensory and mental) or else elided in order to restore order and clarity.

16 Andrew Benjamin, 'Porosity At The Edge: Working Through Walter Benjamin's "Naples"', Architectural Theory Review, 10, no. 1 (2005), 36.

17 Sartre, Nausea, 182.

18 Sartre, Nausea, 181.

19 Sartre, Nausea, 35.

20 Sartre, Nausea, 182–3.

21 Sartre, Nausea, 105, translation modified.

22 Sartre, Nausea, 112, translation modified.

23 Serres, Genesis, 7. One might of course object that binaurality and the concept of the 'sound shadow' cast by the head that helps

rather than hinders spatial localisation proves that this is not the
case (see Prochnik, *In Pursuit of Silence*, 51–9 for a discussion of
the anatomy of hearing; see also Barry Blesser and Lind-Ruth Salter,
Spaces Speak, Are You Listening? (Cambridge, MA: The MIT Press,
2007)). The point made by Serres and others like Nancy, however, is
more phenomenological than technical. What is more, it is important
to note the inconsistency found throughout *Nausea* according to
which noises or sounds seem 'mysterious' or 'suspicious' (*Nausea*,
14) yet able, when the narration turns more to a description of
phenomenological experience rather than mere observation, to lose
these disorienting qualities.

24   Much the same could be said of Jean-Luc Nancy's work *À l'écoute*
that we will encounter at various points through this book. See
Jean-Luc Nancy, *Listening*, trans. Charlotte Mandell (orig. French,
2002; Bronx, NY: Fordham University Press, 2007).

25   Sartre, *Nausea*, 16, translation modified, my italics.

26   Sartre, *Nausea*, 37.

27   Sartre, *Nausea*, 252.

28   Sartre, *Nausea*, 249. Schwartz also comments on this scene, but his
interpretation is entirely at odds with the reading proposed here.
For him, the jazz song is infused with noise rather than being used
as a means to counter noise and nausea, the improvisatory nature of
jazz meaning that the melodic line is itself contingent but attractively
so, inspiring an almost dervish-like ecstasy in Roquentin (Hillel
Schwartz, *Making Noise: From Babel to the Big Bang and Beyond*
(New York: Zone Books, 2011), 652–3). He writes, 'By way of jazz
and its improvisatory "noise", Roquentin feels himself to be dancing;
across from him dip and spin his contingent partners, wave and
quantum, unreachable' (653). A close reading of the novel and the
broader context of the ideas informing this scene, however, make
this reading hard to sustain and counter to the philosophical position
espoused by Sartre here.

29   Jean-Paul Sartre, *The Imaginary: A Phenomenological Psychology
of the Imagination*, trans. Jonathan Webber (orig. French, 1940;
London and New York: Routledge, 2004), 192. Arnold suggests that
here, 'we not only read a more technical description of the nature
of the aesthetic object as conceived by Roquentin; we recognize a
theory which Sartre claims to have formulated between the ages of
eight and ten and which remains fundamentally unchanged through
the writing of *La Nausée* some twenty years later' ('*La Nausée*
Revisited', 213). That there is a close correspondence between this
idea in *The Imaginary* and *Nausea* becomes self-evident when one

examines certain passages of the novel such as when, talking of the refrain, Roquentin says '*It* does not exist. It is even irritating in its non-existence; if I were to get up, if I were to snatch that record from the turn-table which is holding it and if I were to break it in two, I wouldn't reach *it*. It is beyond – always beyond something, beyond a voice, beyond a violin note. Through layers and layers of existence, it unveils itself, slim and firm, and when you try to seize it you meet nothing but existents, you run up against existents devoid of meaning. It is behind them: I can't even hear it, I hear sounds, vibrations in the air which unveil it. It does not exist, since it has nothing superfluous: it is all the rest which is superfluous in relation to it. It *is*' (*Nausea*, 248).

30 Gilles Deleuze and Félix Guattari, *A Thousand Plateaus: Capitalism and Schizophrenia 2*, trans. Brian Massumi (orig. French, 1980; Minneapolis: University of Minnesota Press, 1987), 261.

31 Deleuze and Guattari, *A Thousand Plateaus*, 300. I will return at length to this definition of music in the final chapter of the book when I turn my attention towards the relation between noise and music.

32 Deleuze and Guattari, *A Thousand Plateaus*, 300.

33 Deleuze and Guattari, *A Thousand Plateaus*, 303. It should be noted that this analysis is not in line with Deleuze's own conception of noise for in *The Logic of Sense* he traces the move towards sense between two points, from noise to voice (Gilles Deleuze, *The Logic of Sense*, trans. Mark Lester with Charles Stivale (orig. French, 1969; New York: Columbia University Press, 1990), 194), thereby implying that music (which would reside in the voice) necessitates the leaving behind of noise. It is important to note at this point also that I am not suggesting that noise *is* a haecceity, just as I have stressed and will continue to stress that noise is not coterminous with music. Rather, noise is the transcendental principle according to which a haecceity or relational ontology comes to be in the world via an expressive event.

34 Jean-Paul Sartre, *Les Mots* (Paris: Gallimard, 1964), 204.

35 Sartre, *Nausea*, 252.

36 Sartre, *Nausea*, 251.

37 See Sartre, *Nausea*, 182.

38 Simon Critchley, *Very Little ... Almost Nothing: Death, Philosophy, Literature* (London and New York: Routledge, 1997), 33.

39 Critchley, *Very Little ... Almost Nothing*, 33.

40 Critchley, *Very Little ... Almost Nothing*, 33–4.

CHAPTER THREE

Noise, Horror, Death

Do you see what I see?

* * *

Scream

Noise, in the collective imagination of Hollywood, seems to be indelibly associated with horror. I say this in part, of course, because horror movie soundtracks are often constituted almost entirely of noises of one kind or another: the creak of an old door blowing open in the wind (or being opened by an unwelcome visitor); the noise of a twig snapping in a dark forest as an unseen presence unwittingly makes itself known sonically; the roar of a beast/demon/monster; the gasps of shock and screams of terror of a victim being pursued or devoured; the menacing orchestral rumbles of the soundtrack scored to build tension and menace and which is suddenly punctuated by the dissonant explosion of piercing, screeching violins as suspense gives way to action. It is not really noises such as this that interest me here, however, even if one might suggest that they often point towards the same oppositional order that has been attributed to noise thus far as they signal the presence (or approach) of a being-not-like-us, an alterity perceived of as threatening to the integrity of form, or life. Rather, these are noises because they are sounds that we do not want to hear (even though, of course, as horror movie spectators we *do* want to hear them, but only if they are enclosed in a safe diegetic universe on the silver screen where they are held at a distance and thus able merely to thrill and not kill). This kind of noise and the kind of thrill that it can engender, of course, is not particularly new and can be traced back to earlier cultural forms. The spooky noises from the soundtrack of horror movies, for instance, are closely related to the unexplained sounds that populate Gothic fiction commented on by Schwartz. He writes:

> *The Vampyre* contributed to a definition of noise that was being refined in the darker recesses of the Gothic aesthetic: noise as sounds you do not *want* to identify, unforgettable sounds you try desperately to forget, sounds whose implications so repulse as to demand for sanity's sake a generic masking – sounds that should be so unfamiliar as to be incomprehensible – sounds of cannibalism and necrophilia, of bloodsucking, of sex-unto-death. Such noise was the acoustic underside of the sublime: if the sublime takes your words and breath away, at its most horrifying the sublime becomes noise, sounds you cannot dismiss but will not define, sounds you wish you had never heard.[1]

Noise emanates not only from the horrific site itself, though, but also from those who cross into that space and find themselves face to face with horror, as though noise were infectious. As Simon Reynolds has pointed out, noises and horror go hand in hand because when faced with the chaos and irrationality of horror, the ordered forms of language crumble and leave only one possible noisy response. As he writes:

> Noise is like an eruption within the material out of which language is shaped ... This is why noise and horror go hand in hand – because madness and violence are senseless and arbitrary (violence is the refusal to argue) and the only response is wordless – to scream.[2]

In both of these cases, regardless of whether the noise is emitted from the horrific or the horrified, noise arises out of a troubling of taxonomies, it is the sound of that which does not fit within the bounds of an ordered and safe existence and the only possible response to that which cannot be contained within existing herme-neutic categories. As Reynolds' comments infer, however, the reason why horror is so troubling is perhaps precisely because it allows us to glimpse an alterity that is not absolute but that inhabits us. This is to say that if it is 'like an eruption within the material out of which language is shaped', then it is necessarily a sign of the formlessness out of which language struggles into existence, the noisy background of all expression to which language can return when words fail us, when we stutter, stammer or scream.[3]

In horror movies, though, this troubling of the taxonomic order is by no means restricted to language; on the contrary, this is the very essence of the operations of the horror genre that requires the natural order of things to be disturbed before, in most cases, the hero discovers the means to restore that order, always then maintaining the aesthetic distance necessary to send the viewer back into the real world. Horror movies are then filled with a more generalised form of noise that extends far beyond their soundtrack and operates as a fundamentally destabilising principle. In horror, this is to say, just as in communications systems, noise is that element which disrupts the harmony or desired configuration of the system from within the very materiality or expressive constraints of the system itself. So if the material properties of a communications system pre-determine to a certain extent some of the qualities of the content transmitted by that system, so the generic conventions of horror are always already imbricated in its content, pulling its individual expressions outwards in a move that parallels that taking place in the diegesis itself. What is perhaps surprising – or perhaps it is not surprising at all given this double disturbance – is that this noise is very often explicitly figured as something that we recognise as noise, as something that interferes with the transmission of information. What is more, in a number of films from the genre, this explicit figuration of noise serves also to perform a reflection on the material specificity of the media through which we make sense of the world, obviating the possibility of doing as we have seen Roquentin do and pretending that these mediated expressions are somehow separate from reality.

Poltergeist

The 1982 Steven Spielberg-produced, Tobe Hopper-directed film *Poltergeist* begins with noise. Rather, it begins with the 'Star-Spangled Banner' playing on the soundtrack, but this is accompanied by highly pixelated images whose subject matter or content is unrecognisable and which thus leaves us able only to discern the technological mediation at play rather than the content or meaning of the mediated images. It becomes clear, as the camera slowly tracks away from the object being filmed, that we are witness merely to a television set broadcasting those images of crude patriotic symbolism familiar to insomniacs and which play in the early hours of the morning in various countries around the world once the end of the night's programmed schedule has been reached. However, being shot at first from so close as to be unrecognisable, these clichéd, too well-known images do not instil in the viewer a comforting sense of familiarity as they are intended to but, rather, a certain disquiet. What is more, this disquiet is maintained even after the images become recognisable, classifiable within a semiotic order, the camera sufficiently distanced from the TV set for its medial noise (its pixels) to be elided in our perception as they coalesce into a recognisable image of something – thus allowing us access to the media content rather than the mechanics of the media itself. For no sooner does this happen than all recognisable content suddenly disappears to be replaced by televisual noise (or snow) and sonic white noise as the TV station stops broadcasting any meaningful content at all and thus leaves the interpretative media to express its pure mediality.

Into this shot of a television set broadcasting all that it can in the absence of signal – which is to say noise – wanders a dog scavenging for food. Its quest leads it upstairs into the kids' bedroom where it wakes Carol Anne who gets up, goes downstairs, sits in front of the TV set and strikes up a conversation with the noise, asking what they look like, trying to hear them better, and responding to their questions by saying, finally, 'I don't know. I don't know'.

A sudden cut takes us to more familiar territory as, over the opening credits, a sweeping panoramic establishing shot pans from an idyllic, apparently rural setting to a suburban housing development nestled in a valley. Successive shots bring us closer and closer into this setting as we pass from panoramic vistas to views of a section of the development, to shots which follow an individual car making its way through these streets or show children playing. In contrast to the opening sequence of the film, then, here, as is normally the case with the establishing shots of a film, the closer we get to the objects we are observing, the more familiar and understandable they become, the more the viewer feels oriented in the diegetic space of the film.

The homely, safe, suburban condition depicted here is reinforced by the film's subsequent shots which admit danger, death or monsters into this space in very controlled doses: mischievous kids with remote controlled cars conspire to bring a beer-carrying Dad on a bicycle crashing to the ground (but harm only the beer); a TV set that appears to be mysteriously changing channels of its own accord turns out to be merely affected by a neighbour's remote control clicker which operates at the same frequency; an image of space aliens and monsters that fills the screen turns out to be nothing more than a *Star Wars* bedspread being fluffed by a Mom going about her domestic chores; a dead budgerigar is quickly buried and forgotten by its five-year-old owner in return for a goldfish; and a violent electrical storm is rendered unthreatening for young children firstly by counting the time between lightning and thunder for reassurance that it is indeed moving away and then, when that fails, by the safety, warmth and comfort of Mom and Dad's bed.

It is once this calm has been restored, however, that a much more significant threat to order surfaces again. For in an almost exact replay of the film's opening shot, as the family all sleep in bed together, the TV again plays the 'Star-Spangled Banner' and accompanying patriotic images before cutting, as we now know it will, to visual and sonic noise. Carol Anne wakes up, crawls to the end of the bed, sits in front of the TV as before and watches intently. This time, however, in the midst of the noise, the film's audience hears what sound like voices, and zones of visual noise are concentrated into bright star-like points. Carol Anne reaches out towards the TV and a smoke-like, wispy hand swirls out of the noise, wafts above the bed where the rest of the family still lie asleep and then slams into the wall above their heads in a roaring vortex. The entire house starts shaking, the rest of the family wake up, Carol Anne looks away from the noise-filled TV straight at her loved ones and proclaims, calmly, 'They're here'. From this point on, the poltergeists will merely do as is their nature, like the noise whence they issue, and disrupt the 'right' or desired order of things, sending everyday objects – including some markers of linguistic order, a dictionary and a record which, with the help of a compass, plays the ABC song – into a crazy orbit.

All that remains for this suburban family to do, then, is to restore order, to retrieve Carol Anne from the TV people who take her into the noise with them and, ultimately, to play out a fairly standard battle between good and evil – albeit it with a nerdy team of paranormal investigators in tow and a good dose of horror schlock along the way. Whilst much of this provides fairly standard horror fare, what is particularly interesting about *Poltergeist* is that in this struggle between good and evil or the known and the unknown – which in horror (and often in life) amounts to the same thing – the unknown (figured as noise) is seen always to subtend the known. The Other in whom horror resides, this is to say, is not an absolute alterity, a monster from a faraway place, an alien or an escaped madman; rather, as the film's opening sequence analysed above shows us, the Other or the unknown from which horror issues is always present but revealed only when we look closely enough. For what is revealed progressively in the later stages of the film is that the poltergeists who inhabit this family's home and who kidnap Carol Anne are not monstrous Others encroaching upon the suburban calm of Cuesta Verde but, rather, the rightful inhabitants of the land. For as we discover in the course of the film, this housing development has been built on top of an old graveyard, a plot twist which would again be fairly standard fare were it not for the conversations between Steve Freeling, the family Dad, and his

boss which reveal the underside of large-scale property developments such as this and which are always dependent on a great deal
of noise, of information that people do not want to know and are
thus deprived of or wilfully ignore. This, of course, is once again
the very same movement witnessed in the opening shots of the film
which show us that although the noise of the TV is most obvious
when the broadcast signal is cut, there is always underlying any
TV picture a great deal of noise. Indeed, every TV image is formed
out of non-signifying elements that are markers of the material and
technological specificities of the medium, that are necessary for the
transmission of the broadcast content yet which cannot be read in
the same way and which are thus generally elided entirely in order
to concentrate on the meaningful content being broadcast, on what
we want to see or hear.

Whilst *Poltergeist* thus situates itself squarely in the lineage of
the horror genre in which, almost without fail, disruptive, foreign
or monstrous elements are introduced into a familiar, ordered
space, it puts a slight twist on this scenario by suggesting that the
disruptive other is always present and not necessarily an outsider.
And, whilst this is perhaps not unprecedented, what is interesting for the purpose of the present study is that the ever-present
disruptive threat to order is articulated to a parallel reflection on
noise. Indeed, I believe that each successive iteration of the noise-
filled TV screen functions not only as a spooky event, but also
extends the film's horror out beyond the silver screen, indicating
to us the audience that the message-bearing technologies of the
information age always carry within them the potential to disrupt
the messages they are intended faithfully to transmit. Noise of
this kind has surely become such a common trope in horror films
precisely because of this disruptive or contestatory potential, but
not only because of this. Indeed, what is so horrific about noise
in *Poltergeist* (and this is the case to an even greater degree in
the other movies to be analysed subsequently) is that the possibility for these apparently transparent and self-effacing media to
assert themselves brings with it the potential for them to disrupt
our messages, to make *us* passive and thus admit the possibility
of our death. This is to say, then, that noise in the horror genre
can become a gateway not merely to disruptive others (as it is in
Poltergeist) but, more specifically, to death or, rather, to that which
stands in opposition to life.

Death

Whilst it would undoubtedly be somewhat far-fetched to suggest that the horror genre operates in precisely the same way as literature or writing outside philosophy in the analysis of Blanchot and Schlegel observed at the end of the previous chapter, there are nonetheless many similarities. For if, for them, literature 'interrupts the dialectical labour of the negative, introducing into the subject a certain impotence and passivity that escapes the movement of comprehension, of philosophy's obsession with meaning: the desire to master death and find a meaning for human finitude',[4] much of the time the operations of horror – and indeed noise – are ultimately no different. Indeed, the horror genre often relies upon an absolute passivity from its protagonists, a surrender to the monster or dark force which escapes comprehension and which ultimately leads to the possibility of death – a literal, sudden and gruesome death rather than the metaphorical deaths of Blanchot. This passivity (itself already a kind of death for the Cartesian subjects whose internal perception and agency are necessary for the constitution of both self and the world), this surrender to a force which escapes the subject's transcendent structures of meaning is precisely the condition that is precipitated by noise. Noise then – and this is its function in *Poltergeist* – can act as a gateway or portal to death, its imposing and ineluctable presence only ever offering an absence of meaning, an incommensurability of interior and exterior, form and content and thus an absolute abnegation of the figures of unity and totality.

Given this, it should come as no surprise that, since the early days of the recording, communications or broadcasting technologies which inevitably produced noise as an unfortunate by-product of their primary process, people have believed that there are ghosts in these machines or that these machines would enable the living to communicate with the dead. Indeed, in the 1920s Thomas Edison (and Marconi similarly) conjectured that the machines he was so instrumental in creating might eventually enable personalities from a different sphere or existence to commune with those inhabiting our earthly world. These ideas were elaborated much further, however, by Friedrich Jürgenson and later by Konstantin Raudive, both of whose work forms the basis of the investigations of the great number of enthusiasts (or believers?) who attempt to record and interpret Electronic Voice Phenomena (EVP) – as the presence of otherworldly voices heard in noise, static or recorded media more generally is now referred to.

The history of EVP has been briefly documented by Joe Banks and more fully in the context of spiritualist sound experiments by Anthony Enns.[5] Banks, for his part, argues that there are perfectly rational explanations for the supposedly strange phenomenon of EVP, yet maintains that the practice or pseudo-science of EVP merits critical attention and that it is 'of genuine anthropological interest, not least because the process entails the use of electronic technology to help construct, rationalize and validate a fundamentally anti-scientific belief system'.[6] Enns, meanwhile, links spiritualist sound experiments to psychoanalysis to suggest that 'the spiritualists' attempts to translate these noises into coherent 'messages' simply reveal the utter nonsense generated by the unconscious itself' and that, therefore, 'the voices of the dead represent noises that blur the differences between acoustic signals, psychic phenomena and schizophrenic hallucinations'.[7] Whilst these two positions may appear to be fundamentally opposed to each other, Banks finding the phenomenon perfectly understandable and Enns maintaining that the practice in fact illustrates the resistance of noise to all forms of intellectual assimilation – be it via 'conscious mediation or artistic representation'[8] – both ultimately find common ground when talking of the impetus behind these experiments. For Banks, EVP experiments stem 'from an instinct we all share – the desire to triumph over the tragedy of human mortality and to retain contact with lost friends'.[9] For Enns, meanwhile, even if these experiments are doomed to fail because of the nonsense generated by the unconscious, such practices point to a desire to recuperate the unity and totality of a subject perceived to have been fragmented by both the modern science of psychoanalysis and modern technology itself. As Enns writes:

> Under media-technological conditions, the speaking subject is thus no longer able to speak for herself, as speech is no longer part of the self once it is recorded and broadcast. The notion of electrical noise as a repository for the disembodied voices of the dead seems to provide a vivid metaphor for the loss of the 'self' or the 'soul' within the electric media environment.[10]

In both of these analyses, noise, for practitioners of EVP, seems to operate as a kind of suturing device, a signifier capable of sewing up lacks and absences – whether interpersonal as in Banks' analysis or infrapersonal as in Enns'. To suggest that noise can act in this way is to enact a misprision of noise, however, not necessarily because of the fundamental meaninglessness of the unconscious in Enns' analysis, but because to treat noise in this way is to imbue noise itself with a unifying power that it simply cannot have. Indeed, if the work of suture creates a falsely harmonious whole which appears to reconcile the various aspects of a multiple and contradictory reality, then noise is precisely incapable of this work since it refuses the very possibility of such a division between parts, inside and outside, form and content. This is indeed the way we have seen noise operating in *Poltergeist*, not in the slightest as a suturing device but, precisely, as that which confounds interior and exterior and which quite simply cannot be understood or assimilated into an ordered system and must be gotten rid of. What is then particularly interesting about *Poltergeist* is that, ultimately, it actually proves Enns' point that the dead or the other side to which noise can provide access is a powerful metaphor for a perceived loss of self or soul within the electric media environment. For having finally exorcised the demons from their house (which implodes on itself) and their life (the family leaving Cuesta Verde in the film's final sequence), the film's final shot shows the Father removing a television set from the motel room where they stay for a night *en route* towards a new life. However, whereas for Enns it is the electronic media environment generally that serves as such a metaphor for the loss of self in an electric media environment, I would contend that it is actually the *noise* of the media – and the threat of noise that constantly subtends all such media since they are dependent on it – that serves as a metaphor. This is to say, then, that in this scene it is not ultimately the TV set that is banished as much as its noise, the possibility that it might exceed human control and cease to efface itself in the transmission of content.[11]

Whilst the absolute incommensurability and resistance to containment of noise lead to its exclusion in *Poltergeist*, however, it is perfectly possible to argue that it is these very qualities which make others embrace it. Indeed, it is possible to extend the analyses of critics such as Banks and Ronell (for whom technologies such as the telephone counter death by preserving 'the lost "love object" [...] in a crypt like a mummy'[12]) and suggest that it is a refusal of the absolute posed by death that leads to a concomitant refusal of the absolute posed by noise and a desire to read meaning back into noise. For the subject who refuses the absolute meaninglessness of noise, noise can become simply a site in which there is an absence of meaning (which is not the same thing) and thus a blank space into which to cast one's own projected desires – white noise as *tabula rasa*, in other words. Rather than constituting a site of the unhomely, noise apprehended in this manner can then become a haven of comfort and solace, an accessory to the process of mourning as the subject is able to project their own desire into that space.[13] To embrace noise in this way, however, is to indulge in pareidolia, the attribution of meaning to an inherently complex and chaotic system lacking coherent meaning, a charge which is often levelled at EVP. In spite of its embrace of the phenomenon of EVP for its major plot line, the 2004 film *White Noise* (which begins with an inscription from Thomas Edison) occasionally appears to level this same charge at noise. As in *Poltergeist*, however, noise ultimately resists any containment or pareidolia of this kind, but rather than being merely banished as a consequence and in the interests of a happy ending, noise here retains its disruptive potential right up until the end.

White Noise

Nobody knows whether our personalities pass on to another existence or sphere, but if we can evolve an instrument so delicate as to be manipulated by our personality as it survives in the next life such an instrument ought to record something.

THOMAS EDISON 1928

If the 2004 Geoffrey Sax-directed film *White Noise* ultimately does not allow noise to be integrated into a meaningful structure through pareidolia, at times it nonetheless suggests, somewhat cheekily, that EVP is nothing more than this. Indeed, early on in the film the main protagonist, Jonathan Rivers (played by Michael Keaton), goes to see EVP specialist Raymond Price (Ian McNeice) following the death of the former's wife. Price meets him and introduces him to another of his clients, Sarah Tate (Deborah Kara Unger). Sarah is in tears and having a hard time composing herself because, as Price explains to Rivers, they have finally, eight months after the death of Tate's fiancé, had a breakthrough and understood what he was saying through the noise received and recorded by Price. As Sarah confides to Rivers, after a long period of time she and Price have finally made out what her fiancé was saying through the white noise: 'Sarah, yes'. Sarah explains that Price thinks her fiancé probably will not return again and an obviously sceptical Rivers looks away, letting out an awkward laugh. Unperturbed, Sarah affirms that all is well since, as she explains: 'I've heard what I wanted to hear'. And yet, in spite of her acceptance of this aspect of EVP at this time, as John Rivers becomes more and more obsessed by EVP and convinced that his dead wife is foretelling deaths in the local area before they have happened so that Rivers can prevent them, when he asks Sarah if she understands what he claims is happening she replies, 'I can see how you're putting it together, yes'.

For the most part, however, *White Noise* is far from a tongue-in-cheek sideswipe at EVP: on the contrary, it relies for its effect on the audience's suspension of disbelief and acceptance of the basic premise of this pseudo-science. Indeed, to lend credibility to the semi-'factual' or, rather, real-life basis of EVP, the DVD version of the film contains, as bonus features, a documentary on real-life EVP investigations, 'actual EVP sessions' and instructions on how to make EVP recordings at home.

If *White Noise* does not significantly undercut the science of the practice that gives the film its major plot line, however, nor is it content simply to allow noise to become a comforting resource, a medium through which to access the voices and images of lost loved ones, as it is for EVP practitioners (as evidenced by Banks' analysis). So even though noise is at times imbued with meaning and thus serves to ward off the death or entropy that it represents – literally here since Anna Rivers communicates through noise from 'the other side' in order to prevent others from passing over to that side – it also, as in *Poltergeist*, serves as a portal for a far more unsavoury and destructive form of behaviour. Indeed, it is through the noise generated for EVP sessions that the 'men in the room', or 'the ones who like damage', as they are variously referred to in the film, are able to pass into the ordered world of the everyday reality of human mortals. These 'men in the room' are three ghostly, evanescent, silhouetted figures who love to swear, scream, smash up apartments and schizophrenically command an earthly being to abduct, torture and kill women (including John's wife, as we find out) and who ultimately kill John. As such, they represent not the homely aspect that noise can take on in pareidoliac illusions but, rather, its destructive potential, transgressing the ordered bounds of language through expletives,[14] screams and pain.[15] More than this, though, these 'men in the room' are able to appear as emanations of the noise of recorded media even though separated from that media and also to express themselves as the thoughts of an earthly servant, thus conflating interior and exterior realms, collapsing the strictly demarcated taxonomies of ordered human existence.

This is, of course, entirely understandable for a thriller-cum-horror movie, for this genre, as suggested, is dependent upon the destabilisation of the homely, banal or everyday by an unhomely, disruptive, destructive, evil or monstrous alterity. However, *White Noise* articulates itself to another subgenre of the horror genre, that involving machinery out of control and that includes *Pulse*, *Carrie* and the *Terminator* series,[16] and in doing this extends its reflection on noise out into a commentary on the very recording and broadcasting technologies that populate our contemporary, technology-filled everyday spaces. For instance, before Anna Rivers' death at the very beginning of the film, the Rivers' kitchen radio is heard to broadcast a mix of jumbled channels and between station white noise; when John asks his young son if he has been messing around with the radio, his son denies this. Similarly, later in the film John is unable to tune this same radio properly and at another point it turns itself on and scans through channels of its own free will. More technological devices start to misbehave after Anna's death, of course: her cell phone inexplicably calls John's even though switched off; an elevator with John in it breaks down between floors; and clocks seem to be forever stopping at 2:30 a.m., presumably the time at which Anna died because it is at this time that she makes her attempts to contact John through noise.

More significantly, however, John's own early EVP sessions using analogue audio and video tape technology are accompanied by close-up shots of the internal mechanics of these machines – tape spools turning, playback and recording heads coming into contact with tape. Sequences showing John's later recording sessions once he has made the move to digitised files and computer software for greater possibilities of data manipulation, meanwhile, are shot in such a way as to foreground the software interface and its operations with a much greater eye for detail than the exigencies of plot progression alone would warrant. These shots – especially those of the analogue equipment which, in any case, is always hooked up to the later, more sophisticated computer equipment – seem to echo the dual movement attributed to noise in the film which, as suggested, can act both as a homely site if used for pareidoliac fantasies and self-delusion, but which ultimately expresses a fundamentally unhomely and disruptive force. Indeed, the shots of the internal workings of tape equipment are in themselves somewhat unnerving because of the apparent automatism of technology that they display. Rather than serving as a positivist signifier of progress and modernity, then, technology in *White Noise* – as it was for the Futurists – is presented as an inherently noisy and disruptive force whose indifferent base materiality (when not elided in order for the desired content of the messages it transports to get through) threatens to exceed our control, to refuse complete assimilation into our ordered sphere. For the Futurists, unable to admit this lack of control, the task became to conquer noise regardless and to integrate it within a taxonomic, ordering system. In *Poltergeist*, technology is simply too disruptive and ultimately banished from the family's life. But in *White Noise*, noise and technology ultimately prevail, for whilst John does indeed avert the death of the final victim of 'the ones who like damage', their henchman being shot by police alerted to their whereabouts by John, John himself is killed and his final appearances in the film present him as auditory noise.[17] For after his own funeral, John turns on a car radio to say sorry to his son through broadcast noise and then, in the film's final shot, he appears as a visual emanation emerging out of a noise-filled TV screen, no longer alone but reunited with his wife, the look on their faces indicating not eternal bliss, however, but, rather, continued unease and unhomeliness.

This final shot of *White Noise* articulates itself to the horror genre not only by introducing the crushing meaninglessness of death into the domestic sphere but also, as with *Poltergeist*, by figuring a cyborgian union of man and machine. For if the machines-gone-mad horror subgenre consistently fascinates and terrifies audiences, this fear comes not only from the potential physical damage that machines might do to us in that state but, far more powerfully, from the spectre of bodily possession, the threat of technological colonisation (as is made horrifyingly clear in the 1989 Shin'ya Tsukamoto-directed *Tetsuo*). Noise is, of course, particularly suited to this task, for it is by nature that which dissolves the clear-cut, sharply defined boundaries of any taxonomic order, the *Aufhebung* which brings about the dissolution of the binary. Thus, part of the unsettling feeling created by Carol Anne's voice (which struggles to distinguish itself from the white noise of the detuned TV) and by the final fuzzy, noise-degraded image of John Rivers and his wife (who can only just be distinguished from the visual noise or television 'snow' around them) comes from the same sense of dread that has confronted audiences faced with those cyborgian conjugations that have provided horror (and science fiction) so much fertile ground to exploit in films such as *Metropolis*, *Tetsuo*, the *Terminator* films, *Robocop*, *Videodrome*, *Event Horizon*, *Alien*, *Scanners* ...

This cyborgian horror subgenre is given a particularly interesting twist in the last film to be examined here, Gore Verbinski's *The Ring* (2002), the Hollywood remake of the Japanese *Ringu* (2000, directed by Hideo Nakata) and in which, once again, televisual noise acts both as a portal between the realms of the dead and the domestic spaces of the living, but in which the material logic of technology – which is akin to saying its noise – is seen to overtake the human entirely.[18]

The Ring

The Ring begins at a sleepover, as two teenage girls, Katie and Becca, try to scare each other by telling the story of a videotape containing nightmarish images that, so urban legend has it, kill. Indeed, it would appear that anyone who watches this tape – which starts with televisual white noise, of course – receives, as soon as it has finished, a telephone call from someone who says merely 'seven days', this being the number of days anyone who has watched the tape has left to live. Katie claims, however, that this is not merely an urban legend and that she saw the tape a week before with four friends at a cabin in the woods. She explains that during a weekend away, her friends had tried to record a football game on a tape which, when played back, contained instead 'something else', nightmarish images from another place that they had attributed merely to a bad signal in the cabin. But as soon as the tape had finished, Katie continues, the phone rang. Sure enough, seven days later, which is to say later during the night of the sleepover, the TV in Katie's house turns itself on to a detuned channel broadcasting noise and Katie – along with the three friends who have also seen the tape, as we later find out – dies, her heart simply stopping, inexplicably. Whilst we do not actually see her death, Becca, who does, is driven insane by what she has seen and is subsequently incapable of looking at a television.

Katie, as it happens, is the cousin of a young boy, Aidan, whose mother Rachel (Naomi Watts) is an investigative journalist. Rachel decides to discover precisely what happened to Katie and thus eventually comes across the tape, which she watches. The phone rings, the voice speaks, and Rachel, mysteriously, becomes not so much unphotogenic as unphotographable, her face appearing distended and blurred on any photograph taken of her. Understandably keener than ever to solve the mystery, she shows the tape to Noah, a friend (and father of her son as it turns out) who is a photographer and an expert in audio-visual technology. Noah is puzzled by the tape because it sends the counters of his professional video editing machines haywire, as does a copy of the tape that Rachel has made, a phenomenon that indicates to him that, inexplicably, there is no control track and thus no way of telling where, when or on what kind of equipment the tape was made. Whilst looking at the tape with Noah, Rachel thinks she sees something at the very edge of the frame and so they try manually to manipulate the playback head to stretch the alignment of the tracking out far enough to reveal the very outside portion of the image. The machine – whose automated mechanics do not take kindly to this kind of abuse – resists this manhandling, the recording head spinning wildly and cutting Rachel. Unperturbed, Rachel takes the tape to a professional video laboratory where the machines' tracking capability is much greater. Examining the video frame by frame and pulling the tracking out as far as it will go, Rachel manages to see a lighthouse – a landmark which will eventually allow her to pinpoint this landscape geographically and thus uncover the provenance of the tape. Whilst doing this, however, she also notices a fly on the screen which, strangely, does not seem to be pixelated like the rest of the image, and which seems to move very slightly even when the image is frozen. Puzzled by this, Rachel reaches for the fly and is able to pick it off the screen – our first indication that the noise of the TV (figured here as a pixelated video image) serves here once again as a portal to another realm.

Further investigations reveal a mysterious chain of events resulting in the deaths of many horses on the island where this lighthouse is to be found and Rachel, convinced that the tape is linked to these events and, more specifically, to Richard and Anna Morgan, the stable owners whose horses were dying, sets off to the island (keener than ever to solve this mystery now that her son has also watched the tape) whilst Noah goes to a psychiatric hospital to look up Anna Morgan's medical records. In the end it transpires that Richard and Anna, after years of trying for a baby and numerous miscarriages, eventually left this island to return later with a daughter, Samara, whom they claimed to have adopted. Shortly after this, however, Anna started having nightmarish visions which came, she says, only when she was near Samara and which threatened to drive her insane. In order to separate Samara from her mother, therefore, Richard Morgan built a room for Samara in the attic of the stables where she had only a television set for company and where the whinnying of the horses prevented her from sleeping. Samara thus, we presume from the information given, projected mental images into the horses' minds, images so terrible that the horses bolted from their stables, jumped through fences and ran straight into the sea in order to drown themselves. To try and put a stop to this, Anna and Samara visited the local doctor who referred them to a mental institution on the mainland where Samara was of great interest and the subject of great puzzlement to the doctors because of her ability to create images (similar to those on the videotape) directly onto photographic media, images that are called in the film projected thermographies and which resemble photograms.[19]

The various strands of this story are gradually pieced together by both Rachel (at the Morgan's property on the island) and by Noah (in the mental institution's record room), and both eventually end up in Samara's stable room where they see a charred section of wall through a gap in the wallpaper that turns out to be part of the silhouette of a tree, burnt into the wood by Samara's projected thermic thoughts. Rachel recognises this tree as one she has seen near the cabin where the videotape was first seen by Katie and her friends, and so she and Noah return there.

Back at the cabin, a damp, mouldy patch on the floor alerts them to something mysterious below the cabin and they break through the floor to discover a well covered with a large circular stone. A flashback informs us, as Rachel puts the pieces of the puzzle together, that Samara's mother partially suffocated her daughter before throwing her into this well where she survived for seven days, the last images she saw being the tree near the well and the stone cover being pushed over the well, eclipsing all light until only a ring of light remained (both of these images featuring prominently on the videotape). Realising that this is Samara's final resting place, Rachel considers how to climb down into the well. But Samara beats her to it: the television in the cabin above switches itself on to a channel of noise, Samara seeps out of the screen as water and unscrews the floorboard bolts in such a way as to send the noise-filled television careering down a slope, striking Rachel (who is already unbalanced by a swarm of flies that shot out of the well when they removed the cover) and knocking her into the well.

Down in the well, Rachel finally realises the full extent of Samara's tragic end and cradles the intact body she finds which, at the moment of final revelation, quickly decomposes in her arms. For Rachel this is a sign that the nightmare is over and that her son is safe, but Aidan begs to differ and, indeed, the burn marks on his arm and the death of Noah seven days after he had originally seen the tape suggest that Aidan is right. Rachel thus tries to work out what she had done differently from Noah, why she has not died but he has, and she realises that the only difference is that she had made a copy of the tape and had shown it to Noah. Given her realisation that the images created by Samara were symptomatic only of a desire to be heard and not locked away and ignored, Rachel concludes that if Aidan makes a tape which is then seen by someone else, he too will be safe. The final sequence of the film thus shows Rachel and Aidan making another copy of the tape which ends (as does the film in its final images, except for one final accelerated rush of the nightmarish images on the tape) with a screen full of noise.

By ending in noise, the film of course naturally opens itself up to the possibility of a sequel – and, indeed, the Japanese original now has both a sequel (directed by Hideo Nakata again) and a prequel, whilst *Ringu 2* was remade for American audiences in 2005 (the Hollywood remake also directed by Nakata) – since noise in these films acts in part as a portal to another place. But more than this, by ending in noise, *The Ring*, like *White Noise*, albeit in a different manner, also shows the ultimate triumph of technology in itself (and not technology as a self-effacing medium) over the human, and this in spite of the fact that Aidan's death is averted.

To assert that it is technology that triumphs over the human mortals of *The Ring* may appear somewhat puzzling, since it is not so much the technology of the videotape and television which ultimately kills people in *The Ring* as much as the horror instilled in people at the sight of Samara, a ghost. However, it is important to remember that not only does Samara enter the earthly realm through the portal afforded by televisual noise, but that she is also effectively a technological recording mechanism. This is to say that it is Samara's ability to thermographically project images on to various media (be it photographic plates, videotape, human flesh or barn walls) that instigates the process which ultimately ends in the death of those who watch this tape.

What is more, as Rachel deduces at the end of the film, the only way for an individual to save him/herself from this death is to make a copy of the tape and to show that copy to someone else, which is to say that the individual must submit to the duplicatory logic of recording media in the modern age of technological reproducibility.[20] This very logic, of course, was horrendous for Walter Benjamin because it effectively banished the human (figured in the artwork through the concept of aura) from the artwork, and it is a site of horror for humankind in *The Ring* because the only way to achieve individual salvation is to propagate death as a reproducible or viral entity. This is also why we can say that *The Ring* ends with the triumph of technology or, more specifically, the triumph of the noise of technology: not only because the film literally ends with noise, but also because the ending that is left open promises a further proliferation of death – and therefore meaninglessness which we generally attempt to keep at bay – and the potential or necessity for the singular to become multiple, to become, then, following Serres, noise.

Abject?

If Roquentin's nauseous insights enable him to intuit the noise of existence that ultimately renders life meaningless, in the end he chooses to ignore this noise and to invent a meaning for himself, just as he ignores the noise of the vinyl record in order to transcend the materiality and thus entropy of existence. In the films examined here, noise is not so easily ignored and it comes to act as a force which is fundamentally opposed to the human and thus becomes a site of dread and horror which must be banished entirely if it is not to continue to haunt or terrorise us. That noise should come to occupy such a space in horror films is perhaps not surprising, for horror brings us face to face with what we do not want to see, just as common sense definitions of noise figure it as that part of a signal that we wish to eradicate or as that which we do not want to hear. The links between noise and horror, however, go deeper than this since, as we have seen, horror often performs a dramatization of the dissolution of order, whilst noise is that which reveals the processual nature of all being, which dissolves the (desired) clear-cut division between categories: animate and inanimate matter, self and other, subject and object, form and content, life and death. Pulling any illusory sense of sacrosanct interiority out of itself towards the outside in which it is situated and of which it is but a temporary infolding, noise has much in common with another common horror trope, the abject, and it can thus act as a similar site of repulsion for the subject concerned with the clear delimitation of its own borders – an instinctual, autoimmune response. The points of contact between noise and the abject as presented in the work of Julia Kristeva on this subject, indeed, are potentially so numerous that it is worth pausing for a moment to see if in fact her work already holds the key to understanding how something like noise can be embraced rather than rejected/attenuated.

For Kristeva, the abject describes a state much like that in which Roquentin finds himself before the tree root, since it is 'Neither subject, nor object', but, rather, a transgressive site. She writes:

> There looms, within abjection, one of those violent, dark
> revolts of being, directed against a threat that seems to emanate
> from an exorbitant outside or inside, ejected beyond the scope

of the possible, the tolerable, the thinkable. It lies there, quite close, but it cannot be assimilated. [...]

[...] The abject has only one quality of the object – that of being opposed to *I*. If the object, however, through its opposition, settles me within the fragile texture of a desire for meaning, which, as a matter of fact, makes me ceaselessly and infinitely homologous to it, what is *abject*, on the contrary, the jettisoned object, is radically excluded and draws me toward the place where meaning collapses.[21]

In this description can be found most of the elements of the taxonomy of the ontology of noise that we have proposed. What is more, if we look at other aspects of Kristeva's work we might be tempted to think that the semiotics or *sémanalyse* that she proposes is ultimately little different from the approach to be taken here that sets out to examine the noise of texts and expression. Indeed, laying out her project as an affront or challenge to the prevailing norms of literary, linguistic and semiologic methods of the time, Kristeva begins her work *Séméiotiké*[22] as follows:

> *To make of language a work* – ποιεῖν –, to work in the *materiality* of what is, for society, a means of contact and understanding, is this not already to make oneself a stranger to language? The so-called literary act, by not admitting an *ideal* distance in relation to that which signifies, introduces a radical alterity into the supposed function of language: to convey meaning.[23]

Working on the very materiality of language as opposed to its content, in the face of which language effaces itself entirely in the analytic methodologies critiqued in this passage, Kristeva proposes that language and knowledge be examined not as systems from which meaning can be extrapolated but, rather, through their systemic functionality. What is proposed, then, is 'a *materialist gnoseology*, which is to say a scientific theory of signifying systems in history and of history as a signifying system'.[24]

The difference between what Kristeva sets out to analyse through this *sémanalyse* or *gnoséologie matéraliste* (as her very terminology indicates) and the operations of noise as understood here is that, even though she is at pains to ensure that the system itself never becomes petrified into a *disposition* but remains, rather, only a series of *articulations*, and although she ensures that the influence of the system in the analysis of the enunciations emanating from it is never left aside, these enunciations are always thetic and, as such, always still a carrier of sense or *signifiance*, whereas noise is opposed to meaning. That this is the case for her becomes very clear in her second major work, *La Révolution du langage poétique*,[25] but it is already apparent in *Séméiotiké* where she talks not of semiotics but, rather, 'a semiotic level, which is that of the axiomatization, or formalization of signifying systems'.[26]

Another site of apparent similarity yet ultimate difference can be found in Kristeva's use of Plato's *chora*. Like noise, in Kristeva's use of this concept, *chora* only arises in expression itself for she uses the term to denote 'an essentially mobile and extremely provisional articulation constituted by movements and their ephemeral stases'.[27] Similarly, it is both constitutive of yet resistant to expression since 'discourse – all discourse – moves with and against the *chora* in the sense that it simultaneously depends upon and refuses it'.[28] Like noise, it is possible to talk of a topology (or ontology) of *chora* for it can be situated, but because it is always mobile 'one can never give it axiomatic form'.[29] Once again, however, Kristeva ultimately wishes 'to read in this rhythmic space, which has no thesis and no position, the process by which signifiance is constituted', considering it to be, then, if not a correlate of *signifiance*, then certainly subsumed under it.[30] So even though the semiotic *chora* is the precondition of the thetic,[31] it is figured also as but 'a modality of signifiance in which the linguistic sign is not yet articulated as the absence of an object and as the distinction between real and symbolic'.[32] The reason for this becomes clear later on when Kristeva writes:

> Once the break instituting the symbolic has been established, what we have called the semiotic *chora* acquires a more precise status. Although originally a precondition of the symbolic, the semiotic functions within signifying practices as the result of a transgression of the symbolic. Therefore the semiotic that 'precedes' symbolization is only a *theoretical supposition* justified by the need for description.[33]

The *chora* can only stand as the precondition of the symbolic, then, in abstract theorisations (as we have suggested, perhaps, of white noise), for as soon as it enters into the real it can do so only as part of a signifying regime. To point this out is not to attempt to invalidate Kristeva's analyses, merely to indicate that her approach, situated firmly within psychoanalytic, gnostic and linguistic domains, is unable to move beyond a human disposition, and this is the move that an analysis of noise requires us to make. Thus, the only way for Kristeva to reconcile her promulgation of a non-axiomatic structure and open systems with the fixity of human perception (for the human subject is of fundamental importance in all of her work) is to establish her semiotics, as Toril Moi puts it, 'as a science which seeks to represent that which per definition cannot be represented: the unconscious'.[34]

The abject, however, seems to occupy a somewhat different position in Kristeva's work, for even though it is still used within a psychoanalytic enterprise (especially in the latter half of *Powers of Horror* in which she analyses the work of Louis-Ferdinand Céline), the abject has the potential to effect a far more radical negation than the reformulation of Hegel's *Negativät* found in *La Révolution du language poétique*, to take us far further from the human. Indeed, the abject is said to bring about:

> A massive and sudden emergence of uncanniness, which, familiar as it might have been in an opaque and forgotten life, now harries me as radically separate, loathsome. Not me. Not that. But not nothing, either. A 'something' that I do not recognize as a thing. A weight of meaninglessness, about which there is nothing insignificant, and which crushes me. On the edge of non-existence and hallucination, of a reality that, if I acknowledge it, annihilates me.[35]

Reading this description, one could be forgiven for thinking that it came from Sartre's *Nausea*; if we are to attend to noise, however, we must not do as Roquentin or Kristeva's subject faced with the abject, running away out of fear or turning away in disgust.[36] Rather, we must allow that which annihilates the interiority of the privileged term in any dialectic – self (other), life (death), content (form) – to do precisely this. We must, this is to say, open ourselves up to the abject, become nauseous. Far from returning us to a regime of signification, to do this will place us on a constantly shifting ground with no coordinates, for it will be to attend to the plane of immanence as this becomes perceptible as it is contracted into expression. Neither plane nor contracted form, neither form nor content, medium nor message but, rather, the subsidiary result (not goal) of the assemblage formed between any such dialectical pair in the operation of *Aufhebung*, noise not only resists, subsists, persists, coexists and obsists but also *intersists*.

Ultimately, noise as I wish to engage with it here is not then synonymous with the abject, or rather, the abject does not hold the key to understanding how we might embrace noise, for the very nature of the abject ultimately forces us to reject its operations and to bring it back within some kind of seemingly ordered system. This is the very same movement that we find again and again in the horror genre, indeed it is perhaps the defining aspect of the classical horror movie. As Isabel Cristina Pinedo writes: 'In horror, irrational forces disrupt the social order. The trajectory of the classical narrative is to deploy science and force [...] to restore the rational, normative order'.[37] As we have seen previously, then, in the horror genre noise is ultimately figured as a disruptive element only to be gotten rid of. Or is it? For whilst it is a fairly common trope in horror for the audience to be left with one final indication that the monster is not completely dead, that the threat to order remains even though calm seems to have been restored, *all* of the films examined here show in different ways that noise can never in fact be gotten rid of, and the best we can do is then to try and ignore it, like Roquentin.

This of course is easy to do in the horror movie genre, for even though the noise remains at the end of the film, we, the audience, turn our backs on it and return to our normal lives. It is not surprising that we do so, for we, like Roquentin, are understandably not keen to remain in the state of paranoia, uncertainty and fear that the threat of dissolution and irreducibility of noise represents for the characters in these films. As should be clear by now, however, I believe that it is important and necessary *not* to turn our backs on noise, *not* to figure it as that which we would prefer to elide, sublimate or ignore, *not* to perpetuate the bad faith of Roquentin. I believe, indeed, that it is precisely because of the meaninglessness that it brings to the heart of transcendent beliefs, because of the regime of multiplicity that it brings into being that we must figure noise not as a site of horror or that which we must eradicate but, on the contrary, as a site through which we are able to entertain a more productive relation with the world. I believe, this is to say, that when the operations of noise that are figured in the horror movie are positively valorised, they can be apprehended not as threatening but, rather, able to resonate strongly with the kinds of politics of difference espoused by poststructuralist philosophers such as Deleuze and Guattari, Derrida and Cixous. These thinkers argue for an end to 'meaningful' metaphysics and human-centred perspectives *not* in order to usher in a new era of horror but, rather, as an eminently optimistic move intended to expand the bounds of human experience and possibility beyond the limiting confines that will constrain us for as long as belief in such transcendent structures endures. Thus, what I will attempt to do later in this book is to see how noise can be deployed or apprehended in such a way as to not strike fear or repulsion into the heart of those who hear it or see it.

This, though, will not always be an easy task, for if the abject does not *resist* (in the sense that we have given this term here), noise as I wish to understand it here, conversely, does not always *insist* as the abject seems to.[38] Whilst the kinds of noise described by common sense definitions of noise do indeed insist, desecrating soundscapes or interfering with communications channels, the kind of noise that interests me, not without a little irony, does not generally insist or impose itself in this way. On the contrary, the kind of noise that I am listening for effaces itself all too easily in the service of the contents of expression – some obvious exceptions to this rule being found, of course, in the works to be analysed in later chapters and in which we find a noise that is foregrounded as an invitation to attend to it or a more generalised noisy principle. There are many ways in which this happens, but one of the most frequent comes about due to the ways in which noise takes on a different colour across time.

Notes

1 Hillel Schwartz, *Making Noise: From Babel to the Big Bang and Beyond* (New York: Zone Books, 2011), 165.

2 Simon Reynolds, *Blissed Out* (London: Serpent's Tail, 1990), 60.

3 This is consistent with Elaine Scarry's comments on screams of pain that bring about 'an immediate reversion to a state anterior to language,

to the sounds and cries a human being makes before language is learned' (Elaine Scarry, *The Body in Pain: The Making and Unmaking of the World* (Oxford: Oxford University Press, 1985), 4).

4 Simon Critchley, *Very Little ... Almost Nothing: Death, Philosophy, Literature* (London and New York: Routledge, 1997), 33.

5 Joe Banks, 'Rorschach Audio: Ghost Voices and Perceptual Creativity', *Leonardo Music Journal*, 11 (2001); Anthony Enns, 'Voices of the Dead: Transmission / Translation / Transgression', *Culture, Theory and Critique*, 46, no. 1 (2005).

6 Banks, 'Rorschach Audio', 77.

7 Enns, 'Voices of the Dead', 12.

8 Enns, 'Voices of the Dead', 12.

9 Banks, 'Rorschach Audio', 82.

10 Enns, 'Voices of the Dead', 26.

11 This very idea itself, of course, is the subject of a whole separate horror subgenre populated with various kinds of cyborgian conjugations.

12 Avital Ronell, *The Telephone Book: Technology, Schizophrenia, Electric Speech* (Lincoln: University of Nebraska Press, 1989), 341.

13 It is the phenomenon of projection which forms the basis of Banks' analysis and which renders EVP an understandable phenomenon due to his contention that projection 'underpins the whole process of perception' ('Rorschach Audio', 78). For Ronell, rather than a projection it is more a case of a deferral of the process of mourning in which there is an attempt to negate death entirely (*The Telephone Book*, 59).

14 For a discussion of this phenomenon, see Alphonso Lingis, 'Contact and Communication', in *The Obsessions of Georges Bataille: Community and Communication*, ed. Andrew J. Mitchell and Jason Kemp Winfree (New York: State University of New York Press, 2009), 130.

15 On the relationship between pain and language, see Scarry, *The Body in Pain*, 55.

16 This is the case in *Poltergeist* only to a very limited extent, the loss of control of technology that televisual noise represents being prefigured by the humorous incident involving the neighbour's duel with conflicting TV remotes.

17 It should be remembered that, in all of these examples, I am referring to noise as it is explicitly figured, rather than noise as an operational and ontological principle.

18 Even though the plots of the Japanese original and the Hollywood remake are essentially the same, there being only minor variations, the analysis to follow cannot be applied to the Japanese original which does not employ noise as a trope nearly as consistently as the Hollywood version, nor does it contain the same level of reflection on the material ontology of the technology so integral to the plot development of the Hollywood remake, relying instead on more supernatural elements.

19 The process termed in the film projected thermography is more usually known in English as thoughtography, itself an English equivalent of the Japanese *nensha*.

20 See Walter Benjamin, 'The Work of Art in the Age of Mechanical Reproduction', in *Illuminations*, trans. H. Zohn (orig. German, 1936; Fontana Press, London, 1992).

21 Julia Kristeva, *Powers of Horror: An Essay on Abjection*, trans. Leon S. Roudiez (orig. French, 1980; New York: Columbia University Press, 1982).

22 Published as Σημειωτική: *Recherches pour une sémanalyse* (Paris: Seuil, 1969).

23 Julia Kristeva, 'Le texte et sa science', in Σημειωτική: *Recherches pour une sémanalyse* (Paris: Seuil, 1969), 7; my translation.

24 Kristeva, 'Le texte et sa science', 22; my translation.

25 Julia Kristeva, *La Révolution du langage poétique: l'avant-garde à la fin du XIXe siècle. Lautréamont et Mallarmé* (Paris: Seuil, 1974), published in abridged form as *Revolution in Poetic Language*, trans. Margaret Waller (New York: Columbia University Press, 1984). See also the extract published in *The Kristeva Reader*, ed. Toril Moi, trans. Margaret Waller (Oxford: Blackwell, 1986), 90–136.

26 This chapter of Kristeva *Séméiotiké* appears in translation as Julia Kristeva, 'Semiotics: A Critical Science and/or a Critique of Science', in *The Kristeva Reader*, ed. Toril Moi, trans. Seán Hand (Oxford: Blackwell, 1986). See 77.

27 Kristeva, *The Kristeva Reader*, 93.

28 Kristeva, *The Kristeva Reader*, 94.

29 Kristeva, *The Kristeva Reader*, 94.

30 Kristeva, *The Kristeva Reader*, 94.

31 Kristeva, *The Kristeva Reader*, 103–4.

32 Kristeva, *The Kristeva Reader*, 94.

33 Kristeva, *The Kristeva Reader*, 118.

34 Toril Moi in her introduction to Kristeva, 'Semiotics: A Critical
    Science and/or a Critique of Science', in *The Kristeva Reader*, ed.
    Toril Moi, trans. Seán Hand (Oxford: Blackwell, 1986), 75.

35 Kristeva, *Powers of Horror*, 2.

36 See Kristeva, *Powers of Horror*, 1.

37 Isabel Cristina Pinedo, 'Postmodern Elements of the Contemporary
    Horror Film', in *The Horror Film*, ed. Stephen Prince (Piscataway,
    NJ: Rutgers University Press, 2004), 95. In contrast, as Pinedo
    continues, 'the postmodern narrative is generally unable to overcome
    the irrational, chaotic forces of disruption'.

38 Kristeva writes that abjection 'beseeches, worries, and fascinates
    desire [yet] does not let itself be seduced' (*Powers of Horror*, 1).

PART 2

CHAPTER FOUR

On the Difficulties of Attending to Noise

'Old Vintage Typewriter'. © Alexanderf, Stock Free Images & Dreamstime Stock Photos, http://www.stockfreeimages.com/ October 28, 2012.

* * *

On failing to see noise

There exist today numerous computer fonts already integrated into operating systems or available for download that, at first glance,

AaBbCcDdFfG
gHhJjKkLlM
mNnOoIiSsEe
PpQqRrTtUuV
vWwXxYyZz

appear to be what we might call noisy, which is to say that they draw attention to the materiality of the communicative medium that brings the expression or meaning that they carry to perception. As an example, let us consider the font 'Moms Typewriter' by Christoph Mueller,[1] itself a noisier version of 'Typist', the more common Sierra On-Line, Inc./WSI font found on many PCs. 'Moms Typewriter', as its name suggests, is an eminently nostalgic product, intended to emulate the print of old pre-electric typewriters. Its individual letters are designed to evoke in us a sense of pathos: the filled-in lower bowl of the 'g', the too-thick bowl of the 'b', and the 'e' which sits just above the median line at a slightly rakish angle all proof of the overwork to which this machine has been subject, like Mom. Certainly they are both past their retirement age, but they are somehow more endearing in their slight incompetence as they cannot fail to make us nostalgically recall what they once were. Given this, it is tempting to assume that this nostalgic movement takes us back to a time when things were somehow more real: the ink spatters around each letter's already fuzzy outline seem intended to give an impression of the physicality of the medium, of the finger strength and effort needed to depress each key with sufficient force for it to slam the typebar into the ribbon and make it relinquish some of its inky load onto the paper that it almost embosses in the process. But perhaps this is not the case, perhaps this is a lure. Perhaps this font is tied to simulacrum not only because no such effort is required to produce its forms on a modern-day computer keyboard, not only because the nostalgic past to which it harkens back is one that virtually no modern-day PC user will have lived,[2] but also because the past that it seeks to invoke was itself only ever a simulacrum which was never imbued with the physical reality attributed to it by this hyper-simulacral recreation of it.

By this I mean quite simply that what is now perceived as different from our present, less physical and somehow less real technologies would not have been perceived any differently from how we perceive our own present technology by the original users of the kind of antique typewriter that would have produced the 'genuine' version of a font such as 'Moms Typewriter'. The physical act of typing, that is to say, would not have seemed to require almost superhuman finger strength for fingers trained on an Underwood, and the imperfections of the type produced, the noise that resists by both rendering transmission of the message more difficult and by signalling the material reconfiguration required for expression to come into being, would not have been attended to in this same way. Indeed, the ink spatters and uneven lines reproduced by Mueller as a nostalgic simulacrum would not have caused those reading the text produced by an Underwood in the early twentieth century to pause and reflect on the physical mechanisms that printed the letters on the page because, as Krapp points out, 'it seems entirely intuitive for us in using any artificial channel to separate noise from signal, to filter the transmission'.[3] Hence, precisely as is the case for you reading this now, the physical presence of each letter, the materiality of the medium and its technology, would be entirely effaced and subsumed by a desire to understand the text's less concrete and more elusive aspect, its meaning.[4]

To put this another way, we might use an analogy proposed by Beatrice Warde (or, to use the pen name she adopted at the start of her writing career, Paul Grandjean) in 1932. At this time, arguably the golden age of the Underwood and its competitors, Warde suggested that the book typographer's job was to aim at a kind of total transparency, to create a window 'between the reader inside the room and that landscape which is the author's words'.[5] If the typographer were to create a too-elaborate font that the reader would contemplate for its own inherent beauty, that font would be not so much a plain window as 'a stained-glass window or marvellous beauty, but a failure as a window' since it would become 'something to be looked at, not through'. If destined for a book or text whose interest would lie in the meaning behind its letters, such a font would thus necessarily be a failure. To believe that the font produced by an Underwood in 1932 was intended not to enable the communication of a meaning but to be contemplated for its own characteristics is undeniably a mistaken reaction to it, yet this is precisely the nostalgic reaction that the visual noise of 'Moms Typewriter' elicits. In this font, then, noise is foregrounded in such a way as to suggest a more embodied, physical past era different from our own, a suggestion which is entirely misleading since this noise would in actuality never have been apprehended in this way in the past that is supposedly being reverted to. Put simply, the promise of 'Moms Typewriter' (for all nostalgia implies a promise, the promise of a return to a longed-for past) is a lie since it emulates as noisy (or opaque) a font that was only ever intended to be silent and transparent.

This is not to say, of course, that these ink spatters and other markers of the material system that brings this expression into being are *not* noise; it is to say that in their own time they would not have been recognised as such and that it is, then, only retro-spectively, when a new representational norm has come into being, that this noise becomes perceptible or, rather, that it is consciously attended to. Indeed, if a new technology is able to take hold (and this is the logic of advances in high-fidelity reproduction) and supplant its predecessor, this (up until the advent of the MP3 or other download formats[6]) will be because of its (apparent) success in effacing such medial noise to a higher degree than was previously possible.

A similar mechanism that employs a more literal form of noise can be found in the contemporary musical realm where noises such as vinyl cracks and pops and tape hiss, noises that should theoretically have been totally eradicated by the high-fidelity ideals of the digital age, are added to recordings. Indeed, digital production suites such as Pro-Tools have patches written into them that allow the user to degrade the sound produced with noise, to overlay it with vinyl cracks and pops, and the use of such devices can be found in the full gamut of contemporary popular music, from David Bowie to Biohazard, Everything But the Girl to Type O Negative, Janet Jackson to Jet, Incubus to XTC, Bon Jovi to Madonna. As is the case with 'Moms Typewriter', it is easy to interpret the addition of such counterfeit noise to clean digital products as a nostalgic move that is tied up with a desire to return to a time when the world was less virtual, more concrete and real, music having become as evanescent and virtual as hypertext in the online environment. Such is precisely what is suggested by Yochim and Biddinger who note that 'Throughout both their history and in the contemporary moment, vinyl records have been articulated with human characteristics, such as fallibility, warmth and mortality, which, for record enthusiasts, imbue vinyl with authenticity'.[7] As a result, therefore, 'when vinyl collectors expound upon the aesthetic, tactile and sonic superiority of records, they are not simply romanticizing the past but are articulating an abstract relationship between technology and humanity by grounding it in more concrete qualities'.[8]

Something similar is suggested by Stan Link in his article 'The Work of Reproduction in the Mechanical Aging of an Art: Listening to Noise', where he interprets the use of such noise as an ageing mechanism intended to imbue music with a pseudo-authenticity.[9] The noise that Link analyses is, of course, counterfeit or simulacral noise, added in postproduction as opposed to produced by and in the generation or transmission of musical expressions, vinyl noise being digitally grafted onto content that required no vinyl at any point in its passage into perception. Indeed, if, as John Corbett notes, the sound of vinyl noise 'draws attention to the record's blackness, its roundness, its materiality – in short, to its visual presence',[10] then the grafting of such sounds onto a medium that *looks* so different and whose material processes are so radically different from vinyl's creates a radical disjunct of form and content.

There is then a considerable irony in the fact that such noise is intended to imbue digital products with a certain authenticity and nostalgically hark back to a time when things were different. What is more, as was the case with 'Moms Typewriter', to present this noise as an embellishment to which we as listeners should attend is to forget that, in the nostalgic past this noise aims to evoke, this noise was never intended to be heard. Indeed, like the viewer who tries not to see the glass in front of the painting she wishes to contemplate, the hiss, cracks and pops born of the contact between stylus and vinyl were, for the pre-CD era music lover, merely an unfortunate by-product of the available technology, something to be eradicated, not listened to. Thus, even though such noises might still be heard, they were ignored, deemed to be a mere by-product which listeners would, to the best of their ability, filter out in order to listen to the disk's primary audio content. To believe that the addition of such noise imbues a digital product with a higher degree of authenticity, that it nostalgically casts us back to a time when music was more embodied, is then to wilfully misremember the past, to fool oneself and to posit an incommensurability between the analogue and the digital, to find a radical moment of transition where there is really continuity.

The nostalgia and desire for authenticity signalled by such simulacral noise necessarily implies a supposition that the past recalled was different from our present. Such is indeed what seems to be suggested by Baudrillard in his analysis of the contemporary era of simulation which itself appears to be the last possible step in a series of phases mapped on to a certain history of representation. Baudrillard writes:

> When the real is no longer what it was, nostalgia assumes its full meaning. There is a plethora of myths of origin and of signs of reality – a plethora of truth, of secondary objectivity, and authenticity. Escalation of the true, of lived experience, resurrection of the figurative where the object and substance have disappeared. Panic-stricken production of the real and of the referential, parallel to and greater than the panic of material production: this is how simulation appears in the phase that concerns us.[11]

In terms of noise, however, to suggest that our contemporary era is in actuality less noisy than the past – hence the need to simulate it now, as noise signals a reality and materiality that seem to have been lost in the evanescence and virtuality of digital code – is to ignore the logic of high fidelity, to forget that for past generations *their* own era appeared similarly noise-free because, in relation to the preceding epoch, it *was* less noisy.

As we move into the digital era, the difficulty of recognising the noise of expressions transmitted through digital media is somewhat changed, then, for what we find is not so much a quantitative reduction in the degree of noise transmitted by the medium in comparison to previous technologies but, rather, a qualitative change in the very nature of the noise that is brought into being in the expression emanating from the assemblage of form and content. Indeed, as Aden Evens has pointed out, the very mechanical process employed to record and reproduce sound digitally can only ever simulate in binary code an approximation of the actual physical passage of sound.[12] This is to say, then, that in spite of its greater capacity to eliminate noise and focus on signal and in spite of its ability seemingly to efface itself in the playback of its recorded signal as its analogue ancestors with their hiss and crackle never could, digital recording technology does not render a more faithful reproduction of the original sound that it has recorded than analogue technology. However, Evens goes on to suggest that the elimination of noise in CD technology may go some way towards explaining the paucity of this recording format in the ears of many audiophiles, since 'noise contracted as impli-cation is what holds a piece together, what gives it its force and pushes it forward',[13] or, to put this another way, it is that which constitutes musical *expression* itself. Yet whilst I agree entirely that noise is indeed what constitutes not just musical expression but all expression, I nonetheless do not believe that it is the case that in the CD format noise is eliminated. As Evens' analysis of the sampling process shows, the technological medium through which sound is processed in digital recording and transmission is necessarily one that imbues the expression produced with artefacts, remnants or residues of its own material specificity. If the resulting expression *appears* to all intents and purposes noise-free, then, this is not because it is so but because we have not yet learned to recognise this digital noise as noise – although this is undoubtedly less the case with high compression formats such as MP3 that the online download revolution has brought about and that herald a seemingly anti-progressivist reduction of sound and image quality, an increase in perceptible noise produced by a new technology and thus a reversal of the logic of high-fidelity advances.

Whilst I do not agree, then, that there is less noise in the digital era – indeed, there may actually be more, although the qualitative difference we have noted would render it impossible to quantify this noise and thus verify this suggestion – it may well be our

inability to recognise this noise as such, to classify it and thus
sublimate it that explains the sense of uncanniness or a-naturality
that leads many audiophiles to 'regress' to vinyl and analogue
technologies because of a sense that they are more real.[14] Indeed,
if all expression is contracted from noise and carries noise with it,
then an expression whose noise cannot be recognised would, one
imagines, appear to be somewhat unhomely until such time as
one has become accustomed to the different nature of this noise.
This is the situation described by Lev Manovich when he writes:
'Typical images produced with 3-D computer graphics still appear
unnaturally clean, sharp, and geometric looking. Their limitations
especially stand out when juxtaposed with a normal photograph'.[15]

   Manovich goes on to recount how, in order to combat the problem
resulting from the juxtaposition of two different technologies, the
creators of *Jurassic Park* degraded this film's computer-generated
images, diluting their perfection 'to match the imperfection of
film's graininess'.[16] This was done by softening the straight edges
of the computer-generated images with special algorithms and
then adding 'barely visible noise [...] to the overall image to blend
computer and film elements'.[17] The noise added, of course, is
supposed to emulate the noise of film stock granularity and is then
no different from the addition of simulacral noise to digital fonts
and formats already seen. What this required addition of noise
to the computer-generated elements of the image does not imply,
however, as Manovich infers, is that the CGI itself is noise free,
'too perfect' because it is 'free of grain – the layer of noise created
by film stock and human perception'.[18] Indeed, we might go so far
as to suggest that computer-generated images or sounds exhibit,
according to the definition proposed herein, an extremely high
coefficient of noise insofar as they do not take an external object
to form an expressive assemblage but produce their expression
purely from the inside, from their own technological and material
specificity.

   This, however, is a digression – one to which we will return in
a later chapter on the photography of Thomas Ruff. What is more
important for the present analysis is to note that noise is particularly prone to an attempted annihilation. In the first instance it is
often, like Kristeva's abject, rejected because of its own seemingly
destructive properties, its ability to cut across taxonomic boundaries and instil in us a sense that something is not in its right place.

In the second instance, meanwhile, whilst it is true that noise can produce an unhomely sensation when it is perceived for the first time following a technological shift that alters the nature of the medium carrying an expression into being, we quickly acclimatise ourselves to the nature of this new medium and soon no longer notice the noise that it adds to the expressed content.[19] In brief, noise of the kind that interests me here is easily forgotten or rejected for many different reasons. The danger in doing this, however, the reason why we should attend to noise – no matter how hard it may be to recognise – is because (as is hopefully becoming clear by now) it is not external to being, something that can be sublimated, but is the very condition of possibility for all matter in an expressive state – and the first law of thermodynamics states, indirectly, that there is no other state. Noise situates all expression on a continuum and thus guards against the false historicism of nostalgia's misprision of both the present and the past. For to situate noise not only in the past but in the present also erases the difference between hyperreal and real, past, present and, indeed, future, confounding temporalities just as noise crosses categorical distinctions. Indeed, if noise is always present yet only recognised after the fact, then nostalgia becomes not so much a return to the past as a premonition of the future, a proclamation that today's PC is tomorrow's typewriter and, for instance, that the supposedly noise-free squeaky clean ultimate-fidelity CD is actually full of noise.

On failing to get rid of noise

Even though this assertion goes against the progressivist logic of high-fidelity reproduction which is directly responsible for the development of the CD, I want to suggest that the CD *is* full of noise, and not only because of the sampling technology that the medium relies upon. The history of the development of different audio formats from wax to vinyl to tape to CD (although we must draw a line at that point, as mentioned) is driven by a single-minded, stubborn desire to render the communications system or medium entirely transparent (or inaudible, rather), to eradicate entirely any interference coming from the system or medium itself so that we can instead focus solely on the pure audio content of our choice. As Jonathan Sterne notes, in discussions around sound-reproduction technologies, 'Even when the *sounds* of sound-reproduction technologies were explicitly discussed, it was with an eye toward finding new ways for the medium to erase itself'.[20] The development of high-fidelity recording and playback equipment therefore works by a constant succession of failure, the failure of one format to produce perfect fidelity between original and copy leading to the creation of another format aimed at providing, this time, total equivalence between input and output and, therefore, a more complete eradication of noise.

In the mid-1980s, one may well have been tempted to think that, with the advent of digital technology and the introduction of the Compact Disc, such rhetoric of perfectibility and cleanliness would quickly become superfluous since this new format promised an apparently unsurpassable level of fidelity. Such, however, has patently not been the case. Indeed, a recent magazine advertisement for Bose® QuietComfort® 2 Acoustic Noise Cancelling® headphones states:

> QuietComfort® 2 headphones deliver the best audio performance we've ever developed for headphones. Highs are impressively crisp and clean. Lows are deep and enveloping. Vocals are reproduced with lifelike authenticity. Whether you are looking for noise reduction or high-performance headphones for music, we think you'll agree these headphones capture the essence of serenity and sound.[21]

The rhetoric at work here, with its emphasis on 'lifelike authenticity' and 'essence' may well suggest to us that the high-fidelity reproduction ideal is still striving to regain that loss inimical to all recorded sound for Walter Benjamin, namely aura,[22] or to mend the pathological, 'schizophonic' split between sound and its source lamented by R. Murray Schafer.[23] Such, however, is a lure, for if we examine this rhetoric more closely, we will again see something more complex at play. Firstly, there is an explicit recognition that the authenticity produced here is only 'life*like*', which is to say that it does not equate to the recapture of a lost aura which comes, for Benjamin, only in the live, physical, embodied presence of the performer.[24] Secondly, we are told (as we are consistently when referring to literature on hi-fi systems) that these lifelike, authentic vocals are *reproduced*, which is to say that they are a self-avowed reconstruction that has been mediated by technology and *not* a direct analogue of the 'real' embodied, authentic and auratic original. This, interestingly, seems to signal a shift away from the early days of domestic high-fidelity phonograph advertisements (wonderfully analysed by Jonathan Sterne in *The Audible Past*) – or even the advertisements seen at the time of the introduction of either the cassette tape or the Compact Disc onto the domestic hi-fi market. A 1908 Victor Talking Machine advertisement asks, for instance, 'Which is Which?' and proclaims: 'You think you can tell the difference between hearing grand-opera artists sing and hearing their beautiful voices on the *Victor*. But can you?' – and the answer given is obviously that you cannot.[25] Similarly, a 1927 advertisement for Victor Victrola boldly states that 'The human voice *is* human on the New Orthophonic Victrola'.[26] And this tendency continued right through the 1970s and 1980s, as Mark Katz notes when he writes:

> for more than a century, what I would call a discourse of realism has reinforced the idea of recorded sound as the mirror of sonic reality, while at the same time obscuring the true impact of the technology. Consider the series of television and print ads from the 1970s and 1980s in which the voice of jazz great Ella Fitzgerald was shown shattering glass. While a feat in itself, more remarkable was that it was Fitzgerald's *recorded* voice that had such awesome power. Though the purpose of the ad campaign was to sell cassettes, it also espoused the ideal of realism. 'Is it live, or is it Memorex?' consumers were asked. The implicit answer was that the two were indistinguishable.[27]

Yet in the 2005 Bose advertisement there seems to be an implicit recognition that music is *mediated* by technology, and there is then an implicit recognition of the failure of the system intended as a high-fidelity communications channel since to acknowledge mediation is to acknowledge the system, and to acknowledge the system in its non-transparency is to acknowledge that the system contains noise.

This is perhaps not surprising, since the more one examines the very premise implied by the term 'high-fidelity reproduction', the more it seems to undo itself and expose the term's inherent bad faith.[28] Michel Chion has actually qualified the very idea of high-fidelity as a myth, a purely 'commercial concept' with no interest from the point of view of acoustics. In order to show how this notion undoes itself concretely, one could, as does Eliot Bates, examine the actual recording process used today for digital production and surmise that noise of many kinds will always be an unavoidable part of a recording and that 'the true enemy of mastering is the entire recording process'.[29] One could put a similar argument in a slightly different way and suggest, like Rick Altman, that,

> Recorded sound […] always carries some record of the recording process, superimposed on the sound event itself. Added to the story of sound production we always find the traces of sound recording as well, including information on the location, type, orientation, and movement of the sound collection devices, not to mention the many variables intervening between collection and recording of sound (amplification, filtering, equalization, noise reduction, and so forth).[30]

Or one may suggest, like Sterne, that regardless of whether one operates in an analogue or digital environment, the very fact of producing music for a recorded medium means that,

> we can no longer argue that copies are debased versions of a more authentic original that exists either outside or prior to the process of reproduction. Both copy and original are products of the process of reproducibility. The original requires as much artifice as the copy.[31]

This is to say, as Sterne notes earlier, that,

> the medium does not mediate the relation between singer and listener, original and copy. It *is* the nature of their connection. Without the medium, there would be no connection, no copy, but also no original, or at least no original in the same form. The performance is for the medium itself.[32]

If one wanted, one could even take this argument – according to which all originals whose fate is to be recorded are always already mediated – one step further and claim, as did Rick Altman in 1984, that 'The real can never be represented; representation alone can be represented. For in order to be represented, the real must be known, and knowledge is always already a form of representation'.[33]

For the moment, however, let us stay with Sterne's logic. The importance of Sterne's argument in regards to sound fidelity is that this narrative of original and debased copy which seems to drive both the production and reception of hi-fi equipment can only ever be, as he says,

> a story that we tell ourselves to staple separate pieces of sonic reality together. The efficacy of sound reproduction as a technology or as a cultural practice is not in its keeping faith with a world wholly external to itself. On the contrary, sound reproduction – from its very beginnings – always implied social relations among people, machines, practices, and sounds.[34]

For Sterne, any philosophy of sound reproduction (or mediation more generally) that does not insert its analyses into such a relational matrix, 'ontologizes sound reproduction too quickly. [...] In emphasizing the products of reproduction, it effaces the process'.[35]

Sterne's analysis is very important in its ramifications for all communications theory and, indeed, interpretative systems that set out to analyse a product which deploys itself in a relational matrix – and my contention that everything is expressive means necessarily that *everything* does precisely this.[36] Its implications are especially important for any analysis that sets out to attend to the noise of expression, for noise, as suggested, is always mobile, always resistant, only ever arising in the relation of form and content in the contraction of expression into actuality and, oftentimes, perceptible form. What the parts of Sterne's analysis cited above ultimately show, however, is quite how difficult it has been for commentators on analogue sound reproduction technologies to talk about noise, and, as we will see, many commentaries on such matters in the digital era seem to suggest that this task is not becoming any easier. On the contrary, if my initial assertion in this section that the CD is full of noise seems so counterintuitive, this is not because (or not only because) it is so hard to leave such discourses behind, but, rather, (also) because of the differences that the CD presents in relation to its analogue forebears. For if we do not generally hear the noise of the CD, this may well be because either, like our predecessors listening to vinyl, we automatically erase its noise in order to concentrate on the primary desired content; or else because it is beyond the realm of human perception; or else because we have not yet learned to recognise it; or, as we will see, because this very noise-reduction function is now performed for us, what was previously a cognitive process having been displaced into the technological system in the digital sphere – a displacement given its most blatant and concrete embodiment in the noise-reducing headphones already discussed. Given these multiple sets of conditions that would seem to render it impossible to attend to noise, one might then ask how it is possible to suggest that the CD is full of noise.

The answer, of course, is that the noise of the CD is effaced *under normal conditions*; an artistic movement commonly known as glitch, however, forces the CD to operate outside of this normative framework, and it is then perhaps through this music that we can begin to attend to this noise. But only perhaps.

On failing to identify noise

Glitch, as Kelly points out, is 'the digital tick caused by lost or incorrect binary code';[37] when the sound of this failure is integrated into music either as a generative compositional principle or as a sample inserted into a composition determined by other factors, the result is known as glitch (or sometimes click) music. The history and antecedents of this movement have been ably chronicled elsewhere and do not need repeating here. Kelly in particular inserts glitch into a larger historical survey of what he terms 'cracked media' – although glitch is in many respects his primary concern, 'both the end point and the starting point' for his book.[38] Limited attention has also been paid to the specific styles of certain glitch artists or the philosophical and aesthetic questions that their music raises.[39] In his paper 'Glitch – The Beauty of Malfunction', Torben Sangild traces the etymological origins of the term glitch before defining three distinct categories or subgenres of glitch: conceptual glitch, oceanic glitch and minimal click. Sangild then goes on to argue that these artists use dysfunction or the failure of a system in a productive and positive manner, drawing analogies to both evolutionary processes in which genetic mutations are found to be beneficial and which are thus integrated into a new genetic blueprint via natural selection, and also a grain of sand which enters an oyster shell and is turned into a pearl – a 'biological metaphor for glitch music', according to Sangild.[40] Eliot Bates, meanwhile, grounds his analysis far more firmly in relation to the discourses of fidelity that I have analysed herein. He states, for instance, 'A glitch is that which betrays the fidelity of the musical work – the skipping CD or record, the mangling cassette tape, the distorting PA system'.[41] And he later posits that, 'if [...] we define "high fidelity" in recording as *the pursuit of truth*, then in this context the glitch is *the betrayal of the simulation*'.[42] For Bates, then, 'glitch composition is a meta-discursive practice: rather than writing new music inspired by older recordings, it constructs new music inspired by the technological conditions and limitations in which those recordings emerged'.[43]

For both Sangild and Bates, the promise, beauty or importance of glitch lies in its almost redemptive capacity to deploy positively the failures and shortcomings of the system in which it is born. Or, as Peter Krapp would have it, 'This reminder of the imperfect, noisy, lossy nature of the machine [in glitch music] counters our contemporary digital culture's positivistic faith in technology as providing order'.[44] If one were lazy one would merely reiterate a similar thesis for the present volume, showing how, through a close and detailed analysis of the *modus operandi* of [insert name of preferred glitch-meister], his/her music averts the catastrophe that is foretold by the tarnishing of the apparently infallible sheen of digital technology through a positivistic aesthetic act that finds beauty in apparent horror and thus requires invocation of the Kantian sublime. One could even take solace in the fact that one's analysis had *not* ontologised its objects of analysis too quickly and thus emulated the mistakes of those philosophies of mediation critiqued by Sterne precisely because one had at all times been careful to stress the processual nature of glitch, both its meta-discursivity and its evolutionary ontology when crafted by an artist such as Oval who, according to Sangild, 'more or less invented glitch as a constructive musical technique',[45] and who, as Bates points out, 'doesn't directly control the generation of musical material himself, but instead designs systems and processes in which technology drives the sounds'.[46] This indeed would seem to be the logical way to continue the line of argumentation that I have followed thus far, and yet once again I can only find it lacking in some important respects and can only conclude that this line of reasoning fails when applied to the actual ontology of glitch, and that it must then be succeeded by another attempt at a successful analysis.

For all of their apparent care in pointing up the *process* involved in glitch music, analyses such as Sangild's and Bates' still, ultimately, end up ontologising their objects of study too quickly and thus effacing the process in play in glitch music. (And lest this critique seem unnecessarily unjust to these scholars in particular, let me just add that the line they propose to analyse glitch is now almost universally accepted as a given, so much so that some have long proclaimed the movement to be dead since it is just rehashing the same old (and according to this common line, restrictive) principle again and again.) For even though both Sangild and Bates are absolutely correct in their detailing of the processes used to prepare or (in Yasunao Tone's case) 'wound' the CDs these artists use for source material, in both of these analyses the material ontology of glitch is frozen at this point. So whilst they seem to have described the creation of a material artefact which is imbued with the power to create music which will necessarily be generative, and whilst they acknowledge that this music thus problematizes the high fidelity ideal by exploiting bugs, glitches and failures which will cause a system to react in unpredictable ways, by curtailing their ontological material analysis at the stage of disc preparation, they both imbue the disc itself with an agency that it can never have and, furthermore, bypass the process which actually creates the sound that is termed glitch and which is dependent primarily on the hardware of the system's decoder that reads the data and corrupted data on the disc: the CD player itself. Whilst it is perhaps not a serious error, then, to state that in a glitch piece we hear the sound of a CD skipping, this is much the same as saying (again) that the sun rises in the morning: in both cases the expression serves as shorthand to talk of a process that would require more words to explain fully, but the expression is resolutely false. What is odd in the case of critics talking about glitch is not only that such shorthand should stand in for in-depth analysis, but that this falsehood does not actually appear to be recognised as such most of the time. Rather than dealing in material and ontological givens, then, by stopping their analyses short of the material ontology of the system used to decode the prepared CD, such critics indulge in a self-perpetuating mythology in which the CD itself seems to be imbued with a magical and wondrous power.

One notable exception to this trend can be found in Caleb Stuart's article published in the *Leonardo Music Journal*, 'Damaged Sound: Glitching and Skipping Compact Discs in the Audio of

Yasunao Tone, Nicolas Collins and Oval'.[47] Like Sangild, Stuart begins his article with a familiar scenario, introducing the concept of glitch through an imaginary scene in a café at the moment when one's attention is drawn away from the banal and unattended everyday by the sound of a skipping CD heard over the establishment's speakers.[48] Stuart also traces a brief genealogy of glitch, but draws a much finer line than many, invoking only Cage's *Cartridge Music* and Knizak's *Destroyed Music*.[49] The majority of Stuart's paper, however, is taken up with a very thorough and detailed analysis of the techniques employed by Tone, Collins and Oval to extract sounds from the 'broken' media that they employ, and crucial to the genesis of these works (as becomes clear in Stuart's documentation) is not only the preparation of the Compact Disc itself but also the technological specificities of the player hardware in either a prepared or unprepared state.

Before analysing the work of any of his chosen artists, Stuart does something that is very rare amongst commentators on glitch: he actually explains the mechanics behind the sound that we hear as glitch. He writes,

> The glitches heard from a CD player – the skips and stutters – are not caused by actual skips; the CD player's laser does not actually 'stick' in the way a phonograph needle becomes physically locked in a groove. Instead, the skips and stutters that we hear when playing a CD are errors being emitted from the system as audio. The ticks and pops are due to binary values being read incorrectly – if the level of the error is so great that the error-correction software driving the digital system is not able to cope, it emits false sounds. For a CD to do this it needs to have been handled very badly. Dust and small scratches, especially across the disc, do not normally affect the audio output, as errors are covered by the system's error-correction software, which corrects misreadings and information losses.[50]

Stuart then goes on to detail the experiments carried out on the Compact Disc medium at the time of its commercial inception by David Ranada of *Stereo Review* magazine, which consisted of affixing a thin wedge of laser-opaque tape to the data surface of the CD and exploring the internal circuitry of the player to read the error correction data. As Stuart notes of Ranada's findings:

CD manufacturers and developers had created a new form of technology that was said to be able to correct errors and damage done to discs. While Ranada did not see his process of manipulating CDs as anything more than what a conscientious reviewer would do to provide his readers all possible information about the medium, his testing system would be very close to the technique used by Yasunao Tone to produce his indeterminate compositions.[51]

What is vital here for the purpose of the present analysis is that the production of what is perceived to be noise is merely the result of an intensification of an inherent capacity of the decoding technology that overrides that function when too much strain is placed upon it. It is, then, absolutely not the case that a CD skips, nor could it, for it is not within the capacity of the CD as artefact to exhibit any agency, it is merely a passive carrier of information. As Tone states in a discussion with experimental turntablist Christian Marclay organised by *Music* magazine:

> It's not really skipping. It's distorting information. A CD consists of a series of samples. You know bytes and bits, right? One byte contains sixteen bits of information. So, if I block one or two bits, information still exists – one byte of information – but the numbers are altered so it becomes totally different information. That's the idea. It's not skipping sound. […] Scotch tape enables me to make burst errors without significantly affecting the system and stopping the machine. The error-correcting software constantly interpolates between individual bits of misread information, but if adjacent bits are misread, a burst occurs and the software mutes the output. If a significant number of bursts occur in one frame, the error increases until it eventually overrides the system.[52]

What this means, then, is that the digital technology which is supposedly super clean and noise free is, in fact, merely better at disguising its noise and errors which still, as with analogue technology, always and necessarily form a part of its message.

Whilst Tone is especially interesting for the present analysis since his method consists in manipulating the CD in such a way that digital noise is extracted from the decoding or playback system, thus drawing attention (when analysed fully) to the *resistance* of the technological system that reads and transmits the audio content of the

CD, Nicolas Collins' *modus operandi* is of interest because of the light he sheds on the precise reasons behind our inability to hear this noise under normal conditions. Collins' approach, as Stuart notes, 'differs in that his approach involves tampering with the CD player's internal mechanism rather than a corruption of the disc'.[53] As Stuart explains:

> Without any real knowledge of the workings of the technology, Collins assumed correctly that the CD player's laser never left the disc's surface, reading not only audio information but 'hidden' information such as error-detection and information-coverage data, as well as data defining track locations, lengths and so on. Locating the player's control chip, Collins came across a 'mute' pin, which he removed, resulting in a constantly chattering playback. He states: 'With this pin removed, the CD player never shuts up, and one can hear the sound as the laser "scratches" (a magnificent, cartoonish ripping noise) or "pauses" (fast looping rhythms, possessed of a peculiar stutter and swing). Further modifications to the control system, done in collaboration with engineer Sukandar Kartadinata, opened up more extreme aberrations of digital misbehaviour'. Thus, with no muting, the CD player reads all of the disc's encoded information as audio – even the information that keeps the disc in place while in 'pause' mode.[54]

There are then two particularly significant elements in Collins' work as described here. Firstly, his work shows that the successful reproductive operation of this technology relies on a discrete compartmentalisation of different pockets of encoded data and that it is the hardware that performs this selection in which only certain data content is read as audio. Secondly, Collins' experiments show the extent to which even a CD with no apparent data corruption – be it deliberate or otherwise – is always full of noise since it has errors encoded into it that produce noise when what we might term the noise reduction or error suppression mechanism is itself suppressed or muted, for burst errors which would normally be corrected by the muting function here become audible, avowing the presence of encoding errors on an apparently 'clean' disk.

Rather than being a genre in which the noise of the system (or its failure as a high-fidelity system for communication) is turned to positivistic ends or made to 'succeed' through integration into an aesthetic construct as primary content, it is then rather the case that, through the failure that it foregrounds, glitch shows us the extent to which digital technology *always* relies on a successful integration of noise and failure into its systems. This is of great importance for any historiography of digital audio technologies (and indeed other digital technologies) for it suggests that there is a certain continuum between analogue and digital technologies as opposed to a radical paradigm shift.[55] Thus, Jonathan Sterne's critique of histories of sound fidelity still holds true even in the digital era, and to claim that digital technology represents the apex of high-fidelity reproduction is to practice a kind of inverted historiography in which,

> narratives of technological change and the transformation of technical specifications are folded back into an aesthetic and technological telos: the latest technological innovation equals the 'best-sounding' or 'perfect' sound reproduction. The progress narrative is ultimately untenable: the transformation of practices and technologies stands in for a narrative of vanishing mediation, where sources and copies move ever closer together until they are identical. The nature of what is heard and the very conditions of reproducibility are thereby presented as if they spring forth from the technology.[56]

However, whilst Sterne's analysis here is faultless in respect of the analogue technologies he sets out to analyse and whilst, as I have suggested above, these comments are equally applicable to the digital realm – as is attested to by the development of formats such as SACD and DVD audio which, although they have not yet superseded the humble CD, are still presented as advances in high-fidelity reproduction[57] – there is nonetheless an important difference as we move into the digital era that is pointed up by the analyses carried out above. Sterne's final assertion in the above quotation suggests that the technology itself is attributed with an excessive agency in many histories of sound fidelity, just as I have suggested that many analyses of glitch imbue the carrier of information with an agency that should in fact be attributed to the entire communications system. The difference in the two cases is that, whereas in Sterne's analysis of analogue systems it is human agency that is falsely attributed to the system, in my analysis of studies of glitch, it has become clear that it is technological agency that is falsely attributed to a specific component of the technological system. The reason why this is important becomes clear when we examine Sterne's comments on the members of the Volta Laboratory who 'were some of the few people in this early period focusing on the sound of sound-reproduction technologies',[58] and particularly his comments on Charles Sumner Tainter's attempts to improve the phonograph. Sterne writes:

> Tainter had sought a kind of acoustic transparency in sound reproduction: ideally, the medium would disappear and original and copy would be identical for listeners. In practice, however, this would require listeners to separate foreground and background sounds, to treat the apparatus of sound reproduction as merely incidental to the sounds thereby perceived. In other words, listeners were helping the machines reproduce sound 'perfectly'.[59]

In Tainter's experiments, the listening subject integrates noise into a successful and seemingly noise-free, high-fidelity sonic expression. The listening subject, that is to say, becomes a kind of agent of noise reduction or an error correction mechanism, a function which, as my analysis of glitch has shown, is now carried out by digital playback technology itself. To take the case of Collins once again, for instance, one could suggest that his experiments provide an example of this displacement of agency since it is now the CD player which selects only certain data to be interpreted as the desired audio content and not other data which, whilst essential for the operation of the entire system, needs to be elided or sublimated in some way.

The implications of this sound distinctly cyborgian and, indeed, one could perhaps pursue such an analysis. For instance, it is interesting to note that, when talking of their external noise-reducing function, the Bose® QuietComfort® 2 Acoustic Noise Cancelling® headphones advertisement mentioned earlier in this chapter paints a picture of a seamless man-machine coupling wherein 'The QuietComfort® 2 envelopes [sic] you in blissful sound in the utmost comfort that [sic] it's easy to forget they're on your head'. Achim Szepanski, meanwhile, integrates an apparently cyborgian vision into his discussion of glitch, writing:

> In the binary logic of connections, there is not only the on and off modus but as well the switch which transfers the connection

states. It is the non-representable symbol, the medium or the Ab-Ort [sic] which makes the one and zero state possible. Clicks and Cuts, everywhere connections, shifts, transfer, transductions, trans … Interface policy and music mutate to transfer policy and music. The concept of the 'inter' which maintains the separation between man and machine disappears in the proliferation of transactions where the authority of the artist neither acts nor navigates interactively. It is connected with its subjected machine components and with the technological components of the machine, and so it is its duty to step into processes.[60]

Whilst it is doubtless a little extreme to suggest from these analyses that the Compact Disc or glitch music augurs the arrival of the cyborgian future called for by critics such as Donna Haraway,[61] what it does potentially do is return us to the existential crisis of *Nausea* which is precipitated, of course, by the breakdown of just such a categorical distinction.

On noise failing to remain noise

Born in the reversal or undoing of difference between the terms of the CD's binary code,[62] glitch perhaps reveals to us above all else noise's *intersistence*, the way in which noise dissolves categorical distinctions between historical periods and media formats, form and content, man and machine. We might then apply Kelly's assertion about the difficulty of classifying various types of noise to the operations of noise more generally and suggest that 'it traverses the boundaries between […] categories in chaotic and insensible ways, remaining somehow neither/nor'.[63] This suggestion, however, becomes somewhat fraught when applied to the binary pair of noise and music, for the glitch can be and often is appropriated as a much less resistant and much more banal compositional element, sampled as any other sound and used in an entirely instrumental manner. Indeed, this is the case with Oval who, as Kelly notes, 'once they have found the accidental sounds of the CD skip and stutter, record them to use again and again in a highly controlled digital sequencing environment'.[64] The results of this are precisely as Kelly goes on to describe them:

The unknown of the accident is layered into the known of the pop format, the choruses and verses underpinned with the accidental sounds of stressed digital audio. Through repetition we begin to understand the mistake and aestheticize it. The notion of the crack and break as transgressive is undone in the work of Oval.[65]

However, where I do not agree with Kelly is in the implicit suggestion throughout his argument on Oval that the glitch as deployed by this group remains noise in this use of it.[66] To state, as he does, that 'Oval turned an annoying and distressing sound into something listenable, beautiful, and catchy'[67] is, it seems to me, to recognise that the glitch no longer deploys the resistant qualities of noise, that it no longer intersists, that (somewhat like Russolo's *intonarumori* and Cage's panaurality), far from problematising the categorical distinction between noise and music, the glitch here passes over fully to the side of music, leaving noise behind – to the extent that this is possible.

Some may protest that to suggest this is to infer that one needs to be apprised of the compositional techniques and hardware manipulation required by the genesis of any piece before a judgement can be made as to whether or not the apparent noise of glitch music – or indeed any expression – is indeed noise or something else. I would contend that this is not the case, however, for the simple reason that the experience of listening to Oval is so markedly different from that of listening to, for instance, Yasuno Tone's *Solo for Wounded CD*. For Oval's glitch does (mostly) not plunge us into that uncanny realm where we are no longer able to distinguish between form and content, where we are simultaneously drawn towards this strange sound which gestures towards what we might understand as music yet seems somehow incapable of being contained by such an apprehension of it – as in the moment narrated by Sangild and Kelly when the café's CD player's servomotors fail to interpret the CD's binary code in the proper manner.[68] This is not to say, however, that this noise is subjective, nor is it to claim that a sampled and sequenced glitch could never remain noise and thrust us into this realm. It is rather to suggest that in much glitch music the entire system, including its apparent failure, is co-opted to the service of content, over-determined and therefore unable to give voice to the indetermination of its material ontology as this enters into expression. To put this another way, just as analyses of glitch have often fixated on only one aspect of the technological assemblage and thus oversimplified the operations of the assemblage through which this particular expression comes to be, failing to read the system's noise, so the glitch itself, when sampled and inserted into a composition, offers itself to us not as the artefact of an expression arising out of a complex set of semi-determined relations but, rather, as a seemingly necessary element of a higher order.[69]

Whilst glitch may seem to be one of the most obvious places to look for the kind of noise of interest here, then, doing so is fraught with problems. It is true that, because it exploits the failure of the system out of which it arises and forces that system not to behave in its 'right' manner, glitch can help us to perceive the noise of digital media in its own time. This, as we have seen, is often difficult to do because when a more advanced technological assemblage is put into place and functions correctly, it necessarily seems better and less noisy in relation to what came before it. If we are careful in our analyses and do not proceed too hastily, it is then true that glitch can alert us to the bad faith of discourses of high-fidelity and point up the ineradicability of noise. Yet no matter how careful we are, the vast majority of glitch music does not allow the glitch to express itself, as it were, but, rather, treats it as just another musical element. Something similar is suggested by Kim Cascone in his nostalgic look back over the early days of glitch and the subsequent birth of the .microsound list/community/movement/journal that was necessitated by the co-option of glitch. He writes: 'Once plugins began to emulate the "glitch effect" we saw what was once an exploratory mode of inquiry and critique quickly turn into a cliché'.[70] With glitch, we therefore find ourselves in somewhat of a double bind. As I have suggested, it may well be that in order to attend to the noise of digital media we, as citizens of the digital era, have no choice but to turn to those points when the media breaks down because we have not yet learned to recognise these media forms' noise in its own time when it is cloaked in the simulated perfection of its own logic. And yet practitioners of glitch seem loathe to allow it to remain in that logic of imperfection, preferring to bring it into the order of music in such a way that its own operations are annulled. If we are to be able to attend to noise in the auditory realm, it may then be that we must heed our own advice and cast our ears back to a pre-digital era.

Notes

1 Available for download at http://www.freetypes.com/Font.
jsp?aFontId=649 [accessed 1 May 2012] or from http://www.
oldtype.8m.com [accessed 1 May 2012], a site dedicated entirely to
old typewriter fonts that has almost 100 such fonts displaying varying
degrees of supposed authenticity, noisiness or plain simulacra.

2 Except, perhaps, Christoph Mueller himself who apparently created
this font by typing the alphabet on his mum's old typewriter and then
scanning the characters.

3 Peter Krapp, *Noise Channels: Glitch and Error in Digital Culture*
(Minneapolis: University of Minnesota Press, 2011), 68.

4 On the relationship of noise to handwriting and typefaces, see also
Douglas Kahn, *Noise, Water, Meat: A History of Sound in the Arts*
(Cambridge, MA: MIT Press, 1999), 26.

5 Beatrice Warde / Paul Grandjean, 'The Crystal Goblet, or Printing
Should Be Invisible', http://gmunch.home.pipeline.com/typo-L/misc/
ward.htm [accessed 14 July 2004]. Also available in Beatrice Warde,
The Crystal Goblet: Sixteen Essays on Typography (Cleveland, OH:
World Publishing Co., 1956); and in *Graphic Design and Reading:
Explorations of an Uneasy Relationship*, ed. Gunnar Swanson (New
York: Allworth Press, 2000).

6 For an excellent discussion of the MP3 format, see Jonathan Sterne,
'The MP3 as Cultural Artifact', *New Media & Society*, 8, no. 5
(2006), as well as Sterne's recent book *MP3: The Meaning of a
Format* (Durham, NC: Duke University Press, 2012).

7 Emily Chivers Yochim and Megan Biddinger, '"It Kind of Gives You
That Vintage Feel": Vinyl Records and the Trope of Death', *Media
Culture & Society*, 30, no. 2 (2008), 183.

8 Yochim and Biddinger, 'It Kind of Gives You That Vintage Feel', 183.

9 Stan Link, 'The Work of Reproduction in the Mechanical Aging of an
Art: Listening to Noise', *Computer Music Journal*, 25, no. 1 (2001).

10 John Corbett, *Extended Play: Sounding Off from John Cage to Dr.
Funkenstein* (Durham, NC: Duke University Press, 1994), 41.

11 Jean Baudrillard, *Simulacra and Simulation*, trans. Sheila Faria
Glaser (Ann Arbor: University of Michigan Press, 1994), 6–7.

12 Aden Evens, 'Sound Ideas', in *A Shock to Thought: Expression
After Deleuze and Guattari*, ed. Brian Massumi (London: Routledge,
2002), 174–5.

13 Evens, 'Sound Ideas', 184.

14 This suggestion also leads me to qualify Will Straw's claim that the
demise of the CD is predestined in the 'noiseless invisibility held up as
one of its virtues'. For him, 'when the materiality of music playback
technology no longer shapes music's meanings in recognizable ways,
that technology becomes little more than a temporary host for music'
(Will Straw, 'In Memoriam: The Music CD and its Ends', *Design
and Culture*, 1, no. 1 (2009), 85). I contend, however, that the CD
is not noiseless and that if the demise of the CD is linked to such
considerations, then this has to do with a perceived difference in
the materiality of the media. Even with this qualification, however,
it is difficult to state with any degree of certainty whether this does
ultimately have anything to do with the apparent imminent demise of
the CD. Indeed, reviewing the very first commercially available domestic
CD player in 1983, John Rockwell marvelled at the materiality of this
new medium, noting 'The disks themselves are four and three-quarters
inches in diameter and rather thicker than an LP. They are very pretty
to hold and behold: gold with rainbow reflections, nestling neatly in a
small plastic box that includes a miniature booklet with the program
notes' (John Rockwell, 'How the LP and CD Sounds Compare', *New
York Times*, 31 March 1983, C13). If the CD's demise does not result
from a fundamental difference in its perceived materiality, therefore, it
may well have to do with a constellation of other forces tied up with
music distribution, commercialisation, technological distribution and
changing patterns of musical consumption.

15 Lev Manovich, *The Language of New Media* (Cambridge, MA: MIT
Press, 2001), 201.

16 Manovich, *The Language of New Media*, 202.

17 Manovich, *The Language of New Media*, 202.

18 Manovich, *The Language of New Media*, 202.

19 For instance, when watching a new season of *Survivor* filmed with
updated recording technology, I found it very hard to concentrate on
the game for the first couple of episodes and could only focus on the
difference of the image. This did not last for long, however, and I was
soon used to the new image, to the extent that I am almost certain
that the older seasons would now look strange to me were I to watch
reruns of them.

20 Jonathan Sterne, *The Audible Past: Cultural Origins of Sound
Reproduction* (Durham, NC: Duke University Press, 2003), 283.

21 This advertisement appeared in many different print publications
including the Qantas in-flight magazine, *The Australian Way*, for

a number of months in 2005. See also: Bose® Pty Ltd., 'Acoustic Noise Cancelling® Headphone Technology', http://www.bose.com. au/site/index.aspx?path=products&CTRL=PTCH&pfid=10&tid=6 [accessed 28 March 2006]. It is important to note that headphones such as the Bose® QuietComfort® 2 Acoustic Noise Cancelling® headphones can serve two functions (which may or may not be mutually exclusive depending on which function is desired): to reduce background noise through a self-regulating feedback loop that produces sonic frequencies to counter ambient background noise (in which case they reproduce no musical source) or else to reproduce a musical source (in which case they also reduce background noise). Whilst one could no doubt argue that the former function further advances the high-fidelity aims of the latter by producing a sonically hermetic environment, the two functions must be considered separately, and it is these headphones' reproductive function and the discourse surrounding that function that will primarily concern me here.

22 Walter Benjamin, 'The Work of Art in the Age of Mechanical Reproduction', in *Illuminations*, trans. H. Zohn (orig. German, 1936; Fontana Press, London, 1992), 222.

23 See R. Murray Schafer, *The Soundscape: Our Sonic Environment and the Tuning of the World* (New York: Knopf, 1977; rep. Rochester, VT: Destiny Books, 2009).

24 It should be noted that for Andrew Goodwin, digital technology actually heralds the return of the notion of aura in pop- music, but an aura which can now be mass produced (Andrew Goodwin, 'Sample and Hold: Pop Music in the Digital Age of Reproduction', in *On Record: Rock, Pop, and the Written Word*, ed. Simon Frith and Andrew Goodwin (New York: Pantheon Books, 1990), 258–73); reprinted from *Critical Quarterly*, 30, no. 3 (1998)).

25 Reproduced in Sterne, *The Audible Past*, 217. See also Emily Thompson, 'Machines, Music, and the Quest for Fidelity: Marketing the Edison Phonograph in America, 1877–1925', *The Musical Quarterly*, 79, no. 1 (1995).

26 Reproduced in Sterne, *The Audible Past*, 224.

27 Mark Katz, *Capturing Sound: How Technology has Changed Music* (Berkeley: University of California Press, 2004), 1–2.

28 Michel Chion, *Musiques, médias et technologies* (Paris: Flammarion, 1994), 74.

29 Eliot Bates, 'Glitches, Bugs, and Hisses: The Degeneration of Musical Recordings and the Contemporary Musical Work', in *Bad Music:*

The Music We Love to Hate, ed. C. J. Washburne and M. Derno (New York and London: Routledge, 2004), 280.

30 Rick Altman, 'The Material Heterogeneity of Recorded Sound', in *Sound Theory Sound Practice*, ed. Rick Altman (London: Routledge, 1992), 26.

31 Sterne, *The Audible Past*, 241.

32 Sterne, *The Audible Past*, 226. Mark Katz appears to be making a related point with the use of his term 'phonograph effects' which he describes as 'the manifestations of sound recording's influence' (*Capturing Sound*, 3). His conceptualisation of this term and its implications are not nearly as wide-ranging or coherent as Sterne's, however, and his case studies offer little to tighten up the concept.

33 Rick Altman, 'Sound Space', in *Sound Theory Sound Practice*, ed. Rick Altman (London: Routledge, 1992), 46. Since Altman's sentiment here shows the infinitely specular and self-referential nature of all representation, I deliberately quote Altman quoting Altman here and do not provide the original citation.

34 Sterne, *The Audible Past*, 219.

35 Sterne, *The Audible Past*, 219.

36 Goodwin essentially argues in favour of this kind of situated analysis when he asks, rhetorically, at the end of his essay: 'do we need a postmodern theory of society / aesthetic in order to understand postmodern cultural forms?' ('Sample and Hold', 272).

37 Caleb Kelly, *Cracked Media: The Sound of Malfunction* (Cambridge, MA: MIT Press, 2009), 6.

38 Kelly, *Cracked Media*, 6. On the history of glitch, see also: Caleb Stuart, 'Damaged Sound: Glitching & Skipping Compact Discs in the Audio of Yasunao Tone, Nicolas Collins & Oval', *Leonardo Music Journal*, 14, no. 1 (2004) (an earlier version of a chapter of Kelly, *Cracked Media*); Kim Cascone, 'The Aesthetics of Failure: "Post-Digital" Tendencies in Contemporary Computer Music', *Computer Music Journal*, 24, no. 4 (2000); Kim Cascone and Jeremy Turner, 'The Microsound Scene: An Interview with Kim Cascone', *ctheory*, A101 (2001), http://www.ctheory.net/text_file?pick=322 [accessed 23 January 2003]; Kenneth Goldsmith, 'It Was a Bug, Dave: The Dawn of Glitchwerks' (1999), http://www.wfmu. org/~kennyg/popular/articles/glitchwerks.html [accessed March 28, 2006]; Torben Sangild, *Støjens æstetik*, English summary published as: *The Aesthetics of Noise* ([np]: Datanom, 2002); Torben Sangild, 'Glitch: The Beauty of Malfunction', in *Bad Music*, ed. C. Washburne and M. Derno (London: Routledge, 2004); Eliot

Bates, 'Glitches, Bugs, and Hisses'; Krapp, *Noise Channels*; Philip Sherburne, 'The Art of Noise', *Frieze, 62* (October 2001); Mitchell Whitelaw, 'Inframedia Audio: Glitches & Tape Hiss', *Artlink*, 21, no. 3 (September 2001); Rob Young, 'Undercurrents #12: Worship the Glitch', *The Wire: Adventures in Modern Music*, 190/191 (December 1999 / January 2000).

39 Diedrich Diederichsen, 'Clicks', trans. Judith Funk, in the liner notes to *Clicks and Cuts 2* (Mille Plateaux, 2001); Achim Szepanski, 'Music', trans. Judith Funk, in the liner notes to *Clicks and Cuts 2* (Mille Plateaux, 2001).

40 Sangild, 'Glitch', 270. It should be noted that the same metaphor is used by Philip Sherburne who writes, 'Errors and accidents crystallize. The pearl is an error, a glitch in response to impurity. The error is the aura' ('The Art of Noise', 2).

41 Bates, 'Glitches, Bugs and Hisses', 277.

42 Bates, 'Glitches, Bugs and Hisses', 288.

43 Bates, 'Glitches, Bugs and Hisses', 289.

44 Krapp, *Noise Channels*, 74. To be fair to Krapp I must note that he goes on to state a desire not only to cast the possibilities of this strategy 'in binary terms of either a counterhegemonic art strategy or mere toying with the rubble of our high-tech era' (74), and that the examples he gives throughout his book extend the sites in which glitch and error are deployed in digital culture far beyond what is normally the case.

45 Sangild, 'Glitch', 262.

46 Bates, 'Glitches, Bugs and Hisses', 286–7. According to this definition, Oval, aka Markus Popp, would actually belong to a lineage of process musicians such as Alvin Lucier and Steve Reich, a suggestion which may well be problematic for reasons I do not have time to elaborate here.

47 Reworked in this same author's book *Cracked Media* published under the name of Kelly.

48 Stuart, 'Damaged Sound', 47.

49 Stuart, 'Damaged Sound', 47–8.

50 Stuart, 'Damaged Sound', 48.

51 Stuart, 'Damaged Sound', 48.

52 Yasunao Tone and Christian Marclay, 'Record, CD, Analog, Digital', in *Audio Culture: Readings in Modern Music*, ed. Christoph Cox and Daniel Warner (New York and London: Continuum, 2004), 341–2.

53 Stuart, 'Damaged Sound', 49.

54 Stuart, 'Damaged Sound', 49.

55 This is in entirely in accord with the analyses of critics such as
    Oliver Grau, *Virtual Art: From Illusion to Immersion* (Cambridge,
    MA: MIT Press/Leonardo Books, 2003); Manovich, *The Language
    of New Media*; and Sean Cubitt, Daniel Palmer and Les Walkling,
    'Reflections on Medium Specificity Occasioned by the Symposium
    "Digital Light: Technique, Technology, Creation", Melbourne 2011',
    Moving Image Review and Art Journal, 1, no. 1 (2012).

56 Sterne, *The Audible Past*, 222.

57 See Krapp, *Noise Channels*, 56.

58 Sterne, *The Audible Past*, 256.

59 Sterne, *The Audible Past*, 256.

60 Szepanski, 'Music', 12–13.

61 See Donna Haraway, *Simians, Cyborgs, and Women: The
    Reinvention of Nature* (London: Free Association Books, 1991).

62 Kelly notes how Yasunao Tone's compositions such as *Solo for
    Wounded CD* were initiated by his reading of 'a book entitled
    Science Seminar for the Familiar, where a chapter on digital
    recording included this paragraph: "Digital recording is a wonderful
    audio technique, since it has almost no noise and produces sound
    very faithful to the original. However, when it misreads 1 with 0, it
    makes very strange sounds due to the binary code becoming a totally
    different numerical value"' (Kelly, *Cracked Media*, 234–6).

63 Kelly, *Cracked Media*, 69.

64 Kelly, *Cracked Media*, 218.

65 Kelly, *Cracked Media*, 261.

66 See Kelly, *Cracked Media*, 69, 252–75.

67 Kelly, *Cracked Media*, 275.

68 It would of course be wrong of me to take recourse to the common
    sense shorthand I have critiqued and say the moment when the CD
    skips.

69 I will discuss this notion of the sense of a transcendent higher order
    produced by the musical work more in my final chapter.

70 Kim Cascone, 'Ten Years of Not Being There', *Vague Terrain 15:
    .microsound* (2009), http://vagueterrain.net/journal15 [accessed 10
    April 2012].

CHAPTER FIVE

On the Difficulties of Listening to Noise

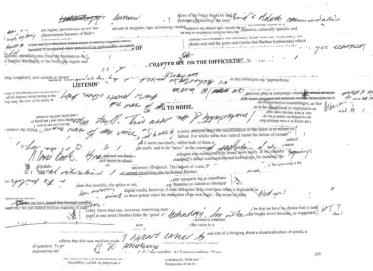

Chapter Five, Concrete Mix, Variations 1–5 (with apologies to Schaeffer).

* * *

Whilst there may be specific reasons why it is hard to hear the kind of noise of interest to us here in its own time, it is not simply by turning our attention back to past, pre-digital media forms that we will be able to do so unproblematically. Indeed, if we have, on numerous occasions, seen that noise has, predictably, often been understood as a primarily sonorous phenomenon, we have also noted how this has regularly led to an abnegation of noise. Indeed, considered as primarily sonorous or auditory, noise is oftentimes doubly negated, either because it is rejected since perceived as undesirable, excessive or even unethical, or else because the common sense apprehension of noise as sonorous seems to lead inexorably to a common sense understanding of noise as merely something that is raucous, inharmonious, dissonant, discordant or unmusical, adjectives which are highly problematic as the basis to consider noise from an ontological point of view because of their subjective, culturally-specific and ephemeral nature.

In this chapter I wish to start by suggesting that the difficulties presented to us when we attempt to attend to the ontology of noise in the auditory realm are similar to those that confronted Barthes when he attempted to attend to the ontology of photography. I will show how Barthes managed to solve his own conundrum through a specific concept, the *punctum*, that allowed him to create something other than a strict formal ontology out of logical operations. What he arrived at instead was a phenomenologically-inflected ontology that shares many similarities with the relational and expressive ontology formulated here. However, as we will see, Barthes failed to distinguish between the separate modes of his ontology and thus fell into the kinds of inconsistencies and contradictions that have plagued many discussions of noise. This problem is found also in his discussion of the grain of the voice that I will go on to discuss, a potentially very useful concept for an analysis of noise yet which remains problematic for this end without some modification. It is not my intention here to dismiss Barthes' ideas outright, although I will claim that it is because many critics of noise fall prey to the same kinds of pitfalls as Barthes that they end up producing such inconsistent conclusions. Rather, I wish to identify precisely where Barthes goes wrong and then (without making those same mistakes hopefully) take my lead from him for an analysis of two musical (or, perhaps better, sonorous) examples.

Punctum

In his work *Camera Lucida: Reflections on Photography*,[1] Barthes, like me, is explicitly concerned with ontology. 'I was overcome by an "ontological" desire', he says, 'I wanted to learn at all costs what Photography was "in itself", by what essential feature it was to be distinguished from the community of images'.[2] When Barthes attempts to pin this ontology down, however, he encounters a number of problems, again similar to mine. Firstly, the existing categories within which Photography is classified are 'external to the object, without relation to its essence',[3] just as I have suggested that oftentimes the various instantiations of what is designated as noise share no common ontological basis. Barthes writes, 'The various distributions we impose upon [Photography] are in fact either empirical (Professionals/Amateurs), or rhetorical (Landscapes/Objects/Portraits/Nudes), or else aesthetic (Realism/Pictorialism)'[4] – categories which might be mapped to the various classifications of noise found in disparate disciplines or the typology of different kinds of noise music and which, in both cases, seem often to be mutually incompatible, removed, therefore, from the ontology of noise since necessarily subjective. More importantly, however, because of the apparently indexical relationship of the Photograph to its referent (an assumption that can be deconstructed in any case),[5] Barthes claims that, in Photography, 'the referent adheres. And this singular adherence makes it very difficult to focus on Photography'.[6] To phrase this in the terms of the present argument, we might then say that Photography suffers the same fate as the vast majority of texts or expressions in the phenomenological act of reception or critique, namely, that the thetic takes precedence over the semiotic to the extent that the latter is obliterated, abnegated or abjected entirely by the former, the content of the medium blinding us to the character of the medium (to paraphrase McLuhan once more).

Determined not to remain blind to the medium but to situate the essence of Photography, to talk of its ontology, Barthes realised that to do this his method would necessarily have to take account not only of the material conditions of the Photograph but also (although these are not his terms) its relational ontology as an expression entering into an assemblage in the phenomenological act of spectatorship. This is to say that he wished to formulate an ontology that would not reduce the possible *affect* of the Photograph, which would not leave aside all of the attendant desires, feelings and nostalgias that Photography can elicit and that are then for him necessarily part of its ontology. Barthes writes:

> I did not escape, or try to escape, from a paradox: on the one hand the desire to give a name to Photography's essence and then to sketch an eidetic science of the Photograph; and on the other the intractable feeling that Photography is essentially (a contradiction in terms) only contingency, singularity, risk [...]. Next, my phenomenology agreed to compromise with a power, *affect*; affect was what I didn't want to reduce; being irreducible, it was thereby what I wanted, what I ought to reduce the Photograph *to*; but could I retain an affective intentionality, a view of the object which was immediately steeped in desire, repulsion, nostalgia, euphoria? Classical phenomenology, the kind I had known in my adolescence (and there has not been any other since), had never, so far as I could remember, spoken of desire or of mourning. Of course I could make out in Photography, in a very orthodox manner, a whole network of essences: material essences (necessitating the physical, chemical, optical study of the Photography), and regional essences (deriving, for instance, from aesthetics, from History, from sociology); but at the moment of reaching the essence of Photography in general, I branched off; instead of following the path of a formal ontology (of a Logic), I stopped, keeping with me, like a treasure, my desire or my grief; the anticipated essence of the Photograph could not, in my mind, be separated from the 'pathos' of which, from the first glance, it consists.[7]

For Barthes, the means to navigate the paradox that Photography embodies for him comes through a decision to explore Photography 'not as a question (a theme) but as a wound',[8] and it is this manoeuvre that in turn mobilises the figure of the *punctum*.

Analysing his own contemplation of photographs of his dead mother, Barthes splits his experience as a spectator into two parts: the *studium* which, as he explains, 'doesn't mean, at least not immediately, "study", but application to a thing, taste for someone, a kind of general, enthusiastic commitment, of course, but without special acuity'.[9] And then there is a second element:

The second element will break (or punctuate) the *studium*. This time it is not I who seek it out (as I invest the field of the *studium* with my sovereign consciousness), it is this element which rises from the scene, shoots out of it like an arrow, and pierces me. A Latin word exists to designate this wound, this prick, this mark made by a pointed instrument: the word suits me all the better in that it also refers to the notion of punctuation, and because the photographs I am speaking of are in effect punctuated, sometimes even speckled with these sensitive points; precisely, these marks, these wounds are so many *points*. This second element which will disturb the *studium* I shall therefore call *punctum*; for *punctum* is also: sting, speck, cut, little hole – and also a cast of the dice. A photograph's *punctum* is that accident which pricks me (but also bruises me, is poignant to me).[10]

In this analysis, the somewhat uncanny affect that the *punctum* is able to effect in him derives from the ontology of Photography which, for Barthes, is situated in this medium's specific relation to time, its strange conflation of different temporalities. For the intractable indexical relationship of the Photograph to its referent[11] combined with its immobility, its freezing of time, means that it embodies both a present which is eternalised and yet (hence its nostalgia) a past which is irrecuperable. He writes:

For the photograph's immobility is somehow the result of a perverse confusion between two concepts: the Real and the Live: by attesting that the object has been real, the photograph surreptitiously induces belief that it is alive, because of that delusion which makes us attribute to Reality an absolutely superior, somehow eternal value; but by shifting this reality to the past ('this-has-been'), the photograph suggests that it is already dead.[12]

In a later chapter on photography, I will problematise some aspects of Barthes' ontology of photography and, in particular, its reliance on the notion of indexicality. This is not what is of concern to me here, however. Rather, what I want to suggest is that the concept of the *punctum* as it is formulated by Barthes might help us understand how to begin attending to noise. For noise, much as we might try to contain it, reduce it, sublimate it, eradicate it, has the potential to affect us, to pierce us in this way – and this could well explain, of course, why it is that we try to control it. In Barthes' terms, noise, like the *punctum*, can bring into being a similar phenomenological event, breaking the *studium*, dissolving the thetic, piercing the perceiving subject who is henceforth unable to contain it or sublimate this part of expression within an aesthetic or hermeneutic apprehension or appreciation. If, in Barthes' ontology of Photography, this affect is produced via the commingling of different aspects of time in the one object, however, this is not the case with noise – even if, as my analyses have shown, noise has much to tell us about nostalgia. Rather, it is the more generalised problematisation of categorical distinctions that will bring about the *punctum*-like effect of noise, our inability to know whether we are dealing with form or content, the thetic or semiotic. It is this moment that instils in the perceiving subject a sense of the abject or uncanny that reveals her own existence to be an expression, that pierces her, precipitating feelings of nausea (or, as in Barthes, 'desire, repulsion, nostalgia, euphoria'[13]) as her sovereign consciousness fails to contain Being.

Barthes' concept of the *punctum*, then, may help us to theorise the peculiar affect of noise as an integral part of its ontology. Unlike Barthes, however, I am not convinced that it is necessary to conflate all aspects of this ontology together into a single moment (as fitting as this might seem when dealing with the ontology of Photography whose affect, for Barthes, comes precisely from this temporal conflation). Indeed, if we posit all ontology as relational, arising only in various expressive assemblages, then the specific attributes of the various partial objects that are carried into expression (as noise) will be expressed differently in different modes. Thus, it may well be that something resembling the *punctum* can be conceptualised as an integral part of the ontology of noise; however, that particular aspect of the ontology of noise might only be expressed in a secondary mode, as noise arises in the in-between of the expressive assemblage formed between the emitter and the receiver. All noise, though, is firstly produced in the very contraction of expression into actuality, in a primary ontological mode, prior to reception. The dangers of not positing such a distinction and attempting to conflate all aspects or modes of such a phenomenologically inflected ontology together are that one can end up making primary ontological claims that are undermined by secondary, more subjective ones. This, I want to suggest eventually, goes some way towards explaining why it is that analyses of noise are subject to the kinds of inconsistencies and contradictions that I have highlighted. But for a specific instantiation of the problem, let us remain with Barthes for a moment and examine another concept in his work that will also be of use to the present investigation of the ontology of noise, albeit indirectly because, precisely, it falls prey to the inconsistency that comes from the failure to make a modal distinction.

Grain

In a very famous essay written in 1970, Barthes sets out to analyse what he calls 'The Grain of the Voice'.[14] In his most basic formulation, Barthes describes this 'grain' as being 'the body in the voice as it sings, the hand as it writes, the limb as it performs'.[15] More than this, though, borrowing from Kristeva (Barthes' pupil at one point) Barthes links the 'grain' of the voice to a different economy of meaning. Rather than drawing on Kristeva's categories of the symbolic and the semiotic, however, Barthes instead reformulates two corollary terms from her vocabulary, the pheno-text and the geno-text (terms that Barthes hyphenates) which he transposes into the terms *pheno-song* and *geno-song* for the purpose of his analysis of the singing voices of Fischer-Dieskau and Panzera. He writes,

> The *pheno-song* (if the transposition be allowed) covers all the phenomena, all the features which belong to the structure of the language being sung, the rules of the genre, the coded form of the melisma, the composer's idiolect, the style of the interpretation: in short, everything in the performance which is in the service of communication, representation, expression, everything which it is customary to talk about, which forms the tissue of cultural values [...], which takes its bearing directly on the ideological alibis of a period [...]. The *geno-song* is the volume of the singing and speaking voice, the space where significations germinate 'from within language and in its very materiality'; it forms a signifying play having nothing to do with communication, representation (of feelings), expression; it is that apex (or that depth) of production where the melody really works

at the language – not at what it says, but the voluptuousness of its sounds-signifiers, of its letters – where melody explores how the language works and identifies with that work. It is, in a very simple word but which must be taken seriously, the *diction* of the language.[16]

Whilst one might imagine that in talking about the 'grain' of the voice Barthes would be talking about something akin to what we have termed noise, it is apparent from the above that this is not necessarily, or not solely the case. For whilst the grain of the voice could indeed be a noisy element, insofar as it might be said to describe the ways in which the materiality of the body is carried into vocal expression via a resistant operation, the 'grain' of the voice for Barthes in fact only arises when certain other conditions are fulfilled that have more to do with a receptive mode. Indeed, somewhat like the *punctum* in his analysis of photography, the 'grain' of the voice brings into focus the possibility of a different receptive mode, one that does not concentrate on the thetic content of the song (the symbolic level or phenotext) but, rather, is drawn to the specificity of the expression that comes from its material (or, in the case of photography, temporal) composition. As with the *punctum*, the experience that comes from an encounter with this 'grain' is both outside of the control of a sovereign consciousness and, concomitantly, seemingly ineffable – indeed Barthes describes his own article as 'the impossible account of an individual thrill that I constantly experience in listening to singing'.[17]

In this respect also, then, the 'grain' of the voice shares many of the characteristics that I have imputed to noise in regards to its effect upon the receiver. However, in conflating these two distinct modes of the relational ontology of the grain, Barthes is forced to make a categorical distinction as to what actually constitutes grain on what are essentially subjective criteria arising only in the secondary phase, a conflation which in turn leads him to negate the liminal aspect of the grain (or, indeed, *punctum*), its ability to dissolve the thetic. For whilst he does indeed talk of the experience of the grain as a 'thrill', as some kind of affective response that would then be situated outside of the economy of the sign, he nonetheless seems to make of the 'grain' or *geno-song* a slave or corollary of the phenotext, of signification. Thus, even though he states that the grain of the voice 'cannot better be defined [...] than by the very friction between the

music and something else, which something else is the particular
language (and nowise the message)',[18] in the exemplifications of
the appearance of the genotext (or its failure to appear) that can be
found in his analyses of Panzera (and Fischer-Dieskau respectively),
the grain of the voice seems to complement the meaning of the
phenotext, reinforcing it rather than piercing it. That this is the case
can be seen in his assertion that 'All of Panzera's art [...] was in the
letters, not in the bellows (simple technical feature: you never heard
him *breathe* but only divide up the phrase)',[19] and this becomes
clearer still in Dunsby's attempt to exhibit (and not merely evoke
rhetorically) the grain of the voice through a musicological analysis
of 'the contextualized musical evidence presented by Barthes before
the general idea rapidly outgrew its particular origins'.[20] Indeed,
commenting on this same assertion that 'you never heard [Panzera]
breathe', Dunsby remarks:

> One would think that breathing can in itself be part of the
> 'grain'. Yet this inflection seems to reinforce how meticulous
> a theorist Barthes was in demanding a corporality in which
> breathing is heard only when assimilated in the poetic diction.[21]

As with Kristeva and the abject, then, in spite of the usefulness
of the idea of the *punctum*, despite the similarities that can be
found between Barthes' idea of the grain of the voice and noise and
in spite of the fact that we can find in his ideas much *resistance* (as
this term has been defined here) when he talks of 'friction between
the music and something else' – that something else being *langue*
or, if you will, the specific assemblage out of which expression
arises –, the potential *obsistence* of these concepts is lost in Barthes'
specific deployments of them and everything is brought back
into the realm of *signifiance*. It may of course be objected that
this is not a problem, that Barthes is quite simply talking about
something different, yet this does not always seem to be the case
as I have intimated. Indeed, the receptive mode that the grain or
genotext brings into play (like noise) would seem to be fundamentally anathema to *signifiance*. Barthes himself suggests that in the
throat, that part of the body which brings grain into expression
in full force, '*signifiance* explodes, bringing not the soul but *jouis-
sance*'.[22] Ultimately, however, his analysis of grain as it stands is
deeply problematic for a study such as this because, in spite of

points of close contact, Barthes – in a similar manner to the critics of high-fidelity technologies already observed and, indeed, those scholars of noise who make ontological claims that are muddied by subjective judgements – does not take enough care when ontologising his object of study, conflating the specific operations and different expressive assemblages he is looking at into one object. This can but lead to internal contradictions in his work, the most heinous of which, for the purposes of this analysis, is the suggestion that the grain can be contained within the economy of the sign, for this makes of it something other than noise.

It should not be thought from this that I am here guilty of the mistake that Dunsby (to my mind falsely) accuses Barthes of and suggesting that the phenotext and genotext are mutually exclusive. Indeed, Dunsby is absolutely right to point out that 'the genotext and the phenotext in human communication are aspects, not separable entities'.[23] What I am suggesting is that whilst they *always* (and not only sometimes, as Barthes' politics of *taste* forces him to claim) accompany each other (noise always *coexisting* let us remember), the genotext is at one and the same time the expression of the material conditions of possibility of the text or communication and yet, concurrently, *in excess of* the phenotext, thus acting against the possibility of its hermeneutic closure. The grain of the voice, this is to say, might indeed be said to constitute its noise, but only if it is not slaved to the phenotext, if it is allowed not so much to '[shift] something in the chain of the signifier'[24] but, rather, to subsist within that chain as a break.

The problem is perhaps greater than this, however, for it is not simply the case that Barthes misconstrues the relation between the grain and the phenotext, he explicitly claims that some singers have no grain on the basis of a subjective perception of the sound they produce. With Fischer-Dieskau, for instance, he writes, 'I seem only to hear the lungs, never the tongue, the glottis, the teeth, the mucous membranes, the nose',[25] which is to say all of those body parts which for him generate grain. All vocal expression, however, necessarily and unavoidably contracts all of these body parts and more together in an assemblage, and they are all then unavoidably present in the expression in some form. Barthes' claim that he does not hear them is, then, not necessarily disingenuous but certainly subjective. And the very same thing can be seen in his analysis of Mélisande's death in which he explicitly links the ideas he has been talking about to the term noise and claims not only that this expression is noise-free, but also, astoundingly, that it is entirely unmediated. He writes:

> Mélisande dies *without any noise* (understanding the term in its cybernetic sense): nothing occurs to interfere with the signifier and there is thus no compulsion to redundance; simply, the production of a music-language with the function of preventing the singer from being expressive. As with the Russian bass, the symbolic (the death) is thrown immediately (without mediation) before us.[26]

Barthes' contention here is no doubt possible because in his aesthetic theory one *can* effect a separation between art and life on an ontological level, because art *is* indeed capable of entertaining a transcendent relation to the world into which it is released. Indeed, in a separate article, 'Introduction to the Structural Analysis of Narratives', Barthes explicitly states that the artwork is an entirely hermetic entity, fully present to itself on its own terms, meaning, effectively, that art is free of noise. He writes:

> Is everything in a narrative functional? Does everything, down to the slightest detail, have a meaning? Can narrative be divided up entirely into functional units? We shall see in a moment that there are several kinds of functions, there being several kinds of correlations, but this does not alter the fact that a narrative is never made up of anything other than functions: in differing degrees, everything in it signifies. This is not a matter of art (on the part of the narrator), but of structure; in the realm of discourse, what is noted is by definition notable. Even were a detail to appear irretrievably insignificant, resistant to all functionality, it would nonetheless end up with precisely the meaning of absurdity or uselessness: everything has a meaning, or nothing has. To put it another way, *one could say that art is without noise* (as that term is employed in information theory): art is a system which is pure, no unit ever goes wasted.[27]

And in a footnote to this proclamation about noise he states:

> This is what separates art from 'life', the latter knowing only 'fuzzy' or 'blurred' communications. 'Fuzziness' (that beyond

which it is impossible to see) can exist in art, but it does so
as a coded element (in Watteau for example). Even then, such
'fuzziness' is unknown to the written code: writing is inescapably
distinct.[28]

This, of course, is the very same ontological division effected by
Roquentin in *Nausea*, although there is no sense in Barthes' text
that the transcendence of the work of art is erected as a defence
against the terrifying contingency, or 'fuzziness' of life. In Barthes'
text, on the contrary, this claim seems instead to be a necessary
artefact of the strict structural stance that he advocates the critic
adopt in relation to the texts or works of art under consideration.
Regardless, it should be clear by now that claims such as this are,
to my mind, untenable. It is simply not possible for an expression
to reach us in its immediacy, hermetic and pure, unmediated, noise-
free, just as it is not possible for a vocal expression to be produced
without the tongue, the glottis, the teeth or the nose. The problem
in both cases, to phrase it in the terminology of information theory,
is that in pretending that this is the case, an ontological claim is
made about the expression emitted on the sole basis of the signal
received, as though these things were necessarily coterminous with
each other or else independent of the systemic relations through
which any act of expression and communication takes place. In
other words, whilst we have seen again and again that noise does
not avail itself to us easily, whilst it can be extremely hard to hear
or attend to, this does not mean that it is not present in those
expressions where we do not recognise it, and the belief that it is
not present arises out of the failure to make a modal distinction
between different ontological phases, the failure to realise that if
expression is relational then its nature will necessarily be unstable.
In other words, to use the same vocabulary as before, whilst a
communicative act contracts together emitter, signal, channel
and receiver in one assemblage, the particular qualities of the
expression produced out of that assemblage, being relational, will
differ in the very expressive act itself.[29]

In his analysis of 'grain', as with his analysis of the 'punctum'
in photography, Barthes thus conflates all moments of a relational
ontology into a single perspective. The problem with this, to an
even greater extent than in his analyses of photography, is that
this leads him to confuse a subjective and aesthetic claim with an

ontological one. This is a shame, for as should hopefully be clear by now, there are elements of his discussion of the genotext and the relationship between 'grain' and *signifiance* that are very pertinent to some of the claims made here in relation to noise. Barthes' glitch, however, opens up a space in which the potential of his ideas can be explored. Indeed, in what remains of this chapter I want to argue that many of the grainy and noisy aspects of the voice talked of by Barthes *can* more usefully be thought of as noise if we do not fall prey to the same lure. However, lest this train of thought become too abstract (and ironically so since 'grain' must, after all, always be grounded in some kind of embodiment), I will not continue this reflection in the same vein. Instead, I want to think through the questions of noise that Barthes' concept of 'grain' (and, indeed, the 'punctum') elicit via two different examples. These examples have the advantage of making more obvious than is normally the case the genetic construction and systematic elements of their expression, meaning that they actively resist the possibility of conflating their various modes and qualities into a single moment or aspect. The examples I will proffer are Alvin Lucier's *I am Sitting in a Room* from 1969, three years before the publication of Barthes' text, and *musique concrète*. The reason why I turn to these examples is because in both of them, albeit in different ways, there is a tension between the genotext and the phenotext, similar in certain respects to that found in Barthes' concept of grain, that might enable us to see how noise exists in the relation between these aspects of a song, sound, text, or any other expression for that matter, and that becomes more perceptible the higher the coefficient of genotext. To put it more succinctly, whilst both of these musical expressions might easily be said to be 'noisy' in the common sense definition of the term, I want to see if in them we can hear noise as it is understood here.

V/Nois/ce

I am Sitting in a Room is, quite literally, self-explanatory, for the process that is used to generate the text forms the basis of the sound material of the text, Lucier reading and recording the following text:

I am sitting in a room different from the one you are in now. I am recording the sound of my speaking voice and I am going to play it back into the room again and again until the resonant frequencies of the room reinforce themselves so that any semblance of my speech, with perhaps the exception of rhythm, is destroyed. What you will hear, then, are the natural resonant frequencies of the room articulated by speech. I regard this activity not so much as a demonstration of a physical fact, but, more as a way to smooth out any irregularities my speech might have.

Lest this not be abundantly clear from this explanation alone, it should be specified that every time this recorded text is played back into the room, that version is recorded, subsequently played back into this same space, this latest version then being recorded, played back, etc.

Whilst the methodology of the piece is then very clearly mapped out by Lucier, what is perhaps not so certain is the extent to which his interpretation of what happens as this piece is performed accounts for what the listener actually hears. For whilst it is indeed the case that 'the natural resonant frequencies of the room [are] articulated by speech' – since it is through the recording and subsequent playback of the contents of speech that the natural resonant frequencies of the room are gradually intensified to the exclusion of those resonant frequencies that are absorbed by and not reflected by the architectural and material qualities of the space in which the piece is performed – this is not all that is going on. Indeed, listening to the piece, what becomes clear as the various iterations roll by is that it is not only the resonant frequencies of the room that are intensified in the heterogenetic production of this work, but the material qualities of both the recording and playback apparatus and the voice itself. Indeed, it does not take many generations before the listener realises that if the voice soon sounds muffled and somewhat distant, then this is in large part because of the loss of high-fidelity reproduction that occurs as we move further and further away from the original expression or, rather, the interpolation of the recording and playback technology's mediality. This is to say, then, that much like those compilation tapes from the 1980s made up of recorded versions of friends' copies of songs originally recorded from the radio, the extra *volume* (by which we mean substance as opposed to intensity) that the piece accrues as it progresses is, and is recognised as, an unavoidable consequence of the impossibility of fidelity.[30] With regard to the materiality of the body in the voice, meanwhile, as the piece progresses what is remarkable is that, whilst it does indeed seem to be the case that the quasi-periodic vibrations of phonation are filtered out in such a way as to express the resonant frequencies of the room, for quite some time the sibilance, pops and clicks produced by frica-tives, plosives and other articulations that implicate the body's musculature (as well as, of course, the tongue, the glottis and the teeth) to a greater degree than most vocal sounds are retained and highlighted through isolation. Abstracted from the meaning or context that would be provided by the intelligible text as originally read, the sounds of these articulations do indeed become rhythmic elements as Lucier suggests, but they are also a perceptible signifier of the body's materiality and the physiological effort required by complex speech.

For this reason it cannot really be said much of the time that Lucier's piece does as he suggests, namely, 'to smooth out any irregularities [his] speech might have' – at least, not if we interpret this literally.[31] And it is because of the long transformation required to arrive at this final stage in which all of the voice's 'irregularities' have returned to what we might call a plane of consistency that we can apprehend what is happening in this piece. For what we hear across the various iterations is the intensification of all aspects of the mediality of the various systems or expressive assemblages responsible for the production and transport of his speech (his body, the recording and playback technologies, and the material and acoustic qualities of the architectural space in which the piece is performed) such that the manifest content of the phenotext (the meaning) is obliterated, it becoming increasingly hard and, in the end, impossible to reconstitute enough of any word's phonemes for it to be recognisable within a linguistic system. Something similar is suggested by Aden Evens who describes the process at work in this piece as follows:

> The text-speech slowly slides from articulate words to a continuous hum of pitch, and eventually – even where there was a silent pause in the original, say, between two sentences – the noise of the tape and the room is selectively reinforced to

produce an unbroken and perpetually evolving chord from an exhausted organ.[32]

Or, as he puts it later,

The most articulate sound is washed into the hum of noise. [...] His piece explodes the transition from inflection into innuendo, the dissolve at which sound melds into noise, inviting its close observation.[33]

In Lucier's piece, then, the noise of many different aspects of the expressive assemblage deployed in space and time is gradually intensified, its mediality, genotext or semiotic level growing in inverse proportion to the eradication of its content, phenotext or symbolic level. Lucier's piece, this is to say, instigates an expression based on *resistance* as the material reconfiguration that is the precondition for the coming into being of any expression is foregrounded through repetition.[34] What we hear as Lucier's piece progresses is the intensification of the noise that always already subsisted in his piece, that necessarily coexisted alongside the utterance that constitutes the start of the piece, that persists and remains noise (or, in this case, becomes ever noisier), and that obsists by pulling apart meaning and signification as its own power increases.

Nor is it only the meaning of the text that is pulled away from a closed hermeneutics in *I am Sitting in a Room*. For, in spite of its title, this is a text in which sovereign subjectivity is pulled beyond itself, in which the self-present expression of the speaking 'I' is revealed to be entirely dependent on and shaped by the outside into which that expression is released.[35] In *I am Sitting in a Room*, then, what we hear in the noise emanating from the assemblage of speaking subject–recording technology–room is the death knoll of Cartesian interiority and the *intersistence* of phenomenological or relational subjectivity. For if, as Sartre and many others have claimed, my own self and being are necessarily tied up with and dependent on those of others, *I am Sitting in a Room* extends this dissolution of ontological boundaries out so that it encompasses apparently inanimate matter. Far from constituting a site of fear as it is for Roquentin, however, something to be sublimated through the reassertion of the primacy of the individual through artistic expression, Lucier's work is born of the pursuit and creation of this noise that links together subject, space and technology in a singular (hence non-reductive) ontology. However, what his work makes us attend to are the modal distinctions between the different kinds of noise that arise across the various relations that the piece conjugates together. Whilst these noises are ontologically linked in regards to the principles and operations according to which they come into being and the secondary effects that they deploy, they are not, nor could they be in a relational ontology, identical to each other. This is not to say that any of them need to be disqualified as noise (as they might be if we were to follow Barthes' methodology). It is to say that we need to be careful about the claims that we make about Lucier's piece. For if noise can be talked of from an ontological perspective, it also inevitably speaks to us of ontology.

Noise, this is to say, arising out of the specific relations of expressive assemblages, tells us something specific about the ontology of those assemblages. In Lucier's piece, the noise that we hear is almost without exception produced by and in-between the technological assemblage and the physical properties of its spatial context rather than by something specific to the sonorous expression itself. What this means (for reasons that will become clear later) is that Lucier's piece tells us little if anything about the relationship between noise and music;[36] it is, rather, a prime example of what Brandon LaBelle would classify as sound art. LaBelle writes: 'Sound art as a practice harnesses, describes, analyzes, performs, and interrogates the condition of sound and the processes by which it operates'.[37] Indeed, this 'activation of the existing relation between sound and space' stands, for him, 'at the core of the very practice of sound art'.[38]

That Lucier's piece does not tell us anything of the relationship between music and noise is, of course, of little matter. Noise, as we have seen and will see in subsequent chapters, arises in many places other than in music, indeed, it is my contention that it arises everywhere, unavoidably. Nonetheless, if we are finally discovering ways to listen to noise, it makes sense to try to listen for it in the musical realm because so many of the debates surrounding noise have been fought on this battlefield. So whilst the going is good, let us consider another kind of sonorous assemblage that actually qualifies itself as music and that, somewhat although not too surprisingly, has much in common with Lucier's piece, to see if it is as full of noise.

Concrete

Intensifying the latent material qualities of both the voice, architecture and recording technologies that are necessary for Lucier's piece to come into expression until the link between signifier and signified or content and meaning is lost, there is arguably a deep filiation between Lucier's *I am Sitting in a Room* and the mechanical period of early *musique concrète*.[39] This is perhaps only the case, though, if we understand precisely why this music takes the appellation *concrète*, for some confusion appears to reign on this point. Thom Holmes, for instance, suggests that this was a term coined by Schaeffer 'to denote the use of sound objects from nature, 'concrete' sounds of the real world'.[40] Such, however, goes against the grain of the widely known fundamental premise of *musique concrète*, which is to say its desire to apprehend sounds in isolation from the source of that sound. Indeed, as Teruggi notes, the primary objective of the early practitioners of *musique concrète* was to use the tools at their disposal or to create new tools to 'strongly affect the essential parameters of sound in order to create a "distorted" perception of them' and, as a result, 'to "erase" from recorded sounds any referential allusion'.[41] In so doing, they wished to present the sounds in their limitless palette as *objets sonores*, sounds to be heard, analysed or studied for their own intrinsic qualities and properties and not, therefore, relegated to the inferior status of signifier always deferring to the more important and essential signified. To claim that the term *concrète* refers to this music's use of 'real', 'concrete' sounds is then to disregard Schaeffer's own pronouncements on the matter. Schaeffer states:

> The word 'concrete' did not designate a source. It meant that we were apprehending all of the characteristics of sound, sound in its totality. Thus, a concrete sound might be thought of as the sound of a violin, but considered in such a way as to account for all of its sensory qualities [*dans toutes ses qualités sensibles*], and not only its abstract qualities, those that are marked down on the score.[42]

If *musique concrète* is called *concrète*, then, it is so firstly because it allows us to apprehend sound as though it were an object, as if it possessed, that is to say, an opaque materiality which enabled the listener to consider it in itself as a being-in-itself (to use the Sartrean concept), divorced from the relational world of language and consciousness. Apprehended 'dans toutes ses qualités sensibles', the *objets sonores* produced by this music were able to act upon the listener in a way that music produced through cerebral and abstract composition techniques did not. It is in this relation to its effect upon the listener that we can grasp the second dimension of the term *concrète*. For if Schaeffer qualified his music with this adjective, it is also because the effect produced by this music was experienced as a bodily, sensual (as opposed to emotive) event whose transmission to the listener was direct and material as opposed to cerebral and abstract. As Abraham Moles writes:

> In an article written for the French musical journal *Polyphonie*, Schaeffer proposed to use the term 'musique concrète' to designate this particular kind of music. This was the word used by the Surrealist poet, Antonin Artaud, in his text *The Theatre of Cruelty* which proposed the ideal of a new music for a new theatre – a new music which would be received directly (concretely) by the spectator's sensorium.[43]

If *musique concrète* was called *concrète*, however, this was also, and perhaps primordially, because it was to an unprecedented degree dependent in its conception, composition and performance or elaboration upon a material support. As Holmes rightly notes, 'Composing a work of *musique concrète* began with the sound material itself rather than with a mental schema laid out by the composer beforehand, such as a score. The *material* preceded the *structure*'.[44] But it is not only in this respect that the creation of *musique concrète* is more material than that of other musics; for Schaeffer, the manual work involved in tape manipulation was an integral part of the process, since it allowed the composer to work directly on the matter out of which the work of art was forged – sound – without a visual interface (such as that which is integral to computer music composition) interfering with or 'colouring' the sound with a sensibility that ultimately had nothing to do with the specificity of the medium in which the composer was working.[45]

Like Lucier's piece, *musique concrète* would thus appear to be a form of expression in which noise is intensified, for it is reliant on the very materiality of the technology which enables it to come into being, and the foregrounding of that material specificity removes the expression's recorded content from an abstract, relational or linguistic structure, pulling the genotext into perception. The extent to which this happens in *musique concrète* as opposed to Lucier's piece is very different, however, for *musique concrète* does not implicate the entire assemblage required for the performance of its expression as a heterogenerative technique of (auto-) composition as does the latter. This is to say that, true to its name, *musique concrète* remains predominantly *music* insofar as the majority of its content is indeed produced through a deliberate compositional act and not as the unintended by-product of an expressive assemblage over which the composer can exercise no ultimate control.[46] This is not to say, as should hopefully be clear by now, that I am positing a dichotomous and mutually exclusive relationship between noise and music and suggesting that noise is here absent because the piece is musical for, as I have suggested, every expression, whether musical or otherwise, is born of and carries noise within it. This is to say that, in spite of the massively technologized nature of *musique concrète*, the coefficient of noise coming from the technological assemblage and deployment of that assemblage for the production of the work in space and time is not sufficient to overwhelm the music's content as it is presented to perception (unlike Lucier's piece therefore). It is for this very reason that *musique concrète* ultimately falls foul of Sean Higgins who writes:

> As a result of his occupation with music, though the sonic event becomes the basis of his artistic vocabulary, *musique concrète* enacted its own noise suppression. Though this music greatly expanded the timbral, structural, and formal vocabulary of music it failed to fully account for the noise that haunts it, the purely sensory noise of sound's empirical mediation that stands in excess of the musical model of recognition. That is, it opened music to the noise of sonic events but it did so only in the terms of irregular sonic events that could be repeated via phonography, and thus eventually structured and recognized. Noise as the difference of each sonic event had been compromised in the name of music, an opportunity was missed to instruct a new sort of listening.[47]

For Higgins, the privileging of Schaeffer's *objets sonores* that makes of them 'an absolutely repeatable, authoritatively standardized, sensible sonic event' means that the transcendental ideal of the musical score is merely replaced by 'the transcendental ideal of the sonorous object profaned by the irregularity of its resounding through concrete media'. For Higgins, then, *musique concrète* presents 'a standardized idea of listening that still suppresses the empirical difference of sound's resounding through media'.[48] This is true up until a point, and what is certain is that the coefficient of noise of this kind in *musique concrète* is far smaller than in Lucier's piece which finds favour with Higgins. It is important to note, however, that such noise is not entirely absent from *musique concrète*, although it is perhaps fairly minimal. Given the nature of this music, however, there is necessarily some noise that emanates from the technological hardware used for the production of this music (such as tape hiss and the technology's material and acoustic impedance, regardless of whether these are actually perceptible as noise or not) in much the same way that there is always some material noise present in the signal emitted by any musical instrument. As Teruggi points out, the very fact that in *musique concrète* 'sounds have to be modelled before being combined' means, invariably, that the tools used to model sound will 'leave "traces" on the sounds that they affect'.[49] More importantly, however, there is in tape-based *musique concr*ète a very specific form of noise which, whilst almost imperceptible, is nonetheless, I would contend, extremely significant for a consideration of the noise of *musique concrète*. This noise is an artefact that comes from the primary *technique* used in tape-based *musique concrète*, namely the splice, this being the specific action employed to enact what is the key principle of *musique concrète*: montage.[50]

Very early experiments in *musique concrète* used shellac records and various performative techniques such as speed transposition, filtering and sound-sample extraction in order to present sound in a different way and to rend the bond between acoustic signifier and signified. Such techniques cannot really be qualified as noise *per se*, however, for their deliberate deployment in a performative setting ultimately draws them close to Russolo's *intonarumori*, which is to say that the turntable here becomes but one more variation on a new breed of musical instruments designed to sound 'noisy' in the common sense definition of the term, yet that remain firmly rooted in the paradigms of conventional musicality and performativity. What is more, early experiments in *musique concrète* were not, as it turned out, very noisy since they were not all that successful in their avowed aim of a bringing about a denaturalisation of sound, a dissolution of the phenotext through the destruction of the denotative and connotative aspects of sound – as Schaeffer himself admitted when looking back on his career.

According to most accounts of *musique concrète*, however, the advent of magnetic tape technology would change this and allow the practitioners of *musique concrète* to wrest sound from its reference and thus achieve this aim far more successfully thanks to the technique of micro-editing that this new medium made possible. As Teruggi explains, 'Tape editing brought a new technique called "micro-editing", in which very tiny fragments of sound, representing milliseconds of time, were edited together, thus creating completely new sounds or structures'.[51] Whilst the content of magnetic tape may be rearranged radically such that its source is no longer recognisable, the technique that renders this possible, the splice or cut, indelibly leaves its own sonic imprint that is (just) perceptible to the ear and that, like the glitch already examined, draws our attention to it as a marker of the technological system's own mediality and also, I would contend, of the mediality of musical expression. This is not a point, however, that I wish to argue further at the present time because it goes so much against the grain that more preparation is needed for the argument to stand up.

Against the grain

In talking about Lucier's *I am Sitting in a Room* and *musique concrète*, we have been dealing with another two examples that reappear almost obsessively in studies that tackle the question of the relationship between noise and music or sound art more generally. The conclusions arrived at here in each case, however, differ quite significantly from much of what has been said on these subjects before (with the exception, of course, of Evens). If ultimately I have contended, for instance, that Lucier's piece ends up awash in noise, this is the very opposite of how most commentators have talked of this piece. Indeed, many see the work progressing further and further towards a musical expression that transmogrifies the noisy elements of the work into something quite strangely beautiful (and thus, in a common sense appreciation, not-noisy). In the entry for Lucier that appears in the volume *Music of the Twentieth-Century Avant-Garde: A Biocritical Sourcebook,* for instance, Warren Burt describes the progression of *I am Sitting in a Room* as follows:

> Over the course of the forty minutes of the piece, the sound of the voice is gradually replaced by a series of glowing resonant tones and chords, purely the effect of the specific frequencies favoured by the room the piece is performed in. By the end of the piece, a gorgeous series of changing sounds occurs, moving, as stated, in the rhythms of the original speech.[52]

Salomé Voegelin, meanwhile, suggests that by the end of the piece Lucier 'is not sitting in a room at all anymore. Instead he is sitting in pure sound',[53] a description that seems to remove us from the realm of noise, at least noise as it is generally understood.

Whilst it may seem an impossible task to reconcile the position adopted here which has much in common with that of Evens and in which *I am Sitting in a Room* ends up awash in noise with that of Burt or Voegelin where it is eminently musical or absolutely sonorous, I believe it is in fact possible to do precisely this and that in doing so we are able to intuit something very important about noise.

The key to this reconciliation comes, for me, as Voegelin unpacks her own statement a little further and describes, in a far more poetic manner, something similar to what has been said here about the operations of Lucier's piece. She writes:

> The place of performance becomes the place of listening, the timespace of production coinciding with the timespace of perception and yet a multiplicity of places are thus produced that erode the notion of an authentic room while offering me the experience of my own temporality. Sound shatters spatial certainty and builds time of fluid rooms. Lucier's voice builds a room that knows no outside and yet it has no boundary. I am in it or it does not exist. It belongs not in language and architecture but in the body of the listener, who takes up the extension of Lucier's body to extend his own. Lucier's voice does not extend

into a space that is already there, realizing the inner necessity of his body, but builds the space of his voice in the time of my perception.[54]

What Voegelin's comments here remind us is that *I am Sitting in a Room* is predominantly a piece that enacts and reiterates or repeats-with-difference a performative act that becomes simultaneously a perceptive and receptive act. To this we can add, of course, that it is also the repeated event of a recording, as noted above. In both cases, however, again somewhat counterintuitively, what is important is to realise that the noise that is described in my account and that of Evens is not really auditory noise, even if it is expressed in sound; it is, rather, the noise of the deployment of an expression in space and time, of a performative and receptive event as well as of a technological assemblage or, as Higgins would have it, there is a deliberate focus here on the noise of the 'particular empirical mediation of sound'.[55] To put this another way, what we are hearing is not so much the noise of the signal but, rather, the noise of the channel in operation and its recording mechanism. This is to say that the noise of the piece indicates that this piece is more about the interrelationship of a subject or, if you will, expression in the world (precisely as its title indicates) than it is about a particular sonic phenomenon (as Lucier's spoken text seems to imply). This is to say, again, that noise can arise in many different kinds of assemblages and in many different modalities or modes, which may or may not relate to noise as a sonic phenomenon. Given that, there is no reason why noise should sound how we might normally expect noise to sound.

Which leads us back to *musique concrète*, which perhaps often seems noisy precisely because, oftentimes, it does indeed sound precisely how people expect noise to sound. Indeed, *musique concrète*, like Cage's *4'33"* and Russolo's *intonarumori*, is often thought of as being noisy because, as we have seen Higgins comment, 'this music greatly expanded the timbral, structural, and formal vocabulary of music'.[56] Cox and Warner suggest something similar and place Schaeffer in a lineage that also includes Cage and Russolo in the introduction to 'Music and Its Others: Noise, Sound, Silence', the first section of their edited volume *Audio Culture: Readings in Modern Music*. They write:

In 1948, Pierre Schaeffer broadcast over French radio a 'Concert of Noises,' a set of pieces composed entirely from recordings of train whistles, spinning tops, pots and pans, canal boats, percussion instruments, and the occasional piano. Schaeffer called his new music '*musique concrète*', in contrast with traditional 'musique abstraite', which passed through the detours of notation, instrumentation, and performance.[57]

What this reminds us, of course, is that it is not surprising that people have often thought of *musique concrète* as little more than a collection of noises attempting to pass for music since Schaeffer himself titled the works performed at the concert Cox and Warner mention *Cinq études de bruits* (*Five Studies of Noises*). The attribution of this common sense definition of noise does not really stand up to scrutiny, however, for the very reasons that Higgins gives. It is precisely for this reason that he kicks against *musique concrète*, wishing that it were able, like Lucier's piece, 'to fully account for the noise that haunts it, the purely sensory noise of sound's empirical mediation that stands in excess of the musical model of recognition'.[58] In Higgins' critique, however, is an (admittedly very common) assumption that music and noise are opposed to each other, indeed he claims that noise is here 'compromised in the name of music'.[59] Whilst representing an inverse position both ideologically and philosophically, this contention actually shares some common ground with Schafer who riles against Schaeffer (and Russolo) because of their sacrilegious integration of noise into the realm of music such that the soundscape of the world is no longer 'divisible into musical and nonmusical kingdoms'.[60] So whilst Schafer hates that Schaeffer has cast a pox on music with noise whilst Higgins hates that Schaeffer has cast a pox on noise with music, both consider these realms or kingdoms to be necessarily in opposition to each other. As should be clear by now, however, and as the tension between Higgins and Schafer shows all by itself, the idea that music and noise are fundamentally opposed to each other, that noise is one of music's 'Others' (to use the term of Cox and Warner's title) is a highly problematic concept given the necessarily arbitrary and subjective nature of the dividing line between the two. Noise and music are, I would suggest, by no means opposed to each other: music is born of noise and carries noise within it just as does any expression. Indeed, what I will suggest in this book's final chapter is that whilst *musique concrète* may have a relatively low coefficient of noise of the kind that is deployed in Lucier's piece (and which has nothing to do with music *per se*), it has an extremely high coefficient of noise pertaining to musical expression.

This though, as we have seen repeatedly, is a hard point to argue because there seems to be so much at stake in this struggle between noise and music for each of the opposing sides. To put this another way, precisely because the common sense definitions of noise relate predominantly to noise as a sonic or auditory concept, this kind of noise is subject to an enormous amount of overcoding that comes from beliefs or positions held for so long and with such conviction that they are imbued with a seemingly incontrovertible rightness or even naturalness. To put it another way still, it is indeed incredibly difficult to listen to noise. And so, for now, let us leave music aside to consider noise as it appears in some other kingdoms, let us move outside of music and sound to pay heed to other kinds of noise, to other moments when the perfect surface sheen of narrative content, hermeneutic closure and high-fidelity are tarnished or punctured by something that troubles the expected reception of expression, when things do not seem quite right.

Notes

1   Roland Barthes, *Camera Lucida: Reflections on Photography*, trans. Richard Howard (orig. French, 1980; New York: Hill and Wang, 1981).

2   Barthes, *Camera Lucida*, 3.

3   Barthes, *Camera Lucida*, 4.

4   Barthes, *Camera Lucida*, 4.

5   See Greg Hainge, 'Unfixing the Photographic Image: Photography, Indexicality, Fidelity and Normativity', *Continuum: Journal of Media & Cultural Studies*, 22, no. 5 (2008).

6   Barthes, *Camera Lucida*, 6.

7   Barthes, *Camera Lucida*, 20–1.

8   Barthes, *Camera Lucida*, 21.

9   Barthes, *Camera Lucida*, 26.

10 Barthes, *Camera Lucida*, 26–7.

11 See Barthes, *Camera Lucida*, 5.

12 Barthes, *Camera Lucida*, 79.

13 Barthes, *Camera Lucida*, 21.

14 Roland Barthes, 'The Grain of the Voice', in *Image – Music – Text*, trans. Stephen Heath (orig. French, 1972; New York: The Noonday Press, 1988).

15 Barthes, 'The Grain of the Voice', 188.

16 Barthes, 'The Grain of the Voice', 182–3.

17 Barthes, 'The Grain of the Voice', 181.

18 Barthes, 'The Grain of the Voice', 185.

19 Barthes, 'The Grain of the Voice', 183.

20 Jonathan Dunsby, 'Roland Barthes and the Grain of Panzéra's Voice', *Journal of the Royal Musical Association*, 134, no. 1 (2009), 128.

21 Dunsby, 'Roland Barthes and the Grain of Panzéra's Voice', 126.

22 Barthes, 'The Grain of the Voice', 183.

23 Dunsby, 'Roland Barthes and the Grain of Panzéra's Voice', 129.

24 Barthes, 'The Grain of the Voice', 187.

25 Barthes, 'The Grain of the Voice', 183.

26 Barthes, 'The Grain of the Voice', 187.

27 Roland Barthes, 'Introduction to the Structural Analysis of Narratives', in *Image – Music – Text*, trans. Stephen Heath (orig. French, 1966; New York: The Noonday Press, 1988), 89; my italics.

28 Barthes, 'Introduction to the Structural Analysis of Narratives', 89.

29 And, of course, the receptive act, if a distinction needs to be drawn, which should serve as salutary warning against the kind of rigid structuralist stance adopted by Barthes in his earlier text, 'Introduction to the Structural Analysis of Narratives', which has none of the subtlety of his later work on the punctum examined above.

30 In light of this assertion, the very term 'high-fidelity' could be taken to be an optimistic avowal of technology's valiant yet ultimately futile attempts at reproduction, the most it can aim for being a high-degree of fidelity.

31 It should of course be noted that his statement, in all probability, is a comment on his stuttering.

32 Aden Evens, *Sound Ideas: Music Machines and Experience* (Minneapolis: University of Minnesota Press, 2005), 53–4.

33 Evens, *Sound Ideas*, 55.

34 And whilst it should go without saying, let me specify that it is not a banal Platonic form of repetition (which, as we have seen, is impossible within discourses of high-fidelity technological reproduction in any case) but the kind of repetition favoured by Deleuze which is based upon difference in itself. See Gilles Deleuze, *Difference and Repetition*, trans. Paul Patton (orig. French, 1968; London: The Athlone Press, 1994; New York: Columbia University Press, 1994).

35 We are here close to the similarly Kristevan-inflected analysis of Brandon LaBelle who writes, 'Lucier's *I am Sitting in a Room* accentuates subjective experience as inherently *in process*' (Brandon LaBelle, *Background Noise: Perspectives on Sound Art* (New York and London: Continuum, 2006), 145).

36 Whilst I am in complete agreement with Kim-Cohen's comments on this piece in many respects, to my mind his analysis does not account for the complexity of the piece and restricts it precisely to a metareflexive commentary on the generative processes of *music*, the score, for instance, 'normally thought to precede the work's materialization, [being] imbricated in the act of materialization' (Seth Kim-Cohen, *In the Blink of an Ear: Toward a Non-Cochlear Sonic Art* (New York and London: Continuum, 2009), 188).

37 Brandon LaBelle, *Acoustic Territories: Sound Culture and Everyday Life* (New York and London: Continuum, 2010), ix.

38 LaBelle, *Acoustic Territories*, ix.

39 For a discussion of the various phases of *musique concrète* and the technological differences between them, see Daniel Teruggi, 'Technology and Musique Concrète: The Technical Developments of the Groupe de Recherches Musicales and their Implication in Musical Composition', *Organised Sound*, 12, no. 3 (2007).

40 Thom Holmes, *Electronic and Experimental Music: Pioneers in Technology and Composition* (New York and London: Routledge, 2002), 91.

41 Teruggi, 'Technology and Musique Concrète', 214.

42 Pierre Schaeffer quoted in Michel Chion, *L'Art des sons fixés ou La Musique Concrètement* (Fontaine: Éditions Metamkine / Nota-Bene / Sono-Concept, 1991), 13–14; my translation.

43 Abraham A. Moles, *Les Musiques expérimentales*, trans. Daniel Charles (Paris: Éditions du Cercle d'Art Contemporain, 1960), 32; my translation.

44 Holmes, *Electronic and Experimental Music*, 93. Something similar is suggested by Jean-Claude Risset who suggests that in *musique concrète* the work is realised 'as a concrete recording rather than an abstract score' (Jean-Claude Risset, 'Foreword', in *Electroacoustic Music: Analytical Perspectives*, ed. Thomas Licata (Westport, CT and London: Greenwood Press, 2002), xiv.

45 Schaeffer has said on this point: 'digital techniques colour sounds far too much to my mind, and they interpolate a visual step, which bothers me enormously, because during my work in the studio I use scores or graphic memory aids as little as possible'. Quoted in Chion, *L'Art des sons fixes*, 86.

46 We should remember that it was Schaeffer's desire to produce *music*. Commenting on one of the fundamental techniques of *musique concrète*, he writes, 'Repeat the same sound fragment twice: you no longer have an event but music' (Pierre Schaeffer, *À la recherche d'une musique concrète* (Paris: Éditions du Seuil, 1952), 230; my translation).

47 Sean Higgins, 'A Deleuzian Noise/Excavating the Body of Abstract Sound', in *Sounding the Virtual: Gilles Deleuze and the Theory and Philosophy of Music*, ed. Brian Hulse and Nick Nesbitt (Farnham: Ashgate, 2010), 70.

48 Higgins, 'A Deleuzian Noise', 70.

49 Teruggi, 'Technology and Musique Concrète', 214.

50 See Paul Hegarty, *Noise / Music: A History* (New York and London: Continuum, 2007), 33.

51 Teruggi, 'Technology and Musique Concrète', 217.

52 Warren Burt, 'Alvin Lucier (1931–)', in *Music of the Twentieth-Century Avant-Garde: A Biocritical Sourcebook*, ed. Larry Sitsky (Westport, CT: Greenwood Press, 2002), 269.

53 Salomé Voegelin, *Listening to Noise and Silence: Towards a Philosophy of Sound Art* (New York and London: Continuum, 2010), 127.

54 Voegelin, *Listening to Noise and Silence*, 127.

55 Higgins, 'A Deleuzian Noise', 70. See also Higgins' somewhat elusive comment that '[Lucier] forcefully shifts listening from sonorous object, or identity, to sonic event, or noise, as if recording the sound of the room's timbre without a note rather than an abstract musical ghost' (72). Whilst there are some similarities between the line taken here and that of Higgins, to my mind he ends up placing too much emphasis on the technological apparatus upon which Lucier's piece depends. Indeed, in Lucier and more generally, what is important for Higgins is that there is a 'creative use of sound technology [that] allows one to shift the frame of attention from its own delivery of a sonorous object to the resonance of the medium itself, to bring the medium to its transcendental exercise, to make the listener aware of its status as producer of sonic events' (73). Thus, in his view, it is only when the medium which acts as a 'prosthetic faculty of sensibility, enters its transcendental exercise and finds itself in the realm which is uniquely its own, producing rather than reproducing, [that] it becomes opaque, a noise' (76).

56 Higgins, 'A Deleuzian Noise', 70.

57 Christoph Cox and Daniel Warner, 'Music and Its Others: Noise, Sound, Silence: Introduction', in *Audio Culture: Readings in Modern Music*, ed. Christoph Cox and Daniel Warner (New York and London: Continuum, 2004), 5.

58 Higgins, 'A Deleuzian Noise', 70.

59 Higgins, 'A Deleuzian Noise', 70.

60 R. Murray Schafer, *The Soundscape: Our Sonic Environment and the Tuning of the World* (New York: Knopf, 1977; rep. Rochester, VT: Destiny Books, 2009), 111.

PART 3

CHAPTER SIX

On Noise and Film. Planet, Rabbit, Lynch

We start in noise. A faint roar, hum, drone, rumble, a sound that seems to have no beginning, end or source but to be only the backdrop out of which other forms are formed. We start with half of Henry's head, horizontal, and half a planet, superimposed on top of each other, fading into each other, the great distance between them reduced to nothing in an impossibly flat depth of field. The head levitates, semi-transparent, an X-ray of Henry's planet brain, until he floats past it and up and around and left out of frame as the planet comes nearer and the noise grows and grows, oblivious to the cut, to our transport to the planet's surface over which we are suspended. Oblivious to every cut or change from this point on, ever-present yet modulating and phasing according to the rhythms of the film, more or less intense, accompanied by screams, cries, static, clanking, banging, grinding, squelching, gurgling, whistling, fizzing, cracking, or not, but always there. A theatre of eternal noise (re)sounding even after the climactic crescendo up to white, present even behind the credits' music as Fats' organ bathes in a sea of vinyl noise on Lenox Avenue.

Twenty-nine years later we pick up where we left off, not that we ever really left, in noise once again, with a clunk and a rumble, drones and vinyl noise. This is what we hear and all we see is light, strobing slightly, in darkness, sound and light, son et lumière, cinema stripped back to its base elements, waiting to be organised and thus to be born from noise, with noise. An assemblage of different elements meeting in order to express something, something out of noise, with noise. A mechanics poetically embodied in the purest simplicity by the sight and sound of a gramophone, in which expression arises as stylus meets vinyl, accompanied, inexorably, by noise. And this we see in close-up, so close that it becomes our entire universe, as though we are witnessing Edouard-Léon Scott's fantasy,[1] as though this mechanics and this noise explained the world or at least this world, this INLAND EMPIRE.

* * *

What do you call the place where ideas originate? The subconscious?

No. Everything – *everything* – originates in the unified field. It's an ocean of pure consciousness. It's the transcendent. And that's what quantum physics says now: Everything that is a thing has emerged from that field. New things are always emerging and bubbling up from it. So an idea will come, but you will not know the idea until it enters your conscious mind. Now, if you expand your consciousness you can catch ideas at deeper and deeper levels, and they'll have more information and more energy.[2]

The cinematic universes created by David Lynch are places where things are not quite right, where categorical distinctions and identities are not stable, where the abject constantly threatens to surge forth and transgress the borders that we draw up in a futile attempt to contain and create meaning. These, then, are universes that share many of the ontological qualities of noise and it is thus perhaps unsurprising that they should be filled with noise. By this I do not only mean that their soundtrack is often populated by all manner of noises (in the common sense meaning of the term) – even if these may serve as an indication of a more generalised form of noise. Rather, I mean that his films seem constantly to dissolve into the noise from which they are constituted, both philosophically and formally, to erase their own form and identity or, perhaps, the possibility of imposing on them anything that would resemble a form, identity or meaning.[3]

Eraserhead

If the opening composite shot of David Lynch's debut feature-length film, *Eraserhead* (1977), seems to present a dialectic of animate (in the form of Henry) and inanimate matter (in the form of the planet), we need only look more carefully to see that this is not the case. Indeed, the shot that superimposes Henry's head over the planet is composed in such a way that the two are conflated in the darkness that conjoins them, the bottom half of the planet (in shadow) merging with Henry's dark hair. Even if the apparent dialectic we may have thought to exist appears to be reinforced as Henry's head floats around the screen whilst the planet remains still, solid, immutable, and even if it appears to be reinforced further still by the next shot (an aerial tracking shot over the planet's rocky, barren surface), both the planet and Henry are quickly revealed to be governed by the same processes. For the tracking shot over the planet's surface (which ends in a dissolve to black created as the camera slowly zooms in on the darkest depths of the cragged valley it has been following) is followed by an aerial shot of a house (that we assume to be on the planet) whose roof has a large hole in it. The camera again slowly zooms down towards this hole until blackness fills the entire screen. Now, from the inside of the house, we pan up to see a man, naked from the waist up and covered in pustules and sores, staring mournfully out of a window. We cut to see Henry once more who opens his mouth. Another composite image makes it seem as though a horrific, embryonic form still attached to a long umbilical cord emerges from his mouth to then float alongside him. We cut back to the man in the house who leans towards three levers in front of him. He pulls the first towards him, an action which, as we cut back, seems to pull the embryo off to another place. He pulls the second lever and we cut to a shot of the planet's surface again, only this time we see a pool of liquid in a crater (or perhaps a mere divot, the scale is not clear). We cut back to the man who pulls the third lever, an action which this time seems to cause the embryo to fall out of the sky into the pool of liquid on the planet's surface. We cut to a close-up shot of the liquid's surface and follow the same path as the embryo, down into the dark depths of the pool, but see only the bubbles that rise from its wake until even these have dissipated and the screen is black once more. A pan brings a brilliant circle of white light formed by a hole above us into the centre of the screen and a zoom takes us up through this hole until we emerge into a brilliant white light that washes out the entire screen. We fade into a shot of Henry in the concrete industrial setting that is his world and pass out of the prologue into the main body of the film.

This opening to *Eraserhead* has provoked a lot of critical commentary, much of which analyses it according to various psychoanalytic paradigms – unsurprisingly, perhaps, as this opening seems to lend itself so easily to interpretation as a dream sequence and seems ostensibly to present us with a birthing sequence seen from both a third and first-person perspective.[4] I believe, however, that such psychoanalytic interpretations of this scene, of the whole film, indeed of Lynch's entire filmic output do not in actuality account for what we are presented with on the screen.[5] Indeed, it might be suggested that the description of the opening to *Eraserhead* provided above is not merely a denotative description of the film's content but already an *interpretation* of it, for I have read across the various shots that make up this opening sequence as though there were indeed cause and effect relations between them. But what if this is not the case? What if the pulling of the levers does not in fact trigger the actions we see subsequently? What if we attribute these cause and effect relations to the shots of this sequence only because of our familiarity with a certain dominant cinematic vocabulary that has trained us in the art of suturing together the disparate fragments of reality that are appended to each other in continuity editing? Indeed, does the second lever pull (unlike the first and third) not trouble our ability to understand the cinematic language and codes we assume to be on display by *not* triggering any action *per se*, only a change of scenery in which we expect something to happen?

For Michel Chion, this is in fact the 'peculiar logic' of Lynch's entire cinematic output, and it requires us 'to renounce all *a priori* interpretations of behaviour and facts, whether taken separately or in succession'.[6] In his reading of Lynch's early work *The Grandmother*, for instance, Chion finds 'unusual cause and effect chains defying the first law of thermodynamics'[7] such that 'there seems to be no link between food and growth'.[8] For Chion, *The Grandmother*, one of Lynch's early shorts, is then governed by what he terms 'an "electro-magical" type of logic'. He continues,

According to this logic, everything occurs by abstract transmission. Bodies are not in themselves whole entities made from
perishable matter (itself moulded out of other bodies which have
been absorbed and transformed) but rather wires, transducers,
conductors of an inexplicable, abstract energy.[9]

This logic is entirely in accordance with the opening composite
shot of *Eraserhead* which, as I have suggested, creates a certain
confluence between Henry and the planet – or, perhaps better,
a zone of indiscernibility. As with Roquentin's existential crisis,
what this scene may suggest is that the division between animate
and inanimate matter no longer exists, and that both of them are
capable of giving rise to *expression*. This, then, is an eminently
machinic universe where everything is always in process, where
matter is never fully formed but embryonic, it is a universe which
exists only as a channel for the transduction of an energy, a noise
field that will be temporarily contracted into semi-stable forms
that seem recognisable whilst simultaneously always escaping
petrification, falling away from sense and back towards the noise
field they carry within them. This process is not governed or given
meaning by a deity or sovereign subjectivity pulling levers that
relinquish answers, it is simply in train, contracted (almost) into
different forms (or not) by the actions taking place within it. Whilst
the circular forms of Henry's head, the planet, the pool and the
hole may then invite us to establish serial relations across these
forms that resonate so strongly with each other, there is no ultimate
meaning to be extrapolated from them as a whole, no way of
stitching these images together in such a way that they will render
an incontrovertible truth – unless, of course, a form is imposed
upon them from the outside.

In this prologue, then, the cuts do not punctuate the cinematic
syntax at work in such a way as to make their content more
readable, they do not have the potential to coalesce into a totality
to be apprehended as an individuated identity. The filmic technique
at work, this is to say, takes on a form analogous to Henry's baby
which, despite having had its umbilical cord cut (even if we never
find out where the child gestated, the prologue suggesting only that
it is an expression of Henry's), does not take on its own individuated form, remaining a site of extreme abjection, only partially
contained by the swaddling clothes that Henry will eventually cut

away. There is here, then, a complementarity between content and
form, or perhaps we might be better advised to say once again that
there is a certain indiscernibility between them. For not only does
the content take on the form implied by the cinematic vocabulary
at work (or vice versa), but the cinematic punctuation of the cut
is, in the majority of cases in this prologue, generated not (in the
first instance) by an actual cut but, rather, by the on-screen content
which comes to engulf the entire frame in blackness or pure white
and thus fulfil the function of a cut as we transition to the next
shot.

What I am suggesting, of course, is that *Eraserhead* is a very
noisy film. This is so not because of the constant noise of machinic
grinding, drones, whirs, thuds and clunks that occupy both the
background and foreground of the film's soundscape at different
times throughout almost the entirety of the film. Nor is it because
we are at times presented with explicit examples of noise, such
as when Henry's gramophone is played, a gramophone which,
strangely but no doubt significantly, seems to produce the exact
same vinyl hiss and rhythmic pop no matter what the sonic content
of the vinyl platter the needle reads – noises which, in some scenes,
also continue long after the song itself has stopped playing. These
are merely clues, indications that this is a noisy universe. The real
noise of *Eraserhead* comes precisely from all of the elements of
the prologue examined: from the resistance that is figured by the
cinematographic technique being pulled into the film's perceptible
content and from the transgression of borders that this entails. This
transgression, as might be expected, brings about massive abjection
in the form of miniature roasted chickens that refuse to remain
dead and instead kick and ooze, foetuses that rain from the sky
only to be hurled into walls or squashed underfoot and, of course,
Henry's baby.

At the end of the film, Henry, of course, kills his baby, cutting
away its swaddling clothes-cum-bandages and poking around in its
now exposed organs with his scissors. Whilst these actions would
seem to imply that his child constitutes a site of abject *horror* for
him, that it is something to be gotten rid of, this reading (once
again) does not really tally with the evidence presented on screen.
Firstly, Henry has cared for this baby, even during a sickness
that made it even more abject and repulsive to most. Secondly,
Henry only attacks the baby once it starts *laughing* at him, his

reaction seeming to be directed against this mockery rather than its abjection. Most importantly, however, Henry's actions do not appear to start out as an *attack*. Rather, his cutting open of the baby's swaddling clothes seems to be motivated by fascination, to come from an attraction towards the abject, and his actions only intensify the abjection, ever more so as he stabs the baby. Finally, if there is any cause and effect link to be found between the final scenes of the film, it is entirely feasible to suggest that, rather than an *attack* on his baby, Henry's actions are nothing more than the pre-condition required for his desired union with the Lady in the Radiator. Indeed, it is only through an intensification of the abject embodied by his baby, a baby whose identity is increasingly conflated with his own, that Henry can erase his own identity and fuse with the object of his desire. As the film reaches its climax, this is achieved once more by the passing of the film's form into its content as the shots of electrical surges in Henry's apartment and the Man in the Planet pulling maniacally on his levers, overloading the machine to the point that sparks fly from its grinding gears, crescendo up to Henry's final embrace with the Lady in the Radiator. If the overloading of the electrical circuits of the apartment and operations of the Planet appear to be brought about by the erasure of individual identity that comes with the killing of the baby, the union of Henry and the Lady in the Radiator in which they are figured as one comes through an excessive intensification of the technology of the cinematic medium itself as the image is overexposed. Dependent on the reaction between light and photochemical agents, overexposure is an intensification of the technological medium that brings with it a great deal of noise. It is this very noise, this excessive assertion of the photochemical ontology of the cinematic medium that dissolves the borders between Henry and the Lady in the Radiator, background and figure, content and form. This, then, is noise that obsists, that pulls meaning away from apparently fixed forms back towards a brute materiality or pure expression, which is to say an expression that exceeds any attempt at synthesis, suture or exegesis.

This kind of noise, as well as its more literal auditory correlate that acts as a sonic clue to this plane that always subsists beneath the film's expression, is present in all of David Lynch's work. What this noise suggests to the viewer is that Lynch's work, both in its content and through the cinematic vocabulary he employs, consistently and deliberately confounds the possibility of ascertaining his films' *meaning*. Rather than search for meaning, the cinemagoer must engage with these texts as properly cinematic objects (or 'pure cinema', to use a term often applied to the work of directors such as Germaine Dulac and who, as we will see, is directly referenced by Lynch), allowing the *strangeness* and *mystery* inherent to the medium for Lynch to come forth. It is this kind of viewing experience that Lynch himself prefers his audiences to have. As he says in his book, *Catching the Big Fish: Meditation, Consciousness and Creativity*:

> Cinema is a language. It can say things – big, abstract things. And I love that about it. [...]
>
> For me, it's so beautiful to think about these pictures and sounds flowing together in time and in sequence, making something that can be done only through cinema.[10]

Lynch's films, then, take us back to the medium itself and figure that medium not simply as something that conveys a signal or meaning in a transparent manner, but as something which resists and interferes with the transmission of the message in its carriage. What we find in his films is a figuration of the ontological specificity of the cinematic medium that forces us to interact with the cinema in a different mode to that with which we are most accustomed in the present era, transporting us instead to the very early days of cinema and what Tom Gunning has termed the cinema of attractions.[11] Rather than pursue this line further (and rehash some things I have already said elsewhere), though, it will be more instructive in relation to noise to turn once again to the analogue–digital divide and see what happens to Lynch's noise as his production techniques shift over to digital in *INLAND EMPIRE*.

INLAND EMPIRE

The thing is, I don't know what was before or after. I don't know what happened first, and it's kind of laid a mindfuck on me.

Nikki Grace / Susan Blue, *INLAND EMPIRE*

Twin Peaks: Fire Walk with Me begins with a screen full of shimmering blues and blacks that, as the camera gradually pulls back, is revealed to be a static-filled television screen. Unlike in *Poltergeist* or the other horror films examined earlier, however, this noise-filled screen does not serve as a signifier of horror, for the horror here is embodied by Bob, Laura Palmer's killer, who smashes a baseball bat through the TV set as he walks towards his victim. This action stands, obviously, as an act of violence intended to set the scene for the rest of the film. More than this, however, it is a metacommentary on this film itself which is a prequel to a long-running popular TV series filmed after the series had run its course. If noise, as I have suggested and as Lynch himself suggests via his comments on the cinema, is medium-specific, then Bob's gesture is not just an act of meaningless violence, but also an indication that the noise of the TV show – which is to say those elements of its stylistics, content and form generated by the specificities of the medium – must be done away with in order to make way for a different kind of noise.[12] Whatever the reasons for Lynch's shift away from 35mm film stock to consumer grade digital video for the shooting of *INLAND EMPIRE*, then, it should not surprise us if there is in this movie a different kind of noise.

The noise to be found in *INLAND EMPIRE* is indeed at times (although by no means always) necessarily different from that found in Lynch's previous films precisely because of this shift away from analogue to digital. More often than not, however, the noise forms in this film have much in common with those found in Lynch's previous films. Indeed, *INLAND EMPIRE* opens with the sound of a dramatic bass note which fades away to reveal a background of what sounds distinctly like the crackle of a stylus in the grooves of an old gramophone record. This is precisely what the sound is, as we understand from the film's first sequence (following the title shot which I will get to soon) that shows an extreme close-up shot of an old phonograph needle on a spinning vinyl platter. This image is (or appears to be) shot in black and white and it is lit by a strobing light that recalls the flashing, electrical pulses and flickering lights seen at privileged moments through nearly all of Lynch's films.[13] Another more focused and constant light is directed onto the black vinyl surface of the disk, turning the area it pinpoints a brilliant white, against which the needle appears in silhouette. Not only does this light bring about a reversal of the normal chromatic qualities of the objects it is directed onto (just as the predominance of audio noise that obscures the content recorded on the disk reverses the normal hierarchy of auditory communications channels), it also enters into an associative resonance with the film's short title sequence that precedes this shot and in which we see 'a dark screen that is explosively ruptured by a beam of light resembling that of an old-fashioned film projector, which slowly illuminates the title', as Martha Nochimson describes it.[14] In many respects it seems to matter little, therefore, that *INLAND EMPIRE* is shot with a different recording technology. So whilst it is true, as Will Dodson writes, that 'More than any other Lynch project, *Inland Empire* calls attention to the tools with which it is constructed, and to itself as a cheaply produced digital film',[15] the technologies explicitly figured in the film's opening are analogue technologies and suggest, then, that there is a continuity between this this film and Lynch's earlier work, that the cinematic noise found in his previous films will persist here and that, ultimately, this noise comes from a particular conception of what the cinema is as an artform or artistic expression and not what it is as a technological assemblage. The revelation of the film's title in the beam of a movie theatre projector is nothing but a literalisation of this statement. What is more, the continuation of this trope into the next shot as a steady spotlight (that comes from the right hand side of the screen, which is to say the same side of the screen via which the projector beam of the title sequence gradually exited as a slow pan drew it to the edge of and then beyond the on-screen space) illuminates the surface of the noise-producing vinyl platter would seem to suggest that, once more, this film will not only be born out of noise but will concentrate (on) it. If this is the case, then these opening shots seem to imply from the outset that this will be an eminently cinematic film in the Lynchian sense of that term, meaning that it will not produce reason or meaning through any kind of standard logic, but that every aspect of the film will conspire to confound the transmission of a clear and transparent narrative content, to allow the cinema to stand as something else, as a place where things happen.

In order to test this hypothesis, let us remain with this opening a little longer to see what other things happen behind the static. For Dodson, 'This needle image is particularly mysterious, for it scratches the record, suggesting that there is something hidden under the surface of both the image and the sound'.[16] But what is happening? Nochimson suggests that the audio content produced by the phonograph consists of 'static, the sound of applause, and a difficult-to-hear voice speaking about an old hotel'.[17] On the first two points she is of course entirely correct. But the voice that we hear through the vinyl's static is not merely someone talking about an old hotel but, rather, a radio announcer who states:

> Axxon N, the longest running radio play in history, tonight, continuing in the Baltic region, a grey winter day in an old hotel.

In many respects, this opening line of the film is itself also nothing but noise, for it confounds so many different things, remains so ambiguous, resists meaning and comprehension on so many levels. For whilst it does indeed seem to prefigure many of the elements that will come later in the film, in which we will indeed see an announcer (played by William H. Macy), the Baltic region, an old hotel, grey winter days and the name $AX^{xo}N_N$ that will appear written (like this) on walls at key points throughout the film, this line proffers no explanation of these elements but, on the contrary, only confusion. The fact that the film begins with talk of a play in the Baltic region, for instance, might lead us to believe that we are dealing here with a *mise-en-abîme*, the film announcing its own content. This cannot be the case, however, for we are specifically told that this is a *radio* play, and yet in *INLAND EMPIRE* the *mise-en-abîme* is provided by a film – itself a remake of a supposedly cursed film from the Baltic region that was never completed (*Vier Sieben* [*Four Seven*]).[18] What is more, further genre confusion arises from the fact that this announcer's voice (which seems to precede the start of a radio play) emanates from a gramophone and not a radio – a technology which is just as capable of producing static. We may then be tempted to think, in spite of all of this, that this opening bears a direct relation to the scene that follows, which does indeed seem to take place in an old hotel, quite possibly in the Baltic region judging from the language the man and woman we see speak and, judging from the quality of the light filtering through the hotel room's net curtains, quite possibly on a cold grey winter's day. Yet this scene in no way seems to be part of a play (even less so a radio play), for apart from the setting (which is obviously a real hotel room and not a stage set), the protagonists' heads are obscured by a digitally imposed blurring, a convention used to hide the identities of people in documentaries or news bulletins, which is to say supposedly real-life situations – and which may also be construed here, of course, as yet another noisy element that both foregrounds the mechanics of the technological system through which this scene is presented at the same time as it inhibits understanding and obscures identity.

The relation of this line to the rest of the film, then, seems to escape any attempt at full articulation. Indeed, listening to it again we realise that the phrasing used to deliver the line suspends the entire phrase in an absolute ambiguity. The pauses before and after the word 'tonight', for instance, as well as the delivery of that word itself, have none of the qualities that might be expected to be given to it by an announcer presenting the content of the show to come – such as when, for instance, Nikki Grace (Laura Dern) and Devon Berk (Justin Theroux) appear on the Marilyn Levens' Starlight Celebrity Show – with the result that it is impossible to know whether the night in question is the night in which the diegesis of the production will be played out (in which case the 'grey winter day in an old hotel' would set the scene for the fiction to come) or whether this entire opening line is simply more of a statement of fact about various unrelated phenomena: Axxon N is the longest-running play in history. STOP. Tonight the cold grey days of the Baltic region continue in this hotel in which I [the speaker of the phrase] find myself.

This impossibility of extricating fact from fiction, of knowing in what level of reality we find ourselves at any one time is, arguably, the major defining characteristic of *INLAND EMPIRE*. Whilst present in many of Lynch's previous work – and notably in his lesser known short work *Absurda*[19] – this confusion is taken further in *INLAND EMPIRE* than ever before. As Matt Murray puts it somewhat poetically on the site *Corn Pone Flicks*,

> *Inland Empire* is a mystery so many layers deep it reminds one of an onion wearing lots of sweaters and cold weather gear; by the time you've gotten all the clothes off, you're left wondering what an onion is doing there to begin with, and peeling back any more layers will likely just make you cry.[20]

Similarly, Geoffrey Macnab qualifies *INLAND EMPIRE* as 'a Russian doll of a film with stories inside stories inside stories' and suggests that 'we are never quite sure whether we are watching the film-within-the-film (being directed by Jeremy Irons) or the film about the film-within-the-film'.[21] Jay Weissberg in *Variety* finds it 'impossible to tell whether [Dern is] Nikki, Nikki playing Sue, or Sue herself'.[22] And Manohla Dargis writing in *The New York Times* states that '*Inland Empire* involves an attractive blond actress who tumbles down rabbit holes inside rabbit holes inside rabbit holes', the end result being that 'this film-within-a-film casts an enveloping shadow over Nikki, leading her real and reel lives to blur'. But, as Dargis continues, 'The reeler it gets the weirder it gets'.[23]

True to the film as a whole, then, every aspect of this opening line has the potential to wrong foot us, and this is the case even with the title given to the radio play, 'Axxon N'. For within the film, 'AX^{xo}N $_N$' is not in fact the longest-running radio play in history as claimed here but, rather, a name that reappears throughout the film written on walls and doors. For those in the know, 'Axxon N' is also the name of one of David Lynch's website projects that was eventually expanded out to become *INLAND EMPIRE*. (The story goes that a long monologue by Laura Dern filmed by Lynch for the first episode of a new online series similar to *Dumbland* or *Rabbits* – which also gets integrated into *INLAND EMPIRE*, of course – and that was to be called 'Axxon N' got Lynch's neurons firing so much that he decided to build it up incrementally into the mammoth project that we now know as *INLAND EMPIRE*.) This is to say, then, that 'Axxon N' refers to the film *INLAND EMPIRE* itself.

Given the noisy context in which this name appears, furthermore, it is not unreasonable to suggest that this name has yet further significance. For an axon is a transmission channel of the nervous system, a projection extruding from a nerve cell that conducts electrical impulses *away* from that cell via synapses. It is then possible to conjecture that here also, with the use of this name that is tied to the film we are watching, Lynch is providing yet another metacommentary about the mode of reception that his film will demand, a mode of reception that will require the cinemagoer to attend to noise rather than attempt to block it out in order to comprehend the content presented. Attending to this noise will necessitate different connections to be made, connections perhaps more akin to the structure of the synapse itself, for a synapse is a gap across which the electrical impulse transmitted by an axon is conducted. Whilst this analogy cannot be stretched too far since the submicroscopic distance across which the impulse has to pass in most synapses leaves little margin for alternate pathways to be formed, it is easy to see how the idea of an electrical signal – the cinema being for Lynch an electrical medium – that is not delivered directly to the receiver through a closed channel but instead reaches its destination across an aporia that can be breached only via the molecular structure of the particular assemblage in play might appeal to Lynch.[24] Indeed, every time the word 'AX^{xo}N$_N$' appears written on a wall in the film, we reach an aporia, a point at which we are required to relinquish our normal modes of understanding and find new connections that are not so obviously causal.

Noisy interlude 1

Perhaps the most striking example of this comes in a back alley of the movie lot where the film within the film is being shot as Nikki sees this name written on a wall in chalk underlined with an arrow. She follows this arrow into darkness. A single strobe flash (a privileged trope in Lynch's work that signals an über-cinematic space) illuminates her momentarily and she then emerges (from out of the darkness and into the focal plane) into the space where the mysterious person who interrupted the early rehearsals for *On High in Blue Tomorrows* had been spotted. From this position she watches herself, Devon, Freddie (Harry Dean Stanton) and Kingsley replay the scene that we have seen earlier. As Devon comes towards her to investigate, she turns and runs, thus explaining (purportedly!) the provenance of the footsteps heard in the earlier scene. Thinking that she sees her husband hidden in the shadows, she cries out 'Billy, Billy' (the name of Devon's character) as though to warn him, then (as a spotlight fades up on her) takes refuge through the (fake) door that Devon had previously been unable to open. She finds herself in a totally different space, a suburban house, and calls out to Billy again (to no avail) as he peers in through the window – as he had previously peered through the set window – before, across a cut, the scene outside her window changes and becomes the actual setting in which this house is situated and before, obviously, Nikki is transported to an entirely different snow-covered streetscape

when, having covered her eyes over as though to snap herself out
of a bad dream, she reopens them.

Metarabbit

If this description seems excessively confusing, this is entirely
normal for this is an excessively noisy scene. (And it is perhaps
then no coincidence that just after this scene we return to a shot of
the vinyl record from the prologue.) This scene, I would suggest,
is one in which we witness an intensification of the technological
ontology of the cinema which, through the primary mode of
construction it is based upon in both its analogue and digital forms,
namely montage, forces different spatiotemporal realities to inhabit
the same space. When this ontological specificity of the cinema is
intensified, as here, the resulting expression is obscured by a high
coefficient of noise, requiring our normal receptive modes to be
rewritten, our axons to be rewired. What this suggests, of course, is
that there are many moments throughout the film that provide the
kind of metacommentary that we are claiming to be the primary
function of the prologue. This may well be true, but for now let us
return to the prologue and what follows the first explicit figuration
of noise as embodied by the gramophone.

If, as I have suggested of the opening of *Eraserhead*, this
prologue is a metacommentary about the film to follow and the
receptive modes that will be required to apprehend its noise, then
this prologue continues beyond these first two shots. It continues,
indeed, into the first part of the hotel room scene in which a
prostitute is ordered to strip (becoming vulnerable) and who
declares in Polish, 'Where am I? I'm afraid'. It would continue
also through the transition into the second half of this scene, shot
in colour, which begins with a composite image showing the Lost
Girl sitting on a couch, clutching a red satin sheet to her body and,
flickering over this image, a shot of a camera lens looking directly
into camera, a lens, furthermore, in which we see multiple reflections of a ceiling light that form a kind of linear *mise-en-abîme*.
Once this self-reflexive image of a movie camera dissipates, we
see that the Lost Girl, now crying, is staring at a TV screen filled
with static – just as we have been, and still are in many respects,

watching a screen full of noise. The camera gradually shifts from its original position in which the Lost Girl and TV screen are portrayed in a shot reverse-shot sequence, to a shot showing both the Lost Girl from behind and, over her shoulder, the TV screen, to a point of view shot on the TV screen now transmitting not static but speeded up scenes from later in the film that we are watching. The TV screen returns to broadcasting nothing but static and a series of ever greater close-up shots eventually fills our entire screen with TV static.

This static dissolves into one of the scenes that the Lost Girl had been watching, presented now not as the diegetic content of the programme she was watching within the film we are watching but, rather, one step closer to us, as the content of our own viewing experience – although the repeated return to close-up shots of the Lost Girl's tear-filled eyes throughout this segment reveal that she is still watching the same thing as us, albeit on a TV and not cinema screen. What we all see is one of the infamous rabbit scenes of *INLAND EMPIRE*.[25] In a minimalist 1950s setting, we see two human figures, each wearing a large rabbit head costume. A female rabbit sits on a leather couch, while another does the ironing at the back of the room. A male man-rabbit enters through a door to the left of the screen, his appearance accompanied by obviously canned applause. The man-rabbit sits down and a conversation full of non-sequiturs ensues with canned laughter cued at seemingly arbitrary points:

> **Sitting Rabbit:** I'm going to find out one day.
> **Ironing Rabbit:** When will you tell it?
> **Man Rabbit:** Who could have known?
> **Sitting Rabbit:** What time is it? [canned laughter]
> **Man Rabbit:** [standing up] I have a secret.
>   *cut to close-up of Lost Girl crying and back to Rabbits interior*
> **Sitting Rabbit:** There have been no calls today.
>   *Ironing Rabbit walks to rear of couch.* [followed by sound of footsteps from outside]
> **Sitting Rabbit:** I hear someone.
> **Ironing Rabbit:** [laughs]
> **Sitting Rabbit:** I do not think it will be much longer now.
>   *Man Rabbit walks over to door through which he entered, opens it and walks through it, shutting it behind him.*

At this point the scene switches and we see the Man Rabbit opening a door and entering into a dark room which seems, even in the half light, to be very different from that of his rabbit companions. He remains standing in front of this door and a spotlight lights it up, showing it to be painted a brilliant gold. More light gradually fills the entire room and, as it does so, the rabbit fades away into nothingness, leaving us contemplating an over-elaborately decorated room filled with antique furniture, a huge Persian rug, mirrors, golden cornices and mouldings and a baroque painted ceiling.

We cut to a very out of focus close-up shot of a man's face. The image struggles into focus and we witness a conversation between two men sitting on chairs in this same room, in Polish once again and subtitled as follows:

Janek: You are looking for something?
Phantom: Yes.
Janek: Are you looking to go in?
Phantom: Yes.
Janek: An opening?
Phantom: I look for an opening. Do you understand?
Janek: Yes, I understand.
Phantom: Do you understand I look for an opening?
Janek: Yes, I understand completely.
Phantom: Good. Good that you understand. That's good! You understand!

The image dissolves once more into a shot of the same room plunged into darkness again, except for the rabbit who is silhouetted against the brilliantly illuminated door. As the image fades to black and the soundtrack to silence for the first time, the prologue ends.

If, as I am claiming here, the prologue to the film is a metacommentary on the noise that the film as a whole will generate and an indication as to the kind of receptive mode or viewing position that we will be required to adopt as we pass into the film proper, and if, what is more, the prologue does indeed finish at this point, the first point in the film, this is to say, when there is a complete break in both the image *and* soundtrack, the question remains as to how the scenes involving the rabbits and Janek and the Phantom can be articulated to the metareflexive commentary of the prologue. The answer is perhaps easier in the case of the latter, for one can indeed reread the above dialogue as a metareflexive commentary on the difficulties of understanding that this film brings into play. For we too are looking for a way into this film, an opening that might give us some traction, some way of understanding what is going on, the irony being, of course, as we are told here, that the only thing that can be understood is that we are indeed trying to understand.

What part the rabbits – who reappear throughout the film – might play in this metacommentary is not so self-evident, however. The rabbit scenes, indeed, seem to stand for many as one of the most incomprehensible aspects of the film. Yet if they are taken to be merely a noisy element as befits their first apparition in this prologue and the privileged role that they seem to occupy, able to exist both in their own, 1950s sitcom universe and yet, occasionally, encroaching into the spaces of the film's main diegesis(/es), their function becomes slightly clearer. For taken as a noisy phenomenon, these scenes become an example of a medium whose functional and mechanical *modus operandi* is stripped so bare that it suddenly appears strange. This is to say that the TV sitcom is a genre in which we find über-familiar settings (a woman ironing, the return home of the working male); that the TV sitcom is a genre which feeds on stereotypes to the extent that identities across different series are effectively inter-changeable (so why not give them all the same heads, rabbit heads at that, to point up the absurdities of the genre?); that the TV sitcom is a genre that requires the active collusion of the audience for its jokes to appear funny, but when they are not all that funny the audience (since nobody wants to miss out on a joke) is coaxed into collusion by the (supposedly) infectious nature of the (canned) laughter of others (so why not cue the canned laughter at points when there is absolutely no humour to be found?). This is not to say that *INLAND EMPIRE* is a film in which these responses are provoked throughout; it is to suggest that these vignettes intensify the very essence of sitcom to such an extent that a strange, incomprehensible result is rendered, just as the film as a whole will intensify those elements that constitute the very essence of cinema for Lynch – namely, electricity, light and noise – up until the point that the viewer is unable to suture these almost elemental forces into any kind of coherent narrative and must instead surrender to a different kind of viewing experience in which the vocabularies of the everyday are rendered strange.

Digital noise

And yet, what the prologue and other aspects of *INLAND EMPIRE* examined here signal to us is perhaps not so much a making strange of the cinema as a return to the origins of cinema. And ironically, the specifically digital noise of *INLAND EMPIRE* that constitutes a major point of difference in relation to Lynch's prior cinematic output can also be seen to return us to the origins of cinema when, oftentimes, things were left to the imagination and not delivered wholesale to the spectator-cum-popcorn-munching consumer. For *INLAND EMPIRE* is shot not on high-definition digital video but, rather, consumer grade digital video. Lynch says of this choice:

> The DV camera I currently use is a Sony PD-150, which is a lower quality than HD. And I *love* this lower quality. I love the small camera.
> The quality reminds me of the films of the 1930s. In the early days, the emulsion wasn't so good, so there was less information on the screen. The Sony PD result is a bit like that; it's nowhere near high-def. And sometimes, in a frame, if there's some question about what you're seeing, or some dark corner, the mind can go dreaming. If everything is crystal clear in that frame, that's what it is – that's *all* it is.[26]

The specific qualities of the image in *INLAND EMPIRE* arising from the artefacts of the digital technology that Lynch decided to use for this film have not been considered in such a positive light by many spectators of the film, however. On the contrary, the lack of clarity or fidelity of this digital image, its opacity as opposed to absolute clarity and thus transparency, is the aspect of the film that has caused even long-time Lynch devotees much consternation. Indeed, for many, the material artefacts of this technology seem to have taken on the intrusive and unwelcome aspects of noise as a non-intentional by-product. For Jay Weissberg, for instance, 'The visual Lynch trademarks [...] are all here, but noticeably missing are the deep, rich colors and sharp images. Instead, they're replaced by murky, shadowy DV, which may give him more freedom but robs the pic of any visual pleasure'.[27] Lee Marshall laments 'the director's conversion to digital film-making', complaining that 'though the format has undoubtedly allowed Lynch greater creative freedom, the result for much of the film is a poor TV-quality image that bleeds color, and lighting that even a Dogme director would blush at'.[28] And Joshua Rothkopf, for his part, qualifies these same aspects of the film as 'an overall fugliness', claiming that 'the film will prove burdensome even to the director's biggest fans'.[29]

For me, though, what the very noticeable qualities of digital video bring to INLAND EMPIRE is yet more noise. By this I mean two things. Firstly, the artefacts of the digital technology bring about a recognition of the technological specificity and materiality of the system that is being used to deliver content to us, the viewer. In other words, as is the case with the rabbits in relation to sitcom in the prologue (and their other appearances throughout the film), the use of digital video performs a laying bare of the technological apparatus through which this film is presented to us. More than this, however, this noise is articulated to the broader noisy principle at work in the film as a whole, for it troubles our ability to engage with the content being presented according to the normative modes to which we are accustomed, to reify the *work* in an act of aesthetic fetishisation. This is to say that whilst Lynch's previous output may also have confounded the possibility of total hermeneutic closure, the possibility of a different kind of totalising receptivity was made possible by the opulence of the image which could be fetishized as an object of desire in itself (as attested to by many of the nostalgic and disappointed comments above). The 'fugliness' of INLAND EMPIRE prevents this from happening and requires the viewer to articulate the strangeness of the image quality to the strangeness of the narrative. Exemplary in this regard is the critique of Drew McWeeny who writes:

> My biggest fear before I saw the film was that I would hate the look of the DV cinematography. This isn't like Michael Mann's MIAMI VICE or Singer's SUPERMAN LIFTS THINGS. This wasn't shot on a high-end piece of equipment. All of this appears to be regular consumer-grade DV, and for the first ten or fifteen minutes, I was disconcerted by just how cheap it looks. But gradually, as I became engrossed in what I was watching, something happened. Not only did I not mind the aesthetic, but it actually started to grow on me. There are things

about video that are completely different than film, and Lynch is canny enough to play to DV's strengths. He seems obsessed with textures and light in the film, like in the very first few shots of the film, with a needle on a record in extreme close-up, and when he pushes things into near-total darkness in the last hour of the film, it becomes much stranger and dreamier than I would have expected. Laura Dern doesn't just step into shadows; she merges with them, bleeds into them. It's like she steps into something tangible, something she can't quite scrape off.[30]

Frustrated by their inability to contain the noise of Lynch's narratives within a coherent scenario – although it must be said that many valiant attempts have been made with all of his films, including *INLAND EMPIRE* –, up until this film, Lynch fans unable or unwilling to relinquish a quest for closure could still entertain a privileged relation to their object of desire, retaining some illusion of mastery over that object through the machinations of fetishism made possible by the film's aesthetic qualities. *INLAND EMPIRE* strips us even of this possibility, however, for Lynch plays to the particularities of this new medium not only in those sections shot in low light where the image quality is markedly different from that rendered by 35mm film, but also in the fully lit sequences of the film through an almost excessive use of extreme close-up shots. For it is in close-quarters that the particularities of the digital image of the PD50 are most apparent.

This difference found in the digital images of *INLAND EMPIRE* in comparison to Lynch's previous 35mm work is perhaps most apparent in the early scenes taking place in Nikki's mansion, especially during her conversation with Visitor #1 (Grace Zabriskie). For not only are we struck by this technology's different treatment of light compared to the 35mm technology we are accustomed to seeing in the cinema, but the focal planes of the image strike us as uncanny, the faces shot in extreme close-up not being rendered in the fine grain detail we expect, seeming almost out of focus – an effect compounded further throughout the film by Lynch's use (already seen in films such as *Lost Highway*) of extremely out of focus images that are gradually pulled into focus – whilst the background remains in tight focus, its definition being more as expected given the focal distance yet still uncanny since the image as a whole presents none of the shallow depth of field blurring that we might expect of shots such as this.

Plus ça change ...

Whilst there is then a certain aspect of *INLAND EMPIRE*'s noise that is generated by the medium-specific content of digital video, even this is articulated to a more general noisy principle that is explicitly signposted in the film's opening shots. This noise, as we see throughout the prologue, is intimately tied to the specificities of the cinematic medium when this is conceived of not as a vehicle for a story but, rather, an assemblage of sound and image generated through electrical means and structured by the cut – which is always and necessarily a breach across which there flows a differential relation that is, in Lynch's films, irreducible. Indeed, if, following the prologue, the main body of the film seems primarily concerned with eradicating the boundaries between the film's supposed reality and the film-within-the-film and conflating all of the film's various geographies, spaces and temporalities into one space of incommensurable multiplicity (in which, across cuts, doors lead to entirely different spaces or countries and different temporal strata coexist within the same frame), in the latter stages of the film we nonetheless return to the prologue's assertion that what we are dealing with is quite simply *cinema*, not so much a film-within-a-film as a film *about* film, a film whose medium is conflated with its content, which is to say then a film with a high coefficient of noise. This transition – if indeed it *is* really a transition – takes place at the exact moment when the viewer is given a key that would appear to allow him[31] to separate out some of the film's various layers again so as to be able, retrospectively, to piece together precisely what has happened.[32]

Noisy interlude 2

After Nikki/Susan has been stabbed in the stomach, collapsed and died on Hollywood Boulevard, leaving us entirely unsure as to whether or not this is fiction or part of (the film's) reality, whether she is actually dead or not, the camera presenting the on-screen diegesis to us pulls away from the tragic scene that we contemplate so that we see a Panavision movie camera on a crane filming this same scene. We hear Kingsley Stewart (Jeremy Irons)

say through a megaphone 'cut it, and print it', and order seems
to be restored as we realise that we are only witnessing a staged
death in the film-within-the-film. But this assumption is troubled
somewhat when Nikki does not move as the other actors get up
and walk away from the scene but instead continues to lie on the
sidewalk, motionless. She does eventually rise to the applause of
the cast and crew, but even at this point order is not restored.
For whilst we might expect Nikki to come out of character and
receive the praise of her colleagues, she instead wanders off in a
daze, rejecting the attention of her entourage and the praise of her
director. She leaves the sound stage where they have been filming
and looks across to the sound stages opposite, stages 5 and 6,
which is to say the numbers in between 4 and 7 which (as Stewart
informed Nikki at the start of the film) are the two numbers that
make up the title of the original film of which *On High in Blue
Tomorrows* (the film-within-the-film) is a remake. Nikki looks
straight into the camera and we cut to a profile shot of the Lost
Girl from the prologue. A reverse-shot shows us the TV this girl
is still watching and on which we now see the image that we have
just been contemplating on our cinema screen as Nikki stares out
from the TV straight at us. We return to the diegetic space of the
film and see Nikki wander off again, passing in front of a red velvet
curtain. She enters into a movie palace from the rear and stops
in the aisles, a puzzled look on her face. A reverse-shot shows us
the cinema screen in this movie palace on which is projected an
extreme close-up shot of Nikki in the movie palace, this appearing
to be, then, a live image feed. We cut back to a shot of Nikki and
then back again to the cinema screen, now shot from behind Nikki
and over her shoulder so as to emphasise the subjective nature of
the point-of-view shot. On the movie palace screen this time we see
one of Nikki's monologues from earlier on in *INLAND EMPIRE*,
specifically the one where she talks of her son's death and how
she experienced the aftermath of this event, 'watching it, like in a
dark theatre, before they bring the lights up'. The on-screen scene
continues then switches to a shot of a silhouetted figure walking
quickly through the arches that flank the movie palace in which
Nikki is standing. Nikki looks off to the side and sees this figure
directly. It is her interrogator from the scene she has just been
watching on screen and he stops and looks directly at her. Nikki
looks back at the cinema screen, as if for verification, and sees this

same man who, still on screen, then turns to walk up the same staircase that Nikki had used to access the room in which these interview scenes were played out. The movie palace cinema screen fills our screen, a *mise-en-abîme* that increases the image's noise, as does the blurring of the image as the shot is pulled rapidly in and out of focus, and on it we see Nikki follow this same path up the stairs. She wanders slowly through a corridor, passing a ticking clock that reads 12:15 (recalling Visitor #1's pronouncements on the confusion of time from earlier in the film) and a door on which is written $AX^{xo}N_N$. Nikki opens this door, goes into a room where she sees a red lamp that has figured repeatedly in the film, and pulls a gun from the chest of drawers in which it is sitting. She follows another corridor and faint vinyl crackles reappear in the soundtrack. The Phantom emerges into this corridor, stalking Nikki stealthily as though in a cat and mouse game. Nikki arrives at a door and turns towards it to see the numbers 4 and 7, numbers that we see in extreme close-up. She turns to see the Phantom walking straight towards her and instinctively she raises her firearm and shoots at him repeatedly. The frame rate is slowed down as the Phantom fills the screen in an extreme close-up shot, the image almost entirely washed out by a brilliant white spotlight trained on his face. He sways gently, refusing to fall, his face an indescribable mixture of pleasure and pain. A reverse-shot shows a much less ambiguous look of horror on Nikki's face but, as we cut back to the space where the Phantom should be, we see instead a hideously morphed image of Nikki's own face. We cut to an extreme close-up and extreme slow-motion shot of the gun discharging again and again and cut to a nightmarish composite shot of a face. This face seems to embody the erasure of identity witnessed throughout the film, for it has had all defining characteristics removed: its eyes are but black blurs on a white screen, its mouth a red fringed black hole from which blood spews out. And then we cut to the rabbits who all look towards the door in their room as it flies open and a flickering white light is projected through it into their space. We cut to a shot of Nikki backing into the room behind door 47 and see that it is painted the same green as the rabbits' lounge. The editing of this sequence suggests that this room is indeed the rabbits' room and, as the camera turns to follow Nikki, we see that it is indeed one and the same space. The rabbits appear to have left now, however, and Nikki turns stage front to see instead a brilliant blue light (that turns out to emanate from, as we find out later, a cinema projector).

It is at this point that we enter the final calming and joyous resolution of the film. The music changes from the threatening menace of Penderecki to the soothing, haunting beauty of Lynch and Chrysta Bell's 'Polish Poem' as we see (on her TV screen) the Lost Girl embrace Nikki before the latter fades away into nothingness. The Lost Girl leaves the room she has been in this whole time (room 205 not 47) and runs through corridors into a room where she is reunited with her husband (who played the various incarnations of Nikki's husband) and son (who is very much alive). This joyous scene dissolves into the brilliant blue-white light of the projector that radiates across our entire screen, diffracted into its separate components as we zoom in towards it until its white heart washes out our entire screen and transitions us back to Nikki.

Nikki, for her part, is still in the rabbits' lounge/room 47 where she stands in the glare of a spotlight, staring straight ahead of her, seemingly dazed by the highly mediated, noised-up canned applause that we hear. Overlaid on this extreme close-up shot of her we see a pirouetting ballet dancer, then a reverse-shot thrusts us into the glare of this spotlight once again, a light that we now recognise for the first time as the light of a cinema projector beamed out into an auditorium. We dissolve back to the reunion of the Lost Girl and her family before we are transported back to the start of the main body of the film as we see Visitor #1 and then Nikki back in her mansion where she turns to look at another, more at peace version of herself sitting on a couch staring back at herself.

Resolution?

From this account of the final 20 minutes of *INLAND EMPIRE*, two things should hopefully be abundantly clear. Firstly, at the very moment when it seems that we will be able to integrate the film's various levels into a logical construct and understand the inter-relations of its parts, the very opposite happens and the various levels of reality in the film and the films within the film, be they infratextual or paratextual – *Axxon N, Four Seven, On High in*

Blue Tomorrows, INLAND EMPIRE[33] – are conflated to a greater degree than ever before. Secondly, if the revelation of the artifice provided by the Panavision camera in our perspective on the final shot of *On High in Blue Tomorrows* does not allow us to understand what is going on in *INLAND EMPIRE*, it is nonetheless only by attending closely to other über-medial and metacinematic moments of this film that we can apprehend what is happening ('something is happening' sings Chrysta Bell in the closing moments of the film, before the final credit sequence). This is to say, then, that *all* of the film's trickery, not only the slow-motion and face morphing, but also the more general principle of confusion of time, place and identity at work throughout every aspect of the film, is only possible within the cinema. Indeed, this is in essence what the cinema is: actors change identities to be filmed and editors splice together various scenes from disparate filmed realities to form a whole in which are juxtaposed different times and places in such a way as to confound Euclidian geometry.[34] By intensifying this logic to the point that the strangeness inherent in the medium surges forth, *INLAND EMPIRE* then obeys that more general principle identified by Eric Dufour in all of Lynch's cinema according to which 'the everyday becomes strange and, in a symmetrical manner, the strange becomes everyday'.[35] To put this in terms more suited to my argument here, Lynch's films are excessively noisy, constantly intensifying the base elements of the expressive assemblage through which cinema comes to be. This noise, like the sonic backdrop in *Eraserhead*, is ever-present and never allows us to remove the narrative content from this background and make of it an autonomous object of understanding (or an autonomous fetish object). This noise is the noise of cinema, the perceptible trace of the material and structural conditions of cinema conceived of as an electrical composition of sound and light assembled via *montage*.

If this is the case, then Lynch's cinema would seem to hark back not only to the cinema of attractions but more generally to the cinema of Eisenstein, Alexandrov and Pudovkin. Indeed, for them too montage is the primordial element of the cinema which is able to account for the effects that the cinema can have on an audience, effects which they feared could easily be compromised by the advent of synchronous sound in the cinema if this were to bring about a more theatrical form of cinema in which sound would be simply adhered to the image and not constructed according to separate, and thus contrapuntal, principles of montage.[36] This is not in the slightest to suggest, of course, that Lynch's is a barren, cold intellectual exercise or a kind of formal archaeology of the cinema, for the very opposite is true as *INLAND EMPIRE*'s closing credit sequence shows. Indeed, this choreographed sequence – danced to the ecstatic strains of Nina Simone's 'Sinnerman' – is a self-reflexive celebration of Lynch's universe that cheekily gestures towards many of his other works. I do not then agree with Nochimson that this scene is a 'carnival vision of a radiant inner unity Nikki has achieved',[37] for to my mind this scene is resolutely not about Nikki and all about Lynch and his cinema. This closing sequence is indeed a carnivalesque celebration, but it is a celebration of cinema and cinema's role as a medium for entertainment. As should be expected by now, this is explicitly signalled to us by a noisy element, for as the music plays and the revellers dance and sing, we notice that this scene is lit by the strobing light that reappears at key, privileged moments throughout *INLAND EMPIRE* as well as Lynch's entire *œuvre* and that returns us to the most basic matter of cinema's noisy (im)material ontology.

Notes

1 See Douglas Kahn, *Noise, Water, Meat: A History of Sound in the Arts* (Cambridge, MA: MIT Press, 1999), 75.

2 Jesse Pearson, 'Interview with David Lynch', *Vice*, 7, no. 9 (2009), 80.

3 As we will see here repeatedly.

4 For psychoanalytic readings of the film, see, amongst others, Martha Nochimson, *The Passion of David Lynch: Wild at Heart in Hollywood* (Austin, TX: University of Texas Press, 1997); Todd McGowan, *The Impossible David Lynch* (New York: Columbia University Press, 2007); Steven Jay Schneider, 'The Essential Evil in/ of *Eraserhead* (or, Lynch to the contrary)', in *The Cinema of David Lynch: American Dreams, Nightmare Visions*, ed. Erica Sheen and Annette Davison (London and New York: Wallflower Press, 2004).

5 As I have argued elsewhere. See Greg Hainge, 'Red Velvet: Lynch's Cinemat(ograph)ic Ontology', in *David Lynch in Theory*, ed. François-Xavier Gleyzon (Prague: Litteraria Pragensia, 2010); Greg

Hainge, 'Weird or Loopy? Specular Spaces, Feedback and Artifice in Lost Highway's Aesthetics of Sensation', in *The Cinema of David Lynch: American Dreams, Nightmare Visions*, ed. Annette Davison and Erica Sheen (London: Wallflower Press, 2004).

6   Michel Chion, *David Lynch*, trans. Robert Julian (orig. French, 2001; London: British Film Institute, 2006), 20.

7   Chion, *David Lynch*, 20.

8   Chion, *David Lynch*, 21.

9   Chion, *David Lynch*, 21.

10 David Lynch, *Catching the Big Fish: Meditation, Consciousness, and Creativity* (New York: Jeremy P. Tarcher/Penguin, 2006), 17.

11 See Tom Gunning, 'The Cinema of Attractions: Early Film, its Spectator and the Avant-Garde', in *The Cinema of Attractions Reloaded*, ed. Wanda Strauven (Amsterdam: Amsterdam University Press, 2006) [first published in *Wide Angle*, 8, nos. 3/4 (1986): 63–70]. For more on the link between Lynch and the cinema of the attractions, see Hainge, 'Red Velvet'. It might also be suggested that the receptive mode his films elicit is more akin to that found in the reception of music, as Lynch himself also suggests in *Catching the Big Fish* when he writes: 'Someone might say, I don't understand music; but most people experience music emotionally and would agree that music is an abstraction. You don't need to put music into words right away – you just listen. Cinema is a lot like music' (20).

12 This may go some way towards explaining the largely hostile reception that the film received from fans of the TV series, although it should be added that many aficionados of Lynch's cinematic *œuvre* were not overly impressed by this film either.

13 Given the close aesthetic proximity, this shot is very likely, as Randolph Jordan suggests, an intertextual reference to Germaine Dulac's 1928 *Disque 957: Impressions visuelles*. Jordan suggested this in a roundtable discussion transcribed in *Offscreen*, 13, no. 9, http://www.offscreen.com/biblio/pages/essays/roundtable_inland_ empire_pt2/ [accessed 19 October 2009]. Such a suggestion is fully in accordance with Robert Sinnerbrink's suggestion that 'The subject matter of *INLAND EMPIRE*, were one to risk such a claim, is something like the contemporary crisis of film that Lynch acutely diagnoses as a "putrefaction" (to use his term) of Hollywood; a failure to acknowledge or renew its creative relationship with the tradition of European cinema to which Lynch, like other Hollywood auteurs, owes a profound debt' (Robert Sinnerbrink, *New Philosophies of Film: Thinking Images* (New York and London: Continuum, 2011), 152).

14 Martha Nochimson, 'Inland Empire', Film Quarterly, 60, no. 4 (2007), 10. It is possible to assert that this principle of resonance characterises the construction of the entire film, different lines of dialogue, details and events being repeated in identical or subtly different forms throughout the film, such as, for instance, the Rabbits scene in the prologue in which the characters hear footsteps coming from offstage, an event that resonates strongly with the scene depicting the first rehearsals for On High in Blue Tomorrows when Nikki, Devon, Kingsley and Freddie also hear some mysterious footsteps.

15 Will Dodson, 'Review of David Lynch in Theory', Screen, 52, no. 3 (2011), 418.

16 Dodson, 'Review of David Lynch in Theory', 415.

17 Nochimson, 'Inland Empire', 10.

18 Whilst this may be a little too contrived, it is worth at least speculating, given the abyssal series of infratextual references set up here, that the title Vier Sieben may resonate not only with the number of a particular room that will appear throughout the film but also provide another coded intertextual reference to Dulac's Disque 957 (9 − 5 = 4; 7).

19 For a commentary on this work, see Hainge, 'Red Velvet'.

20 Matt Murray, 'Inland Empire', http://www.cornponeflicks.com/inland.html [accessed 15 October 2009].

21 Geoffrey Macnab, 'Inspired and Incomprehensible, a Russian Doll of a Film', The Guardian, 7 September 2006, http://www.guardian.co.uk/world/2006/sep/07/filmfestivals.film [accessed 11 May 2012.

22 Jay Weissberg, 'Inland Empire', Variety, 6 September 2006, http://www.variety.com/review/VE1117931480/ [accessed 11 May 2012].

23 Manohla Dargis, 'The Trippy Dream Factory of David Lynch', New York Times, 6 December 2006, http://movies.nytimes.com/2006/12/06/movies/06empi.html [accessed 15 October 2009].

24 To spell out the analogy, the communication channel in the physiology of the body would be: axon–synapse–dendrite; and in Lynch's text's relation to the audience: Axxon N / INLAND EMPIRE aporia viewing/auditory subject.

25 Note that the 'Rabbits' scenes inserted into the film also come from a series originally made for the internet, the difference with 'Axxon N' being that the 'Rabbits' series was actually released on http://www.lynch.com.

26 Lynch, *Catching the Big Fish*, 153. In a question and answer session, Lynch has similarly said that having upped the resolution of the PD-150 digital image and transferred it to film, he found that the end result, as he says, 'had its own feel, not film but a thing that I kind of love. And it reminds me of old 35, where you don't see everything so sharp, and it sort of strangely makes room to dream', https://www.greencine.com/central/node/22 [accessed 19 October 2009].

27 Weissberg, '*Inland Empire*'.

28 Lee Marshall, 'The Inland Empire', *Screen Daily*, 6 September 2006, http://www.screendaily.com/the-inland-empire/4028545.article [accessed 11 May 2012].

29 Joshua Rothkopf, '*Inland Empire*', *Time Out*, http://newyork.timeout.com/articles/film/3423/inland-empire [accessed 19 October 2009].

30 Drew McWeeny, 'Moriarty Visits David Lynch's *INLAND EMPIRE* and Lives To Tell About It!!', *Ain't It Cool News*, 29 October 2006, http://www.aintitcool.com/node/30544. See also Glen Kenny who writes: 'The visual texture Lynch creates in a new medium isn't as immediately beautiful as what he's done in film, but it has its own (sometimes quite ugly) integrity' ('*Inland Empire*', *Premiere*, 6 December 2006, http://www.premiere.com/Review/Movies/INLAND-EMPIRE [accessed 19 October 2009]).

31 I use this term advisedly because of the kind of viewer that it imputes.

32 Note, however, that even though this transition takes place here, it is foreshadowed earlier in the film in the scene examined in this chapter's 'Noisy Interlude 1' in which Nikki sees AX^{XO}N $_N$ written on a wall in chalk.

33 In this regard it should be remembered that *On High in Blue Tomorrows* is a remake of *Four Seven*, a film that was never finished, just as *INLAND EMPIRE* is, in a way, a remake of Axxon N which itself was never finished either.

34 This is a common feature of Lynch's films. As Marina Warner has written on another Lynch film, for instance, 'the plot of *Lost Highway* binds time's arrow into time's loop, forcing Euclidian space into Einsteinian curves where events lapse and pulse at different rates and everything might return eternally' (Marina Warner, 'Voodoo Road: *Lost Highway* by David Lynch', *Sight and Sound*, 7, no. 8 (August 1997), 6).

35 Eric Dufour, *David Lynch: Matière, temps, et image* (Paris: Vrin, 2008), 8; my translation.

36 See Eisenstein, Vsevolod Pudovkin and Grigori Alexandrov, 'Statement on Sound', in *The Eisenstein Reader*, ed. Richard Taylor, trans. Richard Taylor and William Powell (London: BFI Publishing, 1998).

37 Nochimson, *'Inland Empire'*, 14.

CHAPTER SEVEN

On Noise and Photography. Forest, Fuzz, Ruff

One Sunday stroll through the spaces of an art gallery filled with the usual fare, there came a break. I had seen many images of trees, painted with increasing levels of technical prowess and thus, one supposed, indexical veracity, and many photographs of trees also whose veracity as faithful documents of an external reality could not, of course, be contested, given their photochemical nature (or so they say). Here though was an image of another kind, one in which I couldn't see the trees for the image, let alone the forest. The image was large, very large, of a size generally reserved for the Great Masters, or Gursky perhaps. But this was neither of them, obviously, lacking the optical clarity of the latter and metaphysical certainty of the former. An Impressionist painting, perhaps, albeit one with a greater degree of realism than any other I had seen before? Intrigued, I approached (proximity generally bringing greater understanding, as we know from the zero distance viewing habits of the gallery expert so easily picked out from the less attentive viewing practices of the hordes who rush past each image so as to visit the space without actually seeing anything), but as I did so the cognitive dissonance only increased. What I was seeing was not a painting but a photograph, not impasto but pixels, and my failure to seize the image and class it in my well-habituated taxonomic categories for gallery viewing was thus doubled: not only had I mistaken the medium, but now I was faced with a low-resolution image normally found not in the art gallery but, rather, on the internet, and never in these proportions.

* * *

nm 07.1

For a very long time, photography has been considered, and perhaps still is by many, to be the indexical form of visual communication *par excellence*. This has been the case for the viewing public, practitioners and theorists alike, and it is a belief founded on the apparently incontrovertible photochemical material ontology of analogue photographic processes. As André Rouillé has written:

> The theory of the index has given rise to meticulous studies of the 'medium' and the photographic act, but it has spawned a theory which is global, abstract and indifferent to singular practices and productions, to concrete circumstances and conditions. According to this theory, 'photography' is primarily a category whose general laws must be uncovered; it is neither an ensemble of practices that vary according to specific determinations, nor a corpus of singular works. This refusal of singularities and contexts, this exclusive focus on the essence of photography leads this ontological theory to reduce 'photography' to the elementary functioning of its mechanics, to its most basic expression as a luminous imprint, an index, a recording mechanism.[1]

For Rouillé, it is quite simply not possible to talk of photography in relation to ontology since 'photographic practices, on the one hand, and artistic practices on the other, constantly change and exceed ontological principles'.[2] In this chapter, however, I want to suggest that it *is* possible to talk of the ontology of photography in such a way that the *expressive* nature of photography endorsed by Rouillé (and that for him is lost in ontological discussions) is retained.[3] What is more, I want to suggest, again *contra* Rouillé, that when considered through such an expressive ontological framework, 'photography' becomes sufficiently polymorphous as to no longer require an ontological separation between photochemical silver-gelatin and digital photography. This would no doubt be abhorrent for Rouillé for whom the split between photography and digital photography is so great that he is loathe even to allow the term photography to be applied to digital image production. He writes, 'the term "digital photography" is a misnomer, since it is by no means a digital declension of photography. A radical break separates them: they are differentiated not by degree but by nature'.[4] I will contend, however, that this is possible and, as might be expected, that such an ontological theory of photography can be arrived at by examining its noise.

It should not be inferred from this that I am myself defending those theories of the index that Rouillé rejects. On the contrary, I reject them also but I do so for reasons related to my previous rejection of many theories of glitch music. This is to say that the problem with many theories of the photographic index is not a problem with ontology *per se* but, rather, that those theories again ontologise their objects of study too quickly. Indeed, when one examines the photochemical ontology of (traditional film-based) photography, it quickly becomes apparent that there is in fact no direct, immediate and simple analogue relation between the object in the world and the photographic image produced. Rather, the photographic process via which an image is captured and then rendered in a visible form is just that, a process, and as such is subject to a whole host of differential contexts, operations and configurations that complicate the common sense idea that the photographic image entertains an analogous relationship with a radiant reality since light is directly imprinted on a photochemical material or support. This seemingly common sense understanding of photography is reinforced linguistically in French by the fact that the word for the camera lens is 'objectif', a designation that arises precisely because of the supposed objectivity of this technology. This fact is key for André Bazin who writes that with photography:

> For the first time, between the originating object and its repro-
> duction there intervenes only the instrumentality of a nonliving
> agent. For the first time an image of the world is formed
> automatically, without the creative intervention of man.[5]

Whilst such a view entirely bypasses the complex negotiations that are required for the production of a photographic image, Bazin's views on photography are far from being anomalous. On the contrary, Bazin is in good company for similar views have been expressed by many eminent critics, most notably, perhaps, Roland Barthes who writes:

> the *noeme* 'that-has-been' was possible only on the day when a scientific circumstance (the discovery that silver halogens were sensitive to light) made it possible to recover and print directly the luminous rays emitted by a variously lighted object. The photograph is literally an emanation of the referent.[6]

Whilst this may seem to make perfect sense, it does so only if one elides the many intermediary steps of photochemical photography and imagines that the image magically appears on a plate or piece of paper without minute regulation of exposure time and light aperture, and without a multistep chemical immersion process during which the latent image produced by the exposure of a photosensitive surface is amplified or developed in order to become visible, then fixed at an arbitrary point, this whole process being repeated a second time in order to convert the negative into a positive image that might stand some chance of resembling the *noeme* Barthes talks of.

Some critics have of course pointed out the problematic nature of this assumption regarding photography that is based in either an insufficiently detailed understanding of photography's material ontology or else a willed displacement of it.[7] Altman and Manovich, for instance, have commented on some examples of the disruption of the indexicality of the photographic image in various avant-garde artistic practices.[8] More in line with the analysis herein, Hubert Damisch has noted how the fundamental problem for the early pioneers of photography – and, I would contend, the fundamental concept for an understanding of this photochemical ontology of photography – was not in fact the projection of the image via the technological apparatus of the *camera obscura* but, rather, the means to fix or retain that image on a material support.[9] Despite this, however, Damisch maintains that the public and practitioners' 'long familiarity' with the technology of the *camera obscura* led to a continued misprision of the nature of photography, to a persistent belief that its apparently automated (and thus preordained) basis meant that all of its processes could be elided into the apparently indexical moment of projection. As he writes:

This long familiarity with an image so produced, and the completely objective, that is to say automatic or in any case strictly mechanical, appearance of the recording process, explains how the photographic representation generally appeared as a *matter of course*, and why one ignores its highly elaborated, arbitrary character.[10]

For Vilém Flusser, any such posture adopted towards photography and that believes that photographs signify 'states of things that have been reflected onto surfaces' such that 'photographs represent the world itself' is a naïve one.[11] For him, this is because of a much simpler fact than anything to do with the photochemical multistep process of film-based photography; it is because, firstly, 'in the photographic universe one is faced with both black-and-white and coloured states of things', whilst such states of things simply do not exist in the world out there.[12] But secondly, and even more fundamentally, because photography, indeed all images, signify 'something "out there" in space and time that they have to make comprehensible to us as abstractions (as reductions of the four dimensions of space and time to the two surface dimensions)'.[13] What I think is important about these insights is that they enable a reflection on photography as a particular way of producing the image that is able to bridge the divide between film-based and digital photography in a way that cannot be done if one fixates on the photochemical aspects of traditional photography or, on the flipside, the transcoding that takes place in the digitisation of the image. Indeed, what Flusser's points indicate to us, I feel, is that photography, far from being a manifestation of the real, is merely the art of image composition, of arranging colours or tones in two-dimensional space. As such, photography is always concerned with its own status and being as a visual medium, even when it tries to be a *document* and struggles to efface itself in order to tell us something transparent about the world.[14]

nm 07.2

Photography is, and always has been manipulative. The realism of photography and its claims to tell the truth have always been manipulation, not just my interventions, which made it more obvious. But these are of course constantly intertwined. There is the manipulation in what I depict and the manipulation in the photographic technique.[15]

Around 1998, so the story goes, Thomas Ruff was researching nude photography on the internet and stumbled across some internet pornography sites. What he found on these sites was of interest to him not, it would appear, because of the sexual nature of what was depicted in these images' content but, rather, their low-resolution pixel structure which resembled that of images he had produced whilst experimenting with image manipulation software on his computer. Ruff decided to apply the same techniques to these pictures that he had applied to the abstract compositions of pixels that he had been experimenting with, 'processing them so that the pixel structure was only just barely visible [using] fuzziness and other blurring techniques, occasionally modifying the coloring and removing intrusive details'.[16] The results of this manipulation are manifold, as it gives the images a painterly as opposed to photo-graphic quality – an aspect of his images commented on by Carolyn Christov-Bakargiev and which for her is intimately bound up with Ruff's scepticism towards photography and its indexical promise.[17] In addition, however, by 'noising up' the images and obscuring their explicit content to a certain degree, he emphasises not so much the *medium* through which photographs are distributed in the internet age (and indeed to allow oneself to fall into this trap would be to imagine that there were a relation of equivalence between a small, on-screen image and a 122 × 155 cm image printed on high-quality photographic stock and displayed on an art gallery wall) but, rather, the way in which all images are necessarily at some level about the distribution of light and colour, about the process of composition.

This is made abundantly clear in all of the images in this series (*nudes*) in different ways. Very often, for instance, the images are framed in such a way that bodies and limbs bisect the entire image space, sometimes vertically (as in *nudes ga 08* in which an outstretched male nude becomes a white stripe across a dark background), at other times horizontally (as in *nudes noe 09* or *nudes gu 06* where a dildo inserted into a vagina or arsehole at the very centre of the image traces a line out to the left of the frame with a stroke of brilliant red or translucent blue), or even diagonally (such as *nudes ez 14* where the dark space between the profiles of two women about to kiss cuts the image in half from top left to bottom right, through the centre point where their lips and tongues form a yin-yang symbol). At other times geometric arrangements take centre stage, akin to the forms of Kandinsky or Mondrian, lines, colours and forms being exquisitely placed in relation to each other within the frame constituting the whole. In *nudes fee 14*, for instance, the legs of the copulating couple draw the same geometric form as the freemason's square and compasses symbol, and with no less mathematical precision. Meanwhile, *nudes pte 21* and *nudes pei 01* turn mid-female torso shots, underwear and cloth into white, pink and red triangles, rectangles, diamonds and trapezia. This, of course, is something with which we are familiar, for a work such as Gustave Courbet's *The Origin of the World* can be seen to do the very same thing, abstracting the body through truncation and placement within the frame such that it becomes a means to compose the image and foreground a specific form (in Courbet's painting, a black triangle).[18] Other images seem to reference classical studies of form: the figure in *nudes em 05* adopting the same posture as Delacroix's *Odalisque Reclining on a Divan*; the male on the left of *nudes mn 23* holding his arms in a manner similar to that seen in classical representations of discus throwers (even though he could by no means be construed as actually throwing a discus); and to my eye I cannot help but think that the disposition of the two male figures in *nudes an 40* is remarkably similar to that of Adam and God in Michelangelo's Sistine Chapel, even if Ruff reduces the distance between them to nothing and changes the point of bodily contact.

Other images in this series, meanwhile, seem to be studies in colour and contrast, such as *nudes fn 06* where white stockinged legs and panties appear against a vivid bright green couch, *nudes fn 07* which employs the same principle with an orange couch, or *nudes kü 12* where a floating female form, half black half white, is suspended against a fluorescent thulian pink backdrop, the tonal contrast adding to the sense of separation between figure and world, form and background. Other studies take the very opposite approach, subtle gradations of colour and lesser contrast making it hard to separate out figures from each other or to pick out bodies from backdrop (see *nudes tr 08*, *nudes lk 01*, *nudes hm 02*).

In *nudes*, then, we see the beginnings of a particular operation that is to become commonplace in Ruff's work and that takes place within the realm of digital photography but that is about the construction of an image and the severing of representational or indexical ties that takes place as the dimensions of the world are transduced and reduced into those of the photographic image. It is the noise of the image that indicates this to us and suggests what it is that is important in these images, that leads us away from the manifest content of the image to the expressive operations through which the image comes to be. As Matthias Winzen remarks:

> The blurring veil alters the desire of the gaze in a barely discernible but decisive way. The desire of the pornography consumer's gaze is naïve to the extent that it is not visual as it gazes, but graphically imagines depicted contents (enclosed and inaccessible in the depiction). By contrast, when confronted with Ruff's *nudes* the desire of our gaze is challenged, because the fuzziness indicates that there is something here that cannot be precisely grasped. It moves, withdraws, making our gaze even more intense, more curious at the same pre-rational level at which we become aware of pictorial content in the first place.[19]

Or as Ruff puts it somewhat more simply: 'A lot of people look through the photographs at what they want to see. They simply don't see that they are photographic images'.[20]

This operation is seen again most obviously in his series *jpegs* in which Ruff again borrowed images from the internet or other banal sources. The images that he chose for this series depict the aftermath of the 9/11 terrorist attacks, the natural landscapes of the Black Forest in Bavaria, natural and man-made disasters, satellite photos said to prove the existence of weapons of mass destruction in Iraq and burning oil fields during the Second Gulf War. For Bennett Simpson, in a comment that could equally be applied to *nudes*, this series 'is about the way photographs have become most widely experienced today, as digital images on the web, compressed and hyperfunctionalised to the degree that, like the leaves, clouds, and debris these particular images depict, they become ambient and groundless'.[21] However, to believe that this is the case is to fall prey to a materially specific form of ontological determinism that, I would contend, is not present in Ruff since the same operations can be found in *all* of his work, both film-based and digital, and, what is more, to choose to forget the very different phenomenological and material conditions in which his photographic renderings of internet images operate. To believe that Ruff's *jpegs* series is above all a comment on the hypercirculation of images in the internet age, indeed, is to conflate photography as image production with its means of distribution, these being separate facets of the art of photography as a mode of visual communication. As Vilém Flusser writes:

> The process of manipulating information – called 'communi-cation' – is divided into two phases: In the first, information is created; in the second, it is distributed to memories in order to be stored there. The first phase is called 'dialogue', the second 'discourse'.[22]

Like *nudes*, and indeed all of Ruff's photographs, the photographs in the *jpegs* series perform an explicit reflection on both aspects of the communicative function of photography. However, I would suggest, *contra* Simpson once again, that what we are witness to here is *not* a reflection on the distribution of images via a techno-logically-specific means of electronic distribution but, rather, on the general distribution of the image in a communicative assemblage with the spectator, regardless of the medium through which the image's semiotic content is transmitted, which is to say the image as expression.

This suggestion may seem entirely counterintuitive; after all, the very name given to the series is derived from the file name extension given to images that have been compressed with algorithms devised by the Joint Photographic Experts Group with the specific goal of reducing file size for faster online download. It would be tempting to believe, therefore, that the primary interest of these images for Ruff would lie precisely in this functional aspect. Were this the case, however, he would not need to enact the complex opera-tions on these images that he does, for Ruff is not content merely

to download images and blow them up to the oversized proportions they are enlarged to for gallery exhibition (most of the series
measuring 252 × 199 cm or thereabouts, depending on the stock
available). Indeed, before printing these images they are subjected
to a great deal of post-capture manipulation, pixels being moved
in such a way that each pixel is itself regridded and thus expanded,
emphasising the structural properties of the image, and some
colours are altered also. The characteristics of the image that are
emphasised by Ruff's manipulations are then indeed artefacts of an
image compression standard and thus a functional imperative, but
his interest lies not with this functional aspect but, precisely, with
the artefact in and of itself, which is to say that he explicitly sets
out to interrogate the material residues or incidental artefacts of
the expressive assemblage in which these images are born and that
resist the transparent and noise-free transmission of the (normally
desired) expressed content. As he himself says in an interview with
Max Dax,

> The fact that jpegs possess characteristics that give them a
> specific 'aesthetic' or 'look' is a 'collateral phenomenon' – a
> side effect. To me, these characteristics definitely have their own
> appeal. In this sense, my series of jpegs explores this collateral
> phenomenon, the aesthetics of an invention that has made it
> possible for images to be widely distributed via the internet.[23]

Ruff then uses his chosen software here in a similar way to that
seen in his much later series *Zycles*, 'for the opposite purpose to
which it was intended […] in the sense that [he uses] it to build
something non-functional'.[24]

Once more, if we consider the *jpegs* series in this way, it
quickly becomes apparent that the non-functional end to which his
manipulations are put to service is an interrogation of the coming
into existence of the two-dimensional image. Indeed, across all of
the images presented in the *jpegs* series, it becomes apparent that
the geometric gridding effect produced by the high-level pixelation
divides the image into zones in an even more formal manner than
the most geometric of his *nudes*. The image becomes, indeed,
nothing more than a two-dimensional grid in which colour can be
deployed in various zones regimented by a horizontal and a vertical
axis. The heightened two-dimensionality of these images, of course,

reduces the sense of depth that any of the images might have if presented in a different aspect, revealing to us that depth perception is a result not only of stereoscopic vision but also of relative zones of clarity and distortion and the relations and contrast between different shades of the same colour. If these images seem excessively flat, then, it is because there is here no relative difference between any area of the grid, the heightened pixilation rendering each molecule of the image as clear (or unclear) as the next, relative clarity or distortion only coming through the physical movement of the viewer in the gallery space, which means, of course, that this differential relation exists only in relation to the discursive aspect of photography – albeit only when the viewer relinquishes her fixation on content in order to focus on the image itself. What is more, Ruff accentuates the jpegs' artefacts or alters the relative colour tone of his images' pixels in such a way as to create differential relations amongst sectors of the grid, creating in effect a secondary grid at a higher level of organisation on top of the original grid, the individual pixels being grouped together by tonal contrast in 8 × 8 pixel blocks, drawing the false illusion of depth created by shading into the surface of the image and returning it to the strict two-dimensionality that is the preserve of the photographic image.

This process is most apparent in those series of images where the artefacts of the technology being used are brought to the fore such that they become visible, which is to say in those works that are most obviously 'noisy'. However, as has been suggested, this noise is simply a more obvious and explicit manifestation of a more general principle in Ruff's photography, it is indicative of a noisy operation that expresses the coming into being of the image that is present in all of his work and not only in series such as *nudes* or *jpegs* – or other explicitly 'noisy' series such as *Zeitungsfotos* in which Ruff selected images from an archive of newspaper clippings, abstracted the image from its informational context and enlarged them at a ratio of 2:1, rendering the dot matrix of the image much more apparent. This is to say then, again *contra* McLuhan, that the noise of Ruff's photographs may become more perceptible when the technological artefacts of the medium are apparent, but the same principles operate in all of his works. There is then no technological specificity to this noise but, rather, a photographic specificity, when photography is conceived of not as a technologically-determined material practice, as it is for Flusser,[25] but, rather, as the event in which the image passes into actuality in two-dimensional space.

nm 07.3

A striking example of the very same processes we have observed in the *jpegs* series can be found in Winzen's description of *Haus Nr. 7 I*. Winzen writes:

> Two street lamps, one on the left in the front middle ground, the other on the right in the background, arch up over the street from the pathway, yet fail to introduce any real dynamism into the strictly vertical-horizontal composition of the scene as it tapers diagonally along the empty street to the right.[26]

Looking at the images in the *Haus* series as a whole, one is struck by the extent to which this same principle is deployed across all of the photographs, whether the buildings are shot at an angle as is the case with *Haus Nr.7 I* (and *7 II, 8 I, 8 III, 5 III, 2 I, 9 II*, etc.) or straight on, the camera angle being perpendicular to the front of the building (as in *1 I, 3 I, 3 II, 5 I, 12 I, 1 II, 6 I, 12 II*, etc.). What is more, almost every building in this series belongs to a specific kind of post-war to 1970s architecture, remarkable in most cases precisely for its architectural unremarkability. However, as the subject for a study of the translation of volumetric forms into a flat plane in such a way that those forms are disabused of the illusory depth that would shore up their indexical links to the outside world, these buildings are exquisite. Indeed, all of them display a strict geometric rigour, their contours, doors, windows, (minimalist) details and angles all performing a gridding of the image space in a similar way to the pixel grids of the *jpegs* series. *Haus Nr. 8 III*, for instance, presents a brick building built around a steel frame that forms a grid inside of which each brick forms part of a matrix, in exactly the same manner as the pixels of the *jpegs* are gridded together in 8 × 8 blocks through the operations of tone and contrast and the peculiar artefacts of the compression software. What is more, even though this building is shot at an angle, such that we are able to see three walls of this L-shaped building and two corner angles,[27] the absolute neutrality of the background and foreground and the flat light that provides no sense of shading robs this building of any sense of depth or volume. Indeed, the lines of the steel frame do not draw our eyes into an illusory volumetric form, since the spatial depth is not sufficient to bring about a perspectival convergence of parallel lines. Instead, our eyes follow these lines across and up and down the image in a ziz-zag shape, the line between the top of the building and the light grey sky bisecting the upper half of the image into two different zones, two different geometric shapes.

The extreme flatness of these images and the architectural unremarkability of the buildings depicted have led many critics to see in them a socio-political commentary on the conditions of life in certain areas of post-war Germany, or else to describe the images as banal. In both cases, however, such commentaries rely on the retention of an indexical relation that simply no longer exists. These are precisely not photographs *of* something, but photographs. The image here is not subordinated to the referent – as one might at first suspect given the nature of these images which do not appear in the slightest abstract – but vice versa, which is to say that what is of interest here is not the architecture of the building but the architecture of the *image*, the way in which lines, light and colour are deployed within a frame on a two-dimensional plane. *This*, for Ruff, is the essence of photography, the material, expressive elements of it common to all of its manifestations to which we attend through its noise. Indeed, it is by thinking of photography in this way that we can see the continuum in operation across all of his photographic works.[28] For having been made to attend to this aspect of his works by an intensification of their noise, what one realises looking over Ruff's career, from *jpegs* back and indeed forwards, is that his photography has always been about the architectural composition of the image and the frame, about the distribution of light and colour, about the lines of force and relation that draw the viewers' eyes over the surface of his works.

In his *Interieurs* series, for instance, which turns its attention to the interior design and living spaces of various German people (for the most part known to Ruff personally), doorjambs that would generally indicate a threshold leading into a different spatial volume are pushed to the very edge of the image in such a way that they frame one side of the pictorial plane rather than leading into a separate space in the image's content (see, for instance, *Interieur 4C* and *2D*). This same technique can be found with mirrors also, as in *Interieur 3A* where a full-length mirror to the far left of the image is shot in such a way as to enable us to see only its frame at the edge of the image, denying it the ability to double the impression of volumetric space, a function that mirrors are often made to serve. The dressing table mirror shot head on towards the upper right quadrant of the photograph, meanwhile, reflects nothing other than a white surface little different from the white wall on which it is hung, this again denying spatial volume and flattening both object and reflection into a single plane. Through techniques such as these, every element of these interiors, like the bodies, limbs, genitals, sex toys and underwear of *nudes*, is similarly robbed of its functional or utilitarian index to the real space in which it is situated to become instead a geometric shape, a line or a colour bisecting the plane and composing the image. The decorative motifs of tiled surfaces and wallpapers, for instance, are intensified through selective presentation, becoming abstract visual motifs, and all of the objects set against these backgrounds enter into the same logic and visual economy, making of them but a motif, a shape bisecting a plane and not a volume extended in space.

This same principle governs Ruff's *Porträts* also, but extends it out to encompass and suppress the psychology of much portraiture. If good portraits are generally said to tell us something about the personality of the sitter, this link to the 'real' person is consciously rejected by Ruff who shoots his sitters mostly face on, against a plain background (in the early shots against a colour chosen by the sitter, in the later shots a neutral tone), instructing them to retain a blank expression and shooting with a flat light once again to remove any sense of depth from the image such that what we are presented with is not a picture of a person but, rather, a photograph that uses a face to construct its image. As André Rouillé has written of this series:

> Thomas Ruff photographs [...] his models – generally young people – in the most neutral and direct way possible, without diversions or effects. His photographs are always shot head on, with extreme precision, with no shadows or blemishes on the faces so that they appear without depth or contours.

Smooth and transparent, they are lacking in human consistency. Empty, emptied out of their substance, they are the non-faces of individuals who have been reduced to the present of their mere appearance, they are sur-faces [*visages-surfaces*]. Their mute expression betrays a kind of exhaustion, a deaf and fatal erosion of the human.[29]

More surprisingly, perhaps, this noisy analysis of Ruff also enables us to find the same operations at work in his astronomic works, *Sterne* and *Cassini*. In *Sterne*, Ruff used original negatives from the European Southern Observatory archives to produce large scale (260 × 188 cm) images of sections of these negatives. The ambition of Ruff's project is perhaps at its greatest here because the resulting images in effect reduce an infinitesimally large volumetric space measured in light years to a flat plane, making of the universe nothing more than points of light and the absence of light, zones on a plane that enter into relation with each other due to their differential reflective qualities. These photographs no longer refer to the universe or the stars that produced the light they supposedly record, then, but only to the expressive act of (black and white) photography conceptualised in these very same terms, as a distribution of differential reflective qualities. And whilst there may indeed be no reason to restrict this commentary to black and white photography, it is perhaps more apt to make the same claim in relation to colour photography via Ruff's recent series *Cassini*.

In this series, Ruff takes satellite images of Saturn, its moons and its rings from a NASA archive on the internet, and manipulates the colours and framing of the satellite images in such a way as to make of them, once more, merely images, two-dimensional lines, shapes and zones of colour. Technically speaking, *Cassini 04* may then depict one of Saturn's moons, but in actuality it does not for it is merely a black circle containing zones of grey against an olive green background, all of which is bisected horizontally through the centre of the image by a bright light green line, whilst *Cassini 02* is simpler still, presenting a curved line that bisects the image plane vertically into two zones, one of which is black and occupies one-sixth of the plane, the other of which is a light bile yellow and is itself bisected by a horizontal straight line one-sixth of the way up from the bottom of the image.

nm 07.4

More surprisingly still, analysing Ruff's photographs through their noise enables us to include his abstract series *Substrat* and *Zycles* within this same logic and contend that they also display a high coefficient of photographic noise. If this seems so surprising, it is because *Substrat* and *Zycles* are generally considered to be somewhat separate projects to Ruff's photographic *œuvre*, presumably because they contain *no* apparent indexical links to any kind of external real object in the world. In *Substrat*, Ruff takes images from Manga comics found on the internet and layers them over each other, intensifying the colours until all that remain are two-dimensional planes filled with zones of brilliant colour that enter into dynamic relations with each other, each zone bordered by colour gradations that enable it to morph into the neighbouring zone as our eye follows the diaphanous lines that resemble contour lines on a map more than any actual recognisable form – and let us note that, in the light of the present analysis, this is perhaps not surprising since contour lines are a cartographic convention for rendering three-dimensional forms in two-dimensional space through the deployment of a mathematical differential between the lines. Manga comics are particularly suited to this kind of usage since they are themselves one of the most dynamic visual forms imaginable, both in terms of imagined movement projected in the frame and across frames through the dynamic interrelation of lines and forms, as well as in the colour palette and contrasts employed. This is not to say, of course, that I wish to contend that Mangas are somehow photographic nor, conversely, that Ruff's *Substrat* series is in reality a Manga. What I am suggesting is that that Ruff's use of the material provided by Manga comics to produce a photographic image is ultimately no different from his practice in any of the other series examined, even if his tools and techniques may differ.

What is more, if Ruff's photography is extremely true to this term's etymology which designates this art as nothing other than writing with light, and if photography's expressive essence is consti-tuted not by any technological, photochemical specificity, nor by a direct relation of indexicality to the real which one often imagines it must represent, and if indeed its expressive specificity is merely to reduce the dimensions of Euclidean space into the two-dimensional plane of a flat image and to compose an image with lines, forms and colours, in other words to arrange differently reflective zones, then *Zycles* is also a photographic work in the same way as his others. The work is described in *Thomas Ruff: Surfaces, Depths* in the following way:

> the *ZYCLES* are inspired by drawings found in 19th-century literature on electromagnetism. Three dimensional tangles of lines constructed entirely by means of mathematical calculations were processed by the artist using a computer program and then transferred to a two-dimensional virtual image space by means of ink-jet printing. The finished canvasses present detailed views of the linear structures produced by the imaging software.[30]

This same entry notes that this series, in a sense, 'most represents his epistemological interests in representation and mediation techniques', yet nonetheless suggests that it 'seems less photographic than much of Ruff's other work'.[31] Yet, as Douglas Fogle points out, the historical relations between Ruff's *Zycles* and photography run deep. Writing of James Clerk Maxwell, whose book on electromagnetism was fundamental to Ruff's conceptualisation of this series, Fogle explains:

> While Maxwell is often credited for laying the foundation for the emergence of the field of quantum mechanics in the early 20th century, he was also credited, not insignificantly for our purposes, with discovering the process of colour photography in 1861. That he was as preoccupied with the processes of imaging as he was with physics is not surprising as photography itself is nothing more than a visual index of one part of the electromagnetic spectrum.[32]

Fogle's point here is close to mine, for although he reinstates an indexical relation to a phenomenon situated in the real world, it is only to that phenomenon which is fundamental to photography's expressive capacities, namely light. Some may object, of course, that both I and Fogle are at this point no longer talking about photography at all and that, indeed, if photography is nothing other than a composition of light reflecting surfaces in two dimensions that does not need to bear an indexical relation to objects in the outside world, then abstract painting could also qualify as photographic in this definition. The accusation would perhaps be fair, and indeed whilst there is no need I think to be overly techno-logically deterministic about what qualifies as photography and what does not, a move that enables us to talk about film-based and digital photography as different deployments of the same fundamental expressive practice, what we must not lose sight of is precisely the fact that there is always a technological mediation in a photographic work. One could contend, of course, that a paint-brush is also a specific kind of technology, but I would suggest that photography is a different kind of technology with a much higher coefficient of objectivity encoded into it. This is not to say that it harbours an absolute objectivity, as we have seen Bazin suggest or, indeed, as Bernd and Hilla Becher and many others from the Düsseldorf school where Ruff trained might contend.[33] Nor is this to say, as Flusser suggests, that 'we are manipulated by photo-graphs and programmed to act in a ritual fashion in the service of a feedback mechanism for the benefit of cameras'.[34] Rather, photography, I would suggest, is an eminently noisy technology that places human subjectivity and technological objectivity into an expressive relation with each other such that human subjec-tivity is always necessarily machinic and quasi-objective, whilst the objective machinic apparatus of photography is only ever semi-autonomous, always subject to the subjectivity of the photographer (even when the camera is automated).

The point here is no doubt related to Flusser's when he writes,

Every single photograph is the result, at one and the same time, of co-operation and of conflict between camera and photog-rapher. Consequently, a photograph can be considered to have been decoded when one has succeeded in establishing how co-operation and conflict act on one another within it.[35]

For Flusser, the question put to photographs by critics of photog-raphy can therefore be formulated as: 'How far have photographers succeeded in subordinating the camera's program to their own intentions, and by what means?' And, vice versa:

How far has the camera succeeded in redirecting photographers' intentions back to the interests of the camera's program, and by what means? On the basis of these criteria, the 'best' photographs are those in which photographers win out against the camera's program in the sense of their human intentions, i.e. they subordinate the camera to human intention.[36]

Flusser's stance here, however, is far too combative; photography is not a fight. What Flusser is talking about here is the nature of the relation in the machinic assemblage that constitutes the first phase of production of the photographic act, and it is somewhat arbitrary to make value judgements as to the aesthetic or philosophical *worth* of an image according to where on the continuum between human and machine any particular photograph is situated. Rather than the image's *worth*, what does change as we move along this line is the nature and coefficient of the image's noise, either subjectivity or objectivity being more or less resistant to the passage of the photographic expression. This is perhaps close to what Fogle means when he states that '[Ruff] enthusiastically embraces paradox by veering away from the center of visual photographic certitude in order to embrace the shadowy world of photography's dark matter where the collision between subjectivity and objectivity creates a complex explosion of photographic expressivity'.[37] What Fogle refers to as dark matter, however, I term noise.

nm 07.5

Up until this point, I have of course only really talked about half of photography, what Flusser calls the dialogic element, its production of the image, and I have almost entirely left aside the discursive aspect of photography, its distribution. Again, I would contend that in this aspect of photography it is possible to have different coefficients of noise in the assemblages instigated between certain kinds of images with certain kinds of publics and spectators, and that Ruff's work produces a particularly high coefficient of noise in these relations since his photographs often force a recognition of the assemblage in operation for the transmission of the image, which is to say that they are very resistant.

This aspect makes itself manifest in some of his works via their invocation to the viewer that leads to a physical displacement of the viewer in space. As in the narrative beginning this chapter, then, the *jpegs* disrupt our normal viewing practices, and invert the habitual logic of vision in which looking at something closely generally brings about a better understanding and greater clarity. The *nudes* perform this same resistant disruption in regards to the spectatorial practices of the gallery exhibition space, but also invert the logic of the pornographic gaze.[38]

Many of Ruff's series, however, contain a different form of noise that makes us attend to the relationality or expressivity of an object or assemblage that we would generally take to be static, either through a misprision of its ontology or else simply because the expressivity of the relation is generally always elided in order to focus on the assemblage's content and not its expression. And if the *production* of the image very often intensifies the expressivity of the transduction of the image from a four-dimensional space into a two-dimensional plane through a resistant operation, in Ruff's work it is oftentimes the retranslation of the image back into an illusorily three-dimensional form as a mental image through the operations of stereoscopic vision that becomes noisy and seeks out our attention.

That this should be of concern to Ruff is perhaps not surprising if we accept Christov-Bakargiev's suggestion that,

> The sheer abundance of culturally produced flat visual imagery has become so great in the age of mechanical photographic representation that we no longer link the right and the left eye stereoscopically, but constantly exercise our ability to create a purely mental image of depth, due to the double move from reality.[39]

For Christov-Bakargiev, the preponderance of the two-dimensional image produced by photography or generalised dissemination of information via the computer screen has become so great that 'our brains have adapted to the flat agglomeration of bits of information and pixels as if they were forms of volume and depth'.[40] Whilst this claim is somewhat exaggerated, what is no doubt true is that our ability to perceive depth thanks to the mechanics of stereoscopic vision is not something that generally gives us pause for reflection. When we do stop to think about it, however, what we realise is that all impression of depth in vision, whether of two- or three-dimensional objects, is necessarily just that, an impression or illusion since it is produced only through the neurocognitive processing of the difference between two images projected onto the flat screens of the retina. This is a process that seems to be of great interest to Ruff who has created series of stereograms, sets of two almost identical photographs which, when viewed through a stereoscope that presents each image to only one of the viewer's eyes, enhances the illusion of depth and three-dimensionality. This technology, originally invented by Charles Wheatstone in 1838, might itself then be considered to increase the noise of vision, making us aware of that which is generally taken for granted and heightening the artefacts of the very process of vision as an expressive act. For stereograms seem strangely artificial when viewed with the correct technology, and whilst it is undoubtedly true that this unhomeliness is an artefact of that particular techno-logical assemblage, what it is important to remember is that that assemblage itself is an externalised form of the process by which stereoscopic vision itself operates, a doubling up and therefore intensification of the expressive relation between three-dimensional form and two-dimensional shapes, as well as the differential relation between the images produced by our eyes.[41] As Ruff himself says of this technology: 'You have two flat photos, and if you look at them properly you see the one extra dimension. And it is not the eyes that do that; the images are created in the brain'.[42] This is to say, then, that stereoscopic vision results from a neurocognitive interpretation of the differential relation between two flat images. It is then not the case, as Tammer El-Sheikh suggests, that Ruff's *Stereofotos* exploit 'the viewer's perceptual mechanism of reconciling differences',[43] for there is no reconciliation; stereoscopic vision is produced only by the retention of difference such that a differential flow is instigated between the two images in relation with each other. Ruff is aware of this and once again increases the artefacts of this expressive relation not only by this technological doubling, but also by increasing the differential relation between each of the images in his stereograms. As El-Sheikh goes on to explain in his notes on this series, Ruff's innovation in this work

> consists in breaching the technique's prescriptions for realistic effect. Instead of separating the photos by the average distance between a viewer's eyes (6.5cm), he takes the photos at a distance between 1.5 and 150m. This hypothetical giant thereby

surveys the Alps from eyes lodged in a 200 metre-wide head
atop a body that would stand 1,000 metres high.[44]

As is clear from this description of these works, Ruff here breaks
the reality effect that these works were intended to create for early
viewers of stereograms who could be magically transported to
the three-dimensional space of a place they had never visited and
feel like they were actually standing before monuments or scenes
from faraway lands. However, rather than breaking this reality
effect and thrusting us into the body of a giant as is suggested here,
Ruff rather intensifies merely the unreality effect of *normal* vision
by increasing the differential relation that produces stereoscopic
images in the brain. The differential relation between these images is
then not reconciled in such a way as to enable us to effect a synthetic
operation that would provide us with a new stable identity from
which to survey the world; rather, the differential is increased so that
we are all the more unable to effect that work of synthesis, unable
to separate out perception from its objects, unable to maintain the
fiction that there is any such thing as an inanimate, external reality
that would be somehow separate from us as opposed to always
necessarily in a relation of ontological interdependence with us.

A similar operation can be found also in Ruff's series *andere
Porträts* for which he used a Minolta Montage Unit photo
composite machine to combine two portraits from his previous
series in a composite image that has been referred to as a
'phantom image'.[45] Terms such as this, of course, express once
again something of the fear occasioned by the dissolution of fixed
identity put into operation by noise. But they also speak to the
unreality of the image, the extent to which 'the work portrays a
person who does not actually exist'.[46] Yet whilst it is undoubtedly
the case that Ruff's use of the composite image is far removed
from Francis Galton's deployment of a similar photographic effect
through different means for a specific end – namely to create a
typology of the human based on shared physiognomic features[47]
– the unreality effect of these works may again not lie quite where
one might expect. For like the *Stereofotos*, Ruff's *andere Porträts*
also combine two different images into one to produce a noisy
image in which we can almost see the composite image being
produced out of the relation between the images from which it is
formed. Once more, then, if these images are indeed 'unreal' in the

sense that they portray something that does not exist in the real world, they are so only insofar as they constitute a noisier or more intensified version of the world as it is represented in vision (in this instance) or through our senses more generally, which is to say the world as it can only ever be for us.

nm 07.6

If we wish to examine the ontology of photography in and of itself as a mode of material production that takes place through a specific technological assemblage, then photography is necessarily split in two across the silver-gelatin/digital divide, since even though there is a certain amount of consistency in regards to, for instance, the reproducibility of the image that is so important for Benjamin, Flusser and others,[48] the technological and material means through which the photograph comes to be are very different in each case. What is more, if we analyse photography in this way then photography is split once more into two different ontological phases, firstly as the image is produced and secondly as the image is disseminated. If one considers photography in this way, it is perhaps easy to see how one might arrive at the kinds of conclusions drawn by Flusser. For him, technological advances in image production technologies (cameras) and distributions technologies (that have proliferated at an even more exponential rate since Flusser's death in 1991) have led to a complete devaluing or emptying out of the photographic image, such that 'as an object, as a thing, the photograph is practically without value; a flyer and no more'.[49] Or, as he puts it later,

Photographs are silent flyers that are distributed by means of reproduction, in fact by means of the massifying channels of gigantic, programmed distribution apparatuses. As objects, their value is negligible; their value lies in the information that they carry loose and open for distribution on their surface. They are the harbingers of post-industrial society in general: Interest has shifted in their case from the object to the information, and ownership is a category that has become untenable for them. The distribution channels, the 'media', encode their latest significance. This encoding represents a struggle between the distribution apparatus and the photographer. By concealing this struggle, photographic criticism makes the 'media' totally invisible for the receiver of the photograph.[50]

Ultimately for Flusser, then, this leads to a situation in which 'Photographs suppress our critical awareness in order to make us forget the mindless absurdity of the process of functionality',[51] and our job as critics should be to break out of this circular logic.

If we examine these statements more carefully, Flusser's arguments soon seem somewhat counterintuitive, however. It would seem, for instance, that the more successful photography becomes (which is to say the more the technology becomes available to the individual user and the more its products become available to the consumer) the more photography is itself effaced, becoming banal through over production at the same time as photography's own medium is usurped and displaced by the media through which it is distributed. Flusser's invocation to break out of this pattern seems then to suggest that the mediality of photography must be brought back into the fray, highlighting the medium and specificity of photography once more so that the ontological status of photography is reinstated. It is here that we find the crux of the problem in Flusser's analysis, for in actuality, none of the objections that he raises alter the ontological status of the image, which is to say that there is no reason to suppose that an intensification or quantitative increase of one of the technological qualities of photography – its iterability – brings about a fundamental qualitative change in photography. This is not to say that Flusser's comments are entirely without merit, for it would indeed seem to be the case that the speed and volume of photographic images today oftentimes prevent them from being considered in such a way that their noise or (relational) ontological specificity might be apprehended. According to Christov-Bakargiev, Ruff is well aware of this and deliberately produces his works in such a way as to ensure that they are not invisibilised by this speed. She writes,

> Far from being passive, pessimistic and negative, Ruff's art has actually acted systematically and emblematically as a form of resistance to the flood of images that characterize the digital age. He programmatically suspends them out of the speed of this flow, in a way not dissimilar to Marcel Duchamp's strategy when

he created the ready-made, suspending the flow of consumer goods in the new arcades (or early shopping malls) of modernity by removing them from that system of circulation and time, and from their functionality as objects for exchange. If photography became a flood and triumphed in large advertising images, airport posters and back-lit images, which are churned out, put up and substituted at incredible speed as this year's fashion gives way to next year's, Ruff has carefully controlled the number of his images within a relatively small number of series.[52]

Whilst it may then be the case that Ruff's extraction of the photographic image from the blur created by the hyperspeeds of our contemporary mediasphere enable us better to apprehend something about the photographic image itself, it does not necessarily follow from this, as Flusser would have it, that images that do not do this are ontologically different. Rather, the resistant operations of Ruff's photographs (of which this abstraction from the flood of images constitute one – to my mind minor – element) increase his works' coefficient of noise such that this becomes apparent and tells us something about photography (in both its dialogic and discursive modes) that extends far beyond his own work.

The noise generated by Ruff's photographs, however, does not look like what we might expect; it has nothing to do with the grain of the image produced by the size of the silver halide crystals of the film, indeed it has nothing to do with the 'medium' of photography at all and tells us little about the specific material and technological configurations that bring the image into being, even if series such as his *jpegs* may trick us into believing that this is the case. As he says of his *Porträts*, 'The minimalist detail in the photo should not be the grain of the photographic layer, but a pore of the skin or one single hair'.[53] What Ruff's photographs make us attend to, on the contrary, is the way in which the image comes to be as an image, the way in which the image presents information, and how that image is perceived within the medium of photography when this is conceived of precisely not in a technologically reductive manner but merely, true to its etymology, as a means to *write an image*. To view photography in this way is to attend to its noise, the ontological specificity not of the medium but of the middle or in-between, the way in which photography can only ever be a particular kind of expressive assemblage in which light, tone and colour are distributed in differential relations within a certain kind of technological apparatus, this image entering in turn into an expressive relation with a different kind of image-producing apparatus in order to pass into the realm of perception. Conceived of in this way, there is no reason to posit a necessarily indexical relation between an external reality and the photographic image of that reality, nor an ontological divide between silver-gelatin and digital photography, nor any reason to imagine that a photograph viewed on a computer screen is (in the dialogic or production phase) ontologically distinct from a C-type print viewed in a gallery, nor to imagine that the banal snapshot of the photographically illiterate amateur photographer so reviled by Flusser[54] is ontologically different from the art photography of a Cartier-Bresson or Weston or Henson, no justification for the belief that a massification of the production or reception of photography will bring about its demise. Photography in this formulation describes, on the contrary, the ways in which an image is expressed in two-dimensions in a certain kind of (non-prescriptive) technological assemblage characterised by iterability and two-dimensionality, and as such there cannot be an ontological distinction between different kinds of photographs.[55]

This is not to say that all photographic images are equivalent, of course, and if this analysis of photography is made possible through an examination of what we are suggesting might be termed the noise of photographic expression, then we might even go so far as to suggest that the ontological difference between snapshots and art photography that exists for Flusser is in fact a qualitative difference that can be explained by the coefficient of noise expressed by any particular photograph. Noise, of course, is expressed in every photograph, if noise is taken to be the expression specific to the operation by which the image comes to be as a distribution of differential zones. But not every photograph makes us attend to this expressive aspect of the image to the same degree. It has been my contention of course that Ruff's photographs contain a high coefficient of noise that makes us attend to this aspect and that (counterintuitively) enables us to see more clearly the ways in which, for instance, the photographic image necessarily reduces the dimensionality of the world into a flat plane. In Ruff's photography this effect is generated by the excessive flatness of the image and rigorous sense of the two-dimensional architectural composition of the image, but there is no reason why this heightened noise could not come, for instance, from the technologically enhanced depth or shallowness of field in the photographs of, respectively, Cartier-Bresson or Doisneau, both of which similarly point to the two-dimensionality of photography by emphasising the illusion of depth through different means. In all cases, what seems likely is that such a high coefficient of noise would not be found in an average snapshot where the interest comes predominantly if not solely from the captured content.

It might seem, from all of this, that what is being suggested is an equivalence between a high coefficient of noise and the definition of what qualifies as art. Whilst this hypothesis may indeed stand up to some scrutiny, I am nevertheless loathe to claim it as a general principle for all art. What *is* being suggested, however, is that this high coefficient of noise makes us attend to photography (and indeed other forms of expression) differently, in such a way as to be more aware not of the informational content of the medium, nor of the medium as a particular material or technological configuration, but, rather, of the ways in which that content is expressed through a particular medium and, subsequently, of how that impacts upon the secondary expression of the image in a perceptual assemblage. Thus, as with the other examples of noise examined herein, noise reveals to us the necessarily relational nature of photography's ontology at the point of both production and distribution/perception. Far from attenuating our sensory perception, noise here, through the intensification of this relational aspect, becomes that which renders our awareness of the world all the more acute, that insists upon us and calls us to attention – as indeed it does in its common sense definition, which is precisely why it is a problem for many people. As has been written in the catalogue notes to a 1991 touring exhibition of Ruff's work in Germany, 'Art is here intended as a means of intensifying our perception and reflecting on our reality; it is a medium of sensory awareness which can only be wholly realized through the active "collaboration" of the message'.[56]

To say this is not, of course, to mount a defence of the kinds of industrial or other nuisance noises decried by the anti-noisists, as Schwarz likes to refer to the anti-noise lobby. It is, however, to suggest that we should be careful not to apply the same kinds of logics to all forms of noise, precisely because the heightened perception of the unavoidably connected nature of our existence in the world that noise occasions can prevent us from making the kinds of false ontological claims that have haunted philosophies of (in this case) photography for far too long.

Notes

1 André Rouillé, *La Photographie* (Paris: Gallimard, 2005), 248–9; my translation.

2 Rouillé, *La Photographie*, 308; my translation.

3 See Rouillé, *La Photographie*, 610.

4 Rouillé, *La Photographie*, 12; my translation. See also the following passage: 'The passage from a silver-gelatin universe to a digital one does not only change a technique, it affects the very nature of photography. This is so to the extent it is not even certain that "digital photography" is still photography' (614; my translation).

5 André Bazin, 'The Ontology of the Photographic Image', trans. Hugh Gray, *Film Quarterly*, 13 no. 4 (1960), 7.

6 Roland Barthes, *Camera Lucida: Reflections on Photography*, trans. R. Howard (orig. French 1980; New York: Hill and Wang, 1981), 80.

7 See, for instance, Greg Hainge, 'Unfixing the Photographic Image: Photography, Indexicality, Fidelity and Normativity', *Continuum: Journal of Media & Cultural Studies*, 22, no. 5 (2008). The notion of the indexicality of the photograph has of course been problematised even further and much more obviously since the dawning of the digital age.

8 Rick Altman, 'Introduction: Four and a Half Film Fallacies', in *Sound Theory Sound Practice*, ed. R. Altman (London: Routledge, 1992); Lev Manovich, *The Language of New Media* (Cambridge, MA: MIT Press, 2001).

9 Hubert Damisch, 'Five Notes for a Phenomenology of the Photographic Image', *October*, 5 (1978); reprinted in *The Photography Reader*, ed. L. Wells (London: Routledge, 2003), 88.

10 Damisch, 'Five Notes', 88.

11 Vilém Flusser, *Towards a Philosophy of Photography*, trans. Anthony Matthews (orig. German, 1983; London: Reaktion Books, 2000), 44.

12 Flusser, *Towards a Philosophy of Photography*, 41.

13 Flusser, *Towards a Philosophy of Photography*, 8.

14 The tension between what he terms the 'photograph-document' and the 'photograph-expression' is present throughout Rouillé's work *La Photographie*.

15 Thomas Ruff quoted in Matthias Winzen, 'A Credible Invention of Reality: Thomas Ruff's Precise Reproductions of our Fantasies of Reality', in *Thomas Ruff: Photography 1979 to the Present*, ed. Matthias Winzen (New York: Distributed Art Publishers, 2003), 156.

16 Winzen, *Thomas Ruff: Photography 1979 to the Present*, ed. Matthias Winzen (New York: Distributed Art Publishers, 2003), 236.

17 Carolyn Christov-Bakargiev, 'Thomas Ruff at the End of the Photographic Dream', in *Thomas Ruff*, ed. Carolyn Christov-Bakargiev (Milan: Skira, 2009), 14.

18 The resonance with Courbet's painting is noted by Winzen who includes an image of *The Origin of the World* in the middle of his essay on Ruff ('A Credible Invention of Reality', 146). Note also that ironically, perhaps, the image from Ruff's series that most resembles Courbet's in its composition is *nudes re 07* which reinstates the model's modesty by keeping her underwear on.

19 Winzen, 'A Credible Invention of Reality', 149.

20 Ruff quoted in Winzen, 'A Credible Invention of Reality', 147.

21 Bennett Simpson, 'Ruins: Thomas Ruff's *jpegs*', in Thomas Ruff, *jpegs* (New York: Aperture, 2009), np.

22 Flusser, *Towards a Philosophy of Photography*, 49.

23 Max Dax, 'An Interview with Thomas Ruff', in *Thomas Ruff*, ed. Carolyn Christov-Bakargiev (Milan: Skira, 2009), 72.

24 Dax, 'An Interview with Thomas Ruff', 75.

25 Flusser, *Towards a Philosophy of Photography*, 46-4–8.

26 Winzen, 'A Credible Invention of Reality', 135.

27 The corner angles at either extremity of the building cannot be seen since the image is framed in such a way that these lie outside of the image boundaries.

28 The one exception to this is, I feel, his posters which are precisely posters that express a specifically posterly as opposed to purely photographic noise.

29 Rouillé, *La Photographie*, 491; my translation.

30 Tammer El-Sheikh, 'Zycles', in Thomas Ruff, *Oberflächen, Tiefen / Surfaces, Depths*, ed. Cathérine Hug (Vienna: Kunsthalle / Nuremberg: Verlag für moderne Kunst, 2009), 80.

31 El-Sheikh, 'Zycles', 80.

32 Douglas Fogle, 'Dark Matter', in Thomas Ruff, *Oberflächen, Tiefen / Surfaces, Depths*, ed. Cathérine Hug (Vienna: Kunsthalle / Nuremberg: Verlag für moderne Kunst, 2009), 196.

33 On the abolition of self and absence of composition in the Bechers' work, see Rouillé, *La Photographie*, 494.

34 Flusser, *Towards a Philosophy of Photography*, 64.

35 Flusser, *Towards a Philosophy of Photography*, 46–7.

36 Flusser, *Towards a Philosophy of Photography*, 47.

37 Fogle, 'Dark Matter', 194.

38 We have already seen Winzen comment on this phenomenon and the way in which these photographs make us aware of a genetic process inimical to a practice generally thought of as a relatively static given.

39 Christov-Bakargiev, 'Thomas Ruff at the End of the Photographic Dream', 17–18.

40 Christov-Bakargiev, 'Thomas Ruff at the End of the Photographic Dream', 18.

41 Or we might say, conversely, like Maximilian Geymüller, that the photographic medium itself expresses a 'retinal nature' (Maximilian Geymüller, 'Interieurs', in Thomas Ruff, *Oberflächen, Tiefen / Surfaces, Depths*, ed. Cathérine Hug, trans. Nelson Wattie (Vienna: Kunsthalle / Nuremberg: Verlag für moderne Kunst, 2009), 184).

42 Ruff quoted in Christiane Grathwohl-Scheffel, 'Cosmos of Images', in Thomas Ruff, *Schwarzwald.Landschaft*, ed. Christiane Grathwohl-Scheffel and Jochen Ludwig (Freiburg: Museum für Neue Kunst, 2009), 29.

43 Tammer El-Sheikh, '*Stereo Photographs*', in Thomas Ruff, *Oberflächen, Tiefen / Surfaces, Depths*, ed. Cathérine Hug (Vienna: Kunsthalle / Nuremberg: Verlag für moderne Kunst, 2009), 144.

44 El-Sheikh, '*Stereo Photographs*', 144. See also Cathérine Hug's description of the production and reception of these photographs: 'Using a camera with two lenses – at the same distance from each other as our own eyes – two images of the same scene are taken and then shown side by side, so that our eyes automatically combine them to create a single image. However Ruff has so radically altered the relative dimensions of the images that we would theoretically have to be a thousand metres tall to visually unite the images, and yet our eyes, or rather our brains, nevertheless are able to implement the necessary corrections' (Cathérine Hug, 'Surfaces, Depths', in Thomas Ruff, *Oberflächen, Tiefen / Surfaces, Depths*, ed. Cathérine

Hug, trans. Fiona Elliott (Vienna: Kunsthalle / Nuremberg: Verlag für moderne Kunst, 2009), 60).

45 Geymüller, 'Interieurs', 102.

46 Geymüller, 'Interieurs', 102.

47 The catalogue entry for the *anderes Porträt* suggests that these photos 'refer to […] and radically reject the composite portrait developed by Francis Galton in 1878, which aimed at a psychological and moral typology of the human' (Geymüller, 'Interieurs', 102).

48 See Walter Benjamin, 'The Work of Art in the Age of Mechanical Reproduction', in *Illuminations*, trans. H. Zohn (orig. German, 1936; Fontana Press, London, 1992), 211–44; Flusser, *Towards a Philosophy of Photography*, 51.

49 Flusser, *Towards a Philosophy of Photography*, 51.

50 Flusser, *Towards a Philosophy of Photography*, 56.

51 Flusser, *Towards a Philosophy of Photography*, 64.

52 Christov-Bakargiev, 'Thomas Ruff at the End of the Photographic Dream', 19–20. It should be noted that the temporal resistance alluded to here is resolutely not a freezing of time such as that found in those early studies of photographic indexicality examined at the start of this chapter; photography for Ruff is always necessarily inscribed with a temporal dimension, even though this expression takes place within two-dimensions.

53 Ruff quoted in Winzen, 'A Credible Invention of Reality', 139.

54 See Flusser, *Towards a Philosophy of Photography*, 57–8.

55 This definition of photography is in line with Rouillé's who is keen to stress the different *practices* of photography as it is deployed in specific contexts (see Rouillé, *La Photographie*, 16). Rouillé, however, would vehemently reject the idea, as has been suggested above, that the ultimate ramification of this is that there can no longer be an ontological separation between analogue and digital photography.

56 Reinhold Happel, 'Thomas Ruff', in *Thomas Ruff* (Sindelfingen: Kunst + Projekte Sindelfingen, 1991), 61–5; reprinted in *Thomas Ruff*, ed. Carolyn Christov-Bakargiev (Milan: Skira, 2009), 202.

CHAPTER EIGHT

On Noise and Music. Concrete (reprise), Woolly Mammoth

Noise

exploratory sonic surgery by Doctor Merzbow ... sounds elicited from the junk and detritus of his own life, wrapped in cast-off porn ... cut-ups, loops, scavenged sounds and confusion – like a good cathartic brainwashing by your local cult ... a soundtrack for canoodling by a crackling mid-winter fire, sipping a premium shiraz and gazing deep into the eyes of ... Jim Jones ... a compositional ecology employed in the glorious glitches and stuttering synth chatter ... loosing the tethers of studio improv and finding pleasure in the upper reaches of human auditory perception ... impenetrable edifices of white noise and resounding low end drones ... fluttering, flapping puffs of synthesiser flatulence gust over descending whistles and chirps ... a bed rock of factory mumbles and malevolent pulses ... amidst the gyrations of overdriven circuits arises a breathless gargle. growling and gasping, interpretive vocals, a combination of shamanistic grunts, hoarse, impassioned whispers and expressive huffs ... artificially generated jungle drums interspersed with what is possibly an abused baboon with a rumbling ambience ... a clangourous tone fracturing into even more disturbed strings and fervid, jittery electronics ... a single stuttering hum or crackle fizzles to nothing and is promptly replaced by a quizzical string passage or raging pink noise ... spectral keyboard notes, seething with foreboding, dodge pealing effects and the continual percussive pounding ... the clangourous trituration is soothing, tranquil – in a mildly terrifying way ... damp, airless, inky dark, utterly silent ... the sound of tectonic shift and geological groan ... exhaustion, skinned knuckles and the residual claustrophobia ... seething, tempered steel stylings, cold as chrome, and with a similar dazzling finish, circle slamming metallic percussion ... a vocal loop shredded to gibberish floats over a lowered, but insistent and threatening, electronic gale ... the locomotive energy of the rhythmic elements attack and recede between the droop and thrust of a motley collection of quarrelling instruments ... misused microphones creep up on trashy, freaking and periodically startling electrotones ... from amidst a scattershot, improvised drum-roll, a squalling buzz emerges that staggers between something akin to a Theremin solo and a feedback inebriated guitar lead break ... a rounded metronomic pulse in the foreground draws attention away from a background soundscape of what may be strutting peacocks ... an archaic synthesiser whining like a disoriented mosquito ... a sound menagerie ... crunch of percussion panning across channels ... sound-spikes of reverberating metal from a junk glockenspiel intrude arbitrarily ... a disjointed bongo solo ... heralded by a stentorian honk, like the air-horn of some gargantuan conveyance ... electronics accompanied by sparse string plunking ... clipped off-key blurts ... hiccups and gasps ... windy tape loops, breathy snatches of discharging diodes, warped cartoony fusillades and disruptive violin undergo moodswings in the midst of accelerated and braked tape fragments ... selective, spare percussive investigation versus the tinkle and peal of prepared and treated piano strings ... Masami, tearing at his violin, clipped, clangorous cut-ups to punctuate rumbling loops and an electronic grind ... the drum/ scrape interplay moves aside for hollering discordance, an orchestration of protesting brake pads and uncooperative strings immersed in a sound-bath of high-end electronics ... every aural nuance, every clunk, plink and clatter ... the strings struggling to keep pace with the metallic cloudburst ... high-pitched wind instrumentation and tambourine head north for a spot of Morris dancing, spin thrice 'round the Maypole and then bug out upon the arrival of the Nasty Mr Akita ... unadorned generator chatter, portending grief, ultimately accompanied by grating machinic interjections ... Masami is a flurry of fingers, reaching to adjust here, tweak there, scrape, whack, pluck and poke ... the sound of the very incremental

*demise of an ailing piece of equipment, from the initial protestations
of overload to the final violent sputters and sparks ... trotting, then
trickling synth-blorps ... watery effects, scratched and scraped
debris and heavily treated generator refuse ... misused wah creeps
up on trash percussion and freakish, terrifying electro-tones ... this
hail of spent technology set to a score augmented by strings
mirroring the accelerated whine of an earthward descent through
the upper atmosphere ... someone is loose in the studio with a
power drill ... utilised to establish a herky jerky rhythm before
being sent back to maintenance in something less than working
order ... now to be added to the cartload of similarly decrepit metal
items being tipped back and forth between two gigantic hoppers to
fashion the smash/crash/bash elements ... the brittle skin snaps of a
snare drum repeat a call to arms ... the sound of steel shod rats
attacking some poor soul's voice-box while complaining about
tough times ... tumbling, churning electrohowl butted up against
recurrent sound riots and diode distemper ... great destructive
symphonies of minimalist electronics and antiseptic sound
reordering ... unpredictable aural abrasion that seems bent on
planetary obliteration ... the tumult gathers momentum and lumbers
forward ... minute space junk. cosmic debris, the flotsam and
jetsam of the satellite belt, rained down in the proximity of Casa del
Merzbow ... the clamour and tumult inside Hell's garbage disposal
... a cranial catastrophe in danger of consuming your consciousness
... teetering on the brink of the abyss of deconstruction, swirling
aural secretions, brain-pulsing vistas of sound eternal ... the disor-
dered wail of the machinic microcosm ... bellicose discharges
issuing from left and right ... a pitched battle ... a fierce volley
marks the climax and decides the victor ... a sonic battlefield.
crunching cannonade fusillades bludgeon with a near metronomic
consistency ... subsumed by the blare of impact ... an elongated
electronic charge interrupts ... an angle grinder raking the surface
of rusted flaking steel ... tumbling junk-cussion cycles ... the whistle
of shells and muffled faraway thud of cannon fire ... strenuous
metal fatigue trials ... terroriser electronics and heavy histrionics ...
the Noise offensive is less an incendiary barrage and more a surgical
strike ... a nagging radio interference storm, eruptions of pronounced
static and controlled, bleating distortion announce randomly
acquired voice clips inundated in the shudder and chafe of a few
more layers of airwave hum, squeal, twist and shout ... the*

*enervating heat and fumes from primitive diesel engines, the
deafening roar of both motor and cannon debilitate the armoured
division grunts before battle had even commenced ... the horrendous
clang of white hot bullets and shells against tracks and turret and
the shower of sparks that covered those on the receiving end and the
simultaneous colossal report as high velocity projectile meets
stationary tank ... tentative then terrifying, scratches and scrapes
exchange fire from opposite channels. white noise aftershocks cause
further havoc ... elements attack and recede between the lull and
thrust of chattering cartridges ... shouts, gunfire, confusion ... an
utterly destructive beam of concentrated energy ... allow the rushing
wind, harbinger of apocalypse, to gust around you, buffet you
relentlessly and finally sweep you away to an unknown and
unwelcome fate ... just keep your head down ... a revolving cast of
experimental sonics ... staccato burps and jet-propelled menace,
actuating a tainted euphoria; stream of consciousness composition,
kitchen sink – possibly quite literally – instrumentation ... patented
junk extractions ... curt and muffled surges of sound ... unstruc-
tured, nihilistic musical monstrosities ... howling breakers of static
... monstrous discharges of electricity conspire to deflect the atten-
tions of abominable jolts of garish, discordant thwackery ... a
squealing, playful, nonsense vibe ... the soothing strains of chugging,
yowling, all-conquering electronics ... grabs of ruptured announce-
ments ... collisions and wails ... tepid, quivering chirrups and
whistles ... moments of jolting catharsis ... daunting waves of
malevolence ... pulse-pounding electro-acoustic ... wisps of sound
... the fading embers of this Promethean conflagration ... withering
jets of white, pink and grey-green noise, the electronic slush that
engulfs it and the positioning of slab after titanic slab of lo-tech
sound fusion ... formidable distortion and synthetic obstructions ...
unpredictable high-end flatulence ... malignant, dizzying, bleak-
black Noise ... shrill formless masses of sound ... jazzed-out,
spazzed-out sticksmanship ... strident, scrambled, disorienting,
compelling ... a curious, discreet shooshing intrudes ... intermittent,
clanking, percussive taps flesh out a constant machinic buzz and
whirr ... the soothing pulse and hum of loops tracking in reverse ...
cascades of junk percussion ...foreground metal abuse and
background loop wash ... tinkling struck metal, eddies of electronic
interference and the occasional blast of treated voice ... bristling,
unexpectedly, with the crackle and yammer of tape fragments and*

modulated feedback ... speaker cone warping, sputtering sound, sub-frequencies ... oddly timed interjections of a type of locomotive clickety-clack ... low static and multi-layered voices, junked and reshaped into a persistent chirp of disembodied intonations – admonitions from the ether ... distorting feedback and feedback distortion ... a post-traumatic Martin Denny: foreground exotica matched with background curios ... incandescent squeals and chirps shot through with quivering electronics, cheesy organ and drafts of interference ... querulous voices, snare snaps and rim-shots interrupted by anomalous time figures ... rioting barnyard animals smacking four kinds of brick-dust out of Bugs Bunny as their schtick ... auditory turbulence ... brass and bells, broadcast detritus alongside whimsical grunts and growls ... sci-fi soundtrack squeals ... blasts of randomly accessed shortwave ... an electronically manipulated mumble of what could be religious chant or opera ... a mellifluous but giddy whirl ... incoherent female voice uttering unintelligible phrases ... the barely audible tick, tick, tick of a genius at work ... boffin rock is dead ... my Pye 3-in-1 stereo never sounded like this when I was a youngster.[1]

* * *

I have, up until this point, taken what is perhaps the least obvious and most counterintuitive route in order to examine noise as it is manifested in various sites by deciding not to look for noise in musical works. This is because, as has been suggested (and perhaps precisely because music is the most obvious place to start thinking about the operations of noise in a cultural context), there are many weighty assumptions and preconceptions about precisely what noise is in relation to music. Many of these assumptions, as we have seen in the early chapters of this book, have led to various mutually incompatible assertions about what noise in the musical realm sounds like or does, to accounts that either contradict each other or else are, in and of themselves, deeply problematic. These assumptions are hard to shrug off for a number of reasons, as we have also suggested, due to the various difficulties involved in attending to noise, especially in the musical realm. Nonetheless, having suggested what the operations of noise as figured here might look like in some other, less overcoded contexts, I really have no choice but to conclude this study by turning my attention to music, to tackle the elephant in the room head on.

In order to do this I wish to return, firstly, to tape-based *musique concrète*. This is something that I have touched upon already in Chapter Five; however I did not proceed further at that time because of a perceived need to prepare the ground a little further. To have launched straight into an argument that *musique concrète* is both eminently musical and eminently noisy would have been hard without first providing some other examples of the operations of noise outside of the musical realm. For to talk about noise and music in relation to *musique concrète*, one has to struggle to be heard in a very crowded room. This is a heavily territorialised battlefield, on which one side contends that *musique concrète* is noisy primarily because of its use of recorded 'noises' – such as the sounds of trains, creaking doors and whistles – whilst the other claims, as we have seen, that it is in fact not noisy at all but, rather, eminently and resolutely musical. In what follows, I wish therefore to stand the middle ground of this debate and argue that *musique concrète* is both eminently musical and eminently noisy (albeit for very different reasons), to unpack what has already been hinted at and suggest how it is possible to make a claim such as this. In doing so, of course, I will necessarily be reconsidering the relation between noise and music and arguing that these terms are not opposed to each other. By this I do not only mean, as Henry Cowell suggested in 1929, that all music carries noise within it since 'there is a noise element in the very tone itself of all our musical instruments', some of the vibrations issuing from musical instruments being necessarily non-periodic,[2] although this is undoubtedly significant and part of the reason why music is always noisy. Rather, and hopefully somewhat predictably by this point, I want to suggest that noise is the correlate of musical expression just as it has been seen to be the correlate of other forms of expression. Thus, the operations of noise in *musique concrète* will be seen to share many similarities with the way in which noise has been seen to operate in other contexts, its heightened coefficient of noise revealing the nature of the expressive assemblage that brings expression into being, unveiling the organisational principle of expression and, in doing so, showing it to be but an (essentially arbitrary) infolding or actualisation of an expressive field or plane of noise. If *musique concrète* is to be used as a paradigmatic example of where noise is to be found in music and what this tells us about music, however, we must first make a case for it to be considered music in the first place.

Musique

In many accounts, *musique concrète*, in spite of its name, simply cannot qualify as music since it is one of those artistic practices within the sonic realm that desire to integrate 'non-musical' elements into their structure. We have seen examples of this before in the protestations of critics such as R. Murray Schafer, of course, but we can find a similar line taken also in recent works in the philosophy or aesthetics of music. Andy Hamilton, for instance, would seem to prefer that works that integrate 'unpitched or not discretely pitched' sounds be called sound-art as opposed to music.[3] Tracing a familiar lineage from Russolo to Varèse to Schaeffer, Hamilton seems to wish that the latter had considered the possibility of calling his practice sound-art, creating thereby a categorical distinction that would not muddy the waters of the very definition of music so much.

This summary is perhaps a little unfair to Hamilton whose position is more complex and nuanced than these comments might suggest, and he himself critiques what he terms 'the *universalist* position that music is the only art of sound', a position that 'traditionally goes with the assumption that music exploits as material a particular range of sounds, namely tones'.[4] Nonetheless, he goes on to assert, paradoxically by his own admission, that the rejection of instrumental puritanism and incorporation of 'noise elements' into the field of cultural production has actually clarified the tonal basis of music. In doing so, he essentially reasserts the universalist position that he claims to reject, imagining that the creation of a distinct category in which to classify non-tonal works means that his attitude *vis-à-vis* music is somehow different from that of the universalists for whom music is exclusively tonal. He writes:

> Thus I assert that music is the art of tones, while rejecting universalism and recognizing an emergent non-musical sound-art which takes non-tonal sounds as its material. To allow that any sounds can be *incorporated into* music is not, I argue, to say that any sounds can *constitute* music – thus, room is left for my conclusion that music makes predominant use of tonal sounds and that there is also a non-musical sound-art.[5]

Given this conclusion, once he turns his attention to specific musical examples, Hamilton can but make what are to my mind deeply problematic categorical distinctions, suggesting, for instance, that 'The so-called drone musics of Eliane Radigue and Sachiko M are so non-rhythmic that they should be regarded as sound-art rather than music'[6] – and to this list we would surely need to add also Phil Niblock, Sunn 0))), La Monte Young, Tony Conrad, Marian Zazeela ...

For many readers of this book, precisely why a statement such as this is problematic will not need further explanation. For others who are not of the same opinion, let me suggest that the unproblematic assertion of the tonal basis of music is an example of what Ridley terms an autonomanic tendency in much musical scholarship, an intellectual position that begins with an (unfounded or at least unproven or untested) assumption and then carries on to investigate this assumption 'in accordance with a method which reinforces that assumption'.[7] Ridley locates this tendency in the work of those academics or philosophers of music who state that music is essentially autonomous (a position I will turn to later), but it can apply equally to critics who, like Hamilton, mistake a certain (admittedly dominant in many musical traditions) quality of music with its substance, who, on the basis of purely subjective criteria and matters of taste, make ontological claims. There is, this is to say, no reason why non-tonal sounds cannot be organised into forms that would qualify as music, just as, conversely, there is no reason to accept that certain sounds must be excluded from the realm of music simply because some may, on the basis of a common sense assumption, consider them to be noise and thus diametrically opposed to music. A similar problem can be found in the work of Roger Scruton who, in response to the question as to what distinguishes the sound of music, suggests, as I will here, that 'The simple answer is "organization"'.[8] In spite of this, however, he goes on to specify that a qualification is required to distinguish music from other sounds such as, for instance, poetry, and the qualification he provides is that the central instances of the art of music 'each achieve, though not necessarily in the same way, a transformation of sounds into tones'.[9] Whilst the definition of a 'tone' that Scruton provides is perhaps broader than that of many others, it nonetheless imbues music with an internal necessity, an order arising out of the total system that is akin to a grammar or, as he also refers to it, 'a virtual causality of its own'.[10] As he explains later, in a comment that could almost be considered a reversal of Roquentin's stance where instead of the internal necessity of the musical refrain serving to justify his life, the internal necessity of life provides the means to explain the perceived internal coherence of the musical expression,

> This virtual causality is sometimes perceived as physical relations are perceived: namely, as law-like and inevitable. More often, however, the order that we hear in tones is an order of action: one tone does not merely give rise to its successor; it creates the conditions which make the successor a right or appropriate response to it. The order that we hear in music is one that is familiar to us from our own lives: the order of intention, in which one thing serves as the reason for another.[11]

If, from amongst this field of philosophers of music, I appear to side with Ridley more than the others discussed here, however, it should not be inferred from this that I wish to follow his line of reasoning and suggest that we must reject the (for Ridley) autonomanic assumption 'that music is, essentially, pure sound'.[12] This is problematic for him because what this means, for critics such as Pater, is that music 'doesn't trouble with the world outside itself; it doesn't depict or say things or bother itself with psychology; its proper subject matter is, simply, itself – and its glories are the glories of form, design and structure, unsullied by any content not wholly its own. Thus for Pater', Ridley continues,

> music is *sui generis*, self-sufficient – in a word autonomous. And not only for Pater. The view that music is essentially autonomous has been popular for more than a hundred and fifty years.[13]

Clarifying his own position, Ridley later goes on to state that his point

> is not that it is wrong to think of music as sound structure. Music no doubt is that, among other things. The mistake is to assume that music is *essentially* sound-structure, that its character as structured sound is its true, real, ultimate nature.[14]

Whilst it should hopefully be obvious by now that I do not wish to claim in the context of this study in which all ontology is claimed to be relational that music is autonomous, I *do* wish to suggest that ontologically speaking (for it is a matter of ontology in Ridley's book also), music's true nature is indeed nothing other than structured sound. This is not to say, of course, that it cannot express certain qualities that Ridley feels to be excluded by such an absolutist view, it is to say quite simply that all music is necessarily united by this common ontological base condition. Just as it does not follow from this, however, that music is autonomous, this, in and of itself, is not sufficient to account for the ontological singularity of music. If the sole ontological condition of music were that it is structured sound, we would of course not be able to draw a distinction between music and speech. In order to separate out these different categories it is then necessary to suggest in addition that music entertains a different relationship with the world in which it is expressed than speech, that it does not carry meaning in the same way nor relate back to the world as does speech in the relation between signifier and signified. As Hamilton says in relation to the first point,

> Music and speech both impose a structure on sounds, but the structure of speech is semantic while that of music is at most syntactic. [...] A sequence of sounds becomes speech if they are meaningful, and it is not essential, and indeed may be a distraction or barrier to understanding, to appreciate them 'as sounds'. With music, in contrast, it is essential to appreciate the sounds as sounds, in the sense that one does not attend to them for the information that they yield about the world, whether through their natural or non-natural meaning.[15]

With regard to the (non-)representational nature of music, meanwhile, I would suggest, like Hanslick, that the peculiarity of music is 'that it possesses form and content inseparably', and that this

> opposes it absolutely to the literary and visual arts, which can represent [...] thoughts and events in a variety of forms [...]. In music there is no content as opposed to form, because music has no form other than the content.[16]

Again, this is not to say that music is autonomous as Ridley would claim in rejecting such positions, but it is to suggest that the relational aspect of music's ontology arises in the expressive act itself as opposed to arising retrospectively. The latter is what we find in Ridley's analysis in which music is related back to the world via the receptive or interpretive agency of the listener, a facet of music that I do not wish to reject, only to suggest that this is a secondary ontology belonging to a different assemblage that does not then inform an understanding of the ontology of music *per se*.[17] In other words, musical expression is not separate from the world, far from it; on the contrary, it is ontologically conditioned by the expressive assemblage through which it comes into being and thus necessarily expresses the qualities of that assemblage alongside its own musical content.[18]

In brief, the ontology of music as conceptualised here might be characterised by the following conditions:

(i) music is sound that is
(ii) structured,
(iii) eminently expressive since its only form is its expressed content, and hence
(iv) irreducible to a secondary function (such as representation),
(v) conditioned by an assemblage in the real world (and therefore not transcendent or ahistorical).[19]

Having sketched the conditions of this possible ontology of music, I will now turn my attention back to *musique concrète* to see whether it can be qualified as music. Perhaps unsurprisingly, I will surmise that it can and that, what is more, true to the operations of noise which always speaks of ontology, the noisy operations of *musique concrète* make of it a paradigmatic example of this ontological taxonomy. In doing this, I am not simply attempting to ascertain whether *musique concrète* 'is a piece of music rather than mere noise' which, for Dodd, is not an ontological question at all but, rather, a conceptual one[20] – although I have to admit to relishing the irony of tackling the ontological question through the problematic that he raises. What I am suggesting is that *musique concrète*, and, indeed, Merzbow whose music I will go on to consider in the last section of this chapter, can serve as limit cases that severely test the claims made in regards to the ontology of music. What is more, they render deeply problematic not only the type/token theory used by Dodd (due to the exclusivity that arises from the necessary retention of the musical score) but also the whole theory that he critiques (since, as the name implies, whole theory – albeit somewhat synecdochically – infers the possibility of an apprehension of the musical work in its entirety, abstracted off from the world and expression, therefore).[21] These examples, in part because they are so noisy in the common sense definition of the term, enable us to apprehend the philosophical or operational noise of music and to consider music from the perspective of a relational ontology.

Concrete (reprise)

The most common assertion made about *musique concrète* is that it is the musical form which, more than any other, expanded the vocabulary of musical expression, allowing any sound to be integrated into the realm of music.[22] Whilst, as we now know full well, this very fact serves as proof for many of the non-musical status of *musique concrète* and as evidence of the desecration or total destruction of music that this musical form signals, I wish to contend that, on the contrary, the possible integration of all sounds into a structured composition serves in fact to test the limits of music that others would place upon it.[23] To limit music to a set of sonic expressions containing only sounds of a certain quality – whether this be defined in terms of tone, pitch, rhythm, timbre or even mode of production (analogue vs. electronic) – leads one to the kinds of incompossible situations and impasses that similarly subjective definitions of noise have condemned this term to. Quite simply, if one conducts as broad a survey as possible in both space and time of expressions which have, at different times and in different places, been considered 'musical', it quickly becomes impossible to maintain that any one particular subset of sounds holds exclusive rights to the term 'music'. Rather, any such claims are revealed to be merely matters of culture, history or taste and resolutely not matters of musical ontology. *Musique concrète*, due to its ability to integrate quite literally any sound that can be expressed into a musical composition, takes this logic to its most extreme point (although this is a dangerous and ultimately false claim, as we will see later, but one that is perhaps true if projected back into the historical context when Schaeffer's pieces were first being made), reconnecting music with the virtual plane of noise or absolute outside of noise from which any sonic expression is necessarily born and that it carries within it.[24]

As we have noted previously, however, *musique concrète* does not content itself only with recording all possible sounds in the interests of some kind of anthropological or documentary function, it also arranges these sounds in (non-natural or non-realistic) relation to each other. This, indeed, is what converts sound into music, for again, in all music from all times and traditions, the common denominator that unites all musical expression is that sound is organised via a particular kind of expressive event, a musical act. This is the case whether we are dealing with scored music or improvisation, songs or sonatas, jazz or pop, Bach or Bathory, drones or Debussy.

What is particularly significant with *musique concrète*, however, as I started to suggest in Chapter Five, is that a particular noise or artefact of the technological apparatus used to *arrange* sounds in *musique concrète* reveals this organisational imperative to us and shows it to be essentially arbitrary. Very often, and this is certainly the case with Roquentin listening to 'Some of these days' as we have seen, a subjective response to a particular musical line can lead one to believe that music is not merely organised sound but, rather, that there is an internal necessity and unity that accounts for that organisation whilst simultaneously imbuing music with a higher purpose or transcendent essence. Andy Hamilton, for instance, suggests that

> the alleged inseparability of rhythm, melody and harmony poses an aesthetic puzzle. Their fusion seems not to be a merely contingent feature of music but flows from the guiding ideal of the artwork's organic unity – the sense of inevitability and necessity of construction that one experiences with great art.[25]

There is, though, no reason to suppose that this secondary effect that music can at times produce in certain listeners is an ontological characteristic of music, for not all music will produce such a sensation in all listeners all of the time. All music *does always*,

however, obey some kind of organisational principle, it is structured in an expressive and creative act. This is no less the case
in *musique concrète*, as Hegarty points out when he notes that
Schaeffer was quick to point out that the non-traditional aspects
of it did not mean 'that you can string any old sounds together;
this new music would still need organization'.[26] What is more, this
organisational principle is made perceptible in *musique concrète* by
the splice which, whilst it cannot always be heard in and of itself
– because its duration is too short – nonetheless always stands at
the threshold of a moment of transition from one sound to another
that rarely, if ever, seems to obey the same kind of transcendent law
that the purple passages of some other musics can trick people into
imagining. This is to say that the moments of change and transition
across the splice appear to us as precisely that, moments of
transition, they are not sublimated underneath a sense of seeming
perfect and necessary harmony between the separate elements of a
melodic line that fools us into believing that the relations between
different elements could only ever be precisely as they stand.

In suggesting both of these things, however, that music is essentially just sound and that that sound is structured in some way,
let me stress again that I am not merely espousing what Ridley
would consider an autonomanic position and claiming that music
is entirely divorced from the world. I do wish, however, to distance
myself from his formulation of how music relates to the world,
since what the expanded sonic possibilities of tape-based *musique
concrète* and its primary mode of structuration show us is that
all music is necessarily tied to and constrained by the material,
real-world expressive assemblage that brings it into being. Music,
in other words, is always already conditioned in advance by the
technological or corporeal assemblage through which it passes and
it therefore carries that assemblage with it in its very expression.[27]
The point here is similar to that made by Jonathan Sterne, already
examined in Chapter Four, where he suggests that any music made
for a recorded medium is altered by that very fact in advance and
thus can no longer be considered a 'pure' original but, we might
suggest, necessarily a noised-up version of the original. And this
point is made explicitly by Michel Chion who writes:

> It should not be forgotten either, that with electroacoustic
> music, the notion of the sound's *faithfulness* to 'the real' is not

even a consideration. The recording conditions (the type and position of the microphone in relation to the recorded source, the possible movement of the source in relation to the microphone, etc.) can themselves *create* the sound just as much as the actions of the sonorous body itself. The interaction between the recording and the thing recorded is even more radical here than is the case with the photographic image. And there is an entire universe of infinitesimal vibration, unknown to our everyday ears, that can be literally *created* anew by close-micing or the use of a contact microphone (in contact with the vibrating source).[28]

The importance of this for an analysis of *musique concrète* is not only that the sounds it uses are necessarily changed by the technological artefacts of the equipment being used (although this is undoubtedly true, whilst being a slightly different point from that made by Sterne) but, rather, that *musique concrète* provides us with a very clear example of how music is not a transcendent, unconstrained expression that exists in its own self-enclosed autonomous universe but is constrained by the world and its objects in various ways across time. If *musique concrète* is the first musical form to be able *truly* to integrate all possible sounds into the realm of music, this is to say, then this is because the technology that makes this possible only becomes available at a certain point in time. Similarly, if vocal music is only ever scored in the range of E2 to C6 (or 80Hz–1100Hz) this is because this range corresponds to the range that can be expressed by the human singing voice. Music is then resolutely not autonomous and is necessarily connected to the outside from which it is born, it necessarily carries within it something of the material specificity of its expressive assemblage, via which it comes into being in a resistant process. Music, this is to say, is always noisy.

This, though, is a very different point from that made by Ridley when he suggests that music is related to the world, and whilst it may be possible to contend that the stance adopted here would allow for music to be tied to emotions and psychology at the point of enunciation (as Ridley feels music must be), he is more interested in looking at this question at the point of reception and contending that music is representational. Once again, however, the material specificity of *musique concrète* clearly indicates to us that this is not the case. For whilst the sounds used by *musique*

concrète are sounds that emanate directly from the real world,
the whole *modus operandi* of the early practitioners of *musique
concrète* consisted, as we have seen, of manipulating, arranging
or mixing those sounds in such a way that they were placed at a
point of remove from their original sound source, rendered almost
unrecognisable and hence able to be apprehended as a musical
as opposed to documentary element. As Hegarty puts it, 'Each
sound, in manipulation, remains open, potential'.[29] Of course, the
question as to whether or not any recording can in fact perform
a true documentary function is already a vexed one. As we have
seen in Chapter Seven, even in photography, the supposedly most
indexical of all of the arts, there is a necessary transduction of
the object photographed into a specific, technologically-mediated
realm that necessarily makes of a photograph a noisy reproduction
more than a representation.[30] The transduction of any object used
to form the content of a work of art only intensifies this process
and necessarily furnishes us with a new object entirely, for art
necessarily produces a creative expression that results in something
new and not a thing that existed before it – a principle that can
be extrapolated out well beyond the realm of art in a relational
ontology. Or, we might say, in more Deleuzean terms, art is always
a becoming, it is never simply imitative.[31]

What this means, of course, is that music is eminently expressive,
its only form is its expressed content as I have suggested, as has
Hanslick before me, and as Hegarty argues with specific reference
to *musique concrète*, writing:

> Paying attention to the stuff of music – sounds as themselves
> – would reconcile material and form, not, as Adorno saw in
> Beethoven, in terms of a dialectical coming together, but as a
> new immanent body. Form and material would no longer be
> distinguishable, at least in traditional terms.[32]

Musique concrète specifically and music generally, then, are
irreducible to a secondary function that would close them off and
make of them a self-contained, autonomous entity existing in a
defined relation to a stable reality. Music, rather, is heterogenetic,
always relational, constantly differing from itself as it is conjugated
in new assemblages whether at the point of production/perfor-
mance or reception. Music, then, is always noisy and this noise,

in all of these different ways, is intensified and made manifest by *musique concrète.*

Bridge

There is of course a great deal of irony in what I am claiming here, not only because I am suggesting that music, like all expression, is necessarily noisy and thus resolutely not diametrically opposed to noise as it has often been considered to be. In addition, I am claiming that since noise always speaks of ontology, the examination of an excessively noisy (in the common sense definition) form (*musique concrète*), that many consider *not* to be music precisely because it is so noisy (even though it is noisy to them for different reasons than those suggested here) can in fact tell us more about music than other more traditionally 'musical' works – whatever that might mean.[33] As I have suggested, the reason why music does not yield its noisy, messy, material, open self to us, oftentimes, is perhaps because it is easy to adopt Roquentin's stance towards it, to enter into a reverie induced by a seemingly perfect musical line that makes one imagine the essence of music to exist on a higher plane than the messy, base, nauseous and noisy worldly, material and corporeal ontology in which we are unavoidably immersed. If we do not adopt this stance towards music, however, and eviscerate it of its 'aesthetic connotation', as Achim Szepanski writes, it reveals itself to be something else entirely, 'purely operative' and able to grow only 'metastatically'.[34]

In the final section of this chapter, I wish therefore to extend my perverse logic out even further and see whether there are even more extreme examples of works that are universally acclaimed to be 'noisy' in a common sense definition of the term and that, firstly, can be considered noisy in the way that this term is figured here; that, secondly, can confirm the hypotheses I have formulated about musical ontology; and that, finally, might also tell us something about the secondary ontology of music in the discursive phase when it enters into a new assemblage with a listener, about its relational ontology not at the moment of conceptualisation or composition but, rather, performance and reception. I want to see, in other words, whether noise music can leave us not in the reverie of Roquentin as he listens to jazz but, rather, a state that has more in common with his nausea, whether music, this is to say, can transmit its noise to us.

In order to do this, I feel that I have little choice but to turn my attention to the behemoth of noise music, 'the paragon of noise, its "godfather", its master', as Hegarty would have it:[35] Masami Akita, aka Merzbow.

The woolly mammoth in the room

There comes a problem when one tries to write about Merzbow, for such is the nature of this music that the difficulties of writing descriptively about music generally are multiplied a million-fold. As Hegarty writes, even though 'Merzbow's position is as the ultimate example, the reference point, for Japanese noise music and for the consumption of and writing on noise', for any who wish to take up the challenge of doing precisely this and write on Merzbow, 'It is impossible to avoid a vocabulary based on excessiveness, extremity and harshness'.[36] Or, as Brett Woodward puts it, both framing the problem and proving the point simultaneously,

> It's almost the inability to definitively describe Merzbow's music with the limitations of the written word that is the testament to its thrill and power, intricacy and convolution. Music as a densely layered hermetic and alchemic exegesis, a seminal text meant to be combed for clues – often misinterpreted – and argued over. A sound scripture both infuriating, vexing and liberating.[37]

Despite his own pronouncements, Woodward, of course, blithely ignores his own warning and does an absolutely magisterial job of trying to encapsulate something of Merzbow's music in words for the descriptions that he writes of the fifty compact disks in the *Merzbox* retrospective. It is excerpts from these descriptions, heavily 'remixed', that form the prologue to this chapter, and I will at no point from here on either repeat any of these descriptions nor try to outdo them – in part because there is no way that I could. What I wanted to do in that prologue was to provide the reader unfamiliar with Merzbow's music some glimpse into how one might try and describe this music and do justice to its density and volume – in all senses of the term; I recognise, however, as would Woodward, that any attempt to render Merzbow's music in words will necessarily be insufficient, and I would therefore exhort any reader who has not heard a Merzbow CD or track to do so before proceeding further.

If it is ultimately a futile exercise to try and account for music like this in words, to describe it, this means also that I will not be able here to analyse in depth any particular work, piece or track. Rather, I will be responding to what I consider to be some general characteristics and principles of Merzbow's music, which is not to say by any means that I am suggesting – as some do – that all of his releases sound the same, for this is absolutely not the case. Rather, I want to respond here to this body of work as an (open) whole, following to a certain extent Hegarty when he suggests that 'the openness of the work encourages thought'.[38] Like Hegarty, then, I wish to understand how Merzbow's 'noise' (in the common sense definition) relates to music, whether, as he suggests, 'its extremity suggest[s] the limits of all music and all that defines music'.[39] Or whether, in fact, as Thacker suggests (and many others albeit for different reasons), it is rather the case that

> The music of Merzbow is of course not music at all, but rather the intensive expenditure of sound and silence in a whirlpool of electronic catharsis.[40]

> the pieces of Merzbow can only insufficiently be analysed or legitimised on the basis of method or traditional musical language – there is only the experience of and in music itself. [...] as the name implies, noise music is just that – intensive, outpouring noise; in many ways anything but music.[41]

Unsurprisingly perhaps, I want to suggest something different from both Thacker and Hegarty and argue that if one perseveres with a common sense definition of noise when thinking about Merzbow, one can but end up in the kind of double binds, logical impasses and apparent contradictions that reappear consistently in their writing on this subject. This is not to suggest, of course, that I believe the 'meaning' of Merzbow needs to be tied down to one particular thing, it is to suggest that the openness of the work can be retained within a critical discourse that is nonetheless consistent

in the kinds of claims that it makes about the work. As excellent
as they are in many ways, this is not something that can be said
of Hegarty and Thacker's writings on this subject. Whilst Hegarty,
for instance, suggests that 'the openness of the work encourages
thought', for him the work simultaneously stands as 'a negation of
thought'.[42] And for Thacker, meanwhile, whilst Merzbow's noise
is 'not music at all', it nonetheless returns as 'exactly this display
of the excess of music, or the overflowing disintegration of music's
forms and contours',[43] which is to say that it does unavoidably
form part of something that is called music but that its operations
are such that it is concomitantly the disavowal of that very thing.

The problem in both cases, I would suggest, is not only the
unproblematic retention of a common sense definition of the term
noise, but a similar problem in regards to the term music. Indeed,
music seems to be linked for both Thacker and Hegarty to musicality.
For the former, 'the extreme, excessive fullness and density of the
sound, its total flow of uneven pulses, and its delirium of juxtaposi-
tions and transitions from one sound-world to the next [denies] the
language and technique of musicality and rhythm'.[44] And Hegarty,
for his part, suggests that '[Merzbow's] releases make something
out of noise that approximates music, while refusing most ideas
of musicality'.[45] As we have seen with noise, then, an ontological
category (music) is here confused or conflated with a subjective
value (musicality). If we do not do this, if we hold music apart from
musicality or what might generally be considered 'musical', I would
suggest that we can claim that Merzbow absolutely *is* music and
not, as Hegarty has suggested, the 'destruction of music'.[46] More
than this, if we also release noise from its common sense definition
and figure it once again as the residue of an expressive act, I believe
we are able to contend that Merzbow contains an extremely
high coefficient of *this* kind of noise also and that this noise, far
from proving that Merzbow is *not* music, proves in fact quite the
opposite, that it is, if you will, a kind of über-music.

Noise music

Thus far, I have gone about the analysis in this chapter in a slightly
different way to previously, for rather than looking at the noise of

the particular expressive assemblage in order to see what it might tell us about the ontological specificity of that assemblage, I have instead tackled the question of the ontology of music head on. Now, however, as I have done with *musique concrète*, it will be necessary to see if indeed there are in Merzbow extreme, or noisy examples of the kind of relational attributes that I have suggested might be used to draw up a taxonomy of music, whether there is indeed here a higher coefficient of the kind of noise that would point towards the contraction of the different elements of a musical assemblage into expression. So let us recap to see precisely what it is that we are looking for. I have suggested that:

(i) music is sound that is
(ii) structured,
(iii) eminently expressive since its only form is its expressed content, and hence
(iv) irreducible to a secondary function (such as representation),
(v) conditioned by an assemblage in the real world (and therefore not transcendent or ahistorical).

In relation to point i), it hardly seems necessary to point out that there is in Merzbow a great deal of sound. His work seems to spring, indeed, from a desire not only to make a great deal of sound, but to make so much sound that the physical properties of sound are physicalized, to increase the decibel volume to such an extent that his music is able to create a volumetric space whose physical properties are tangibly different to what exists in time and space outside of the music's particular duration. This is to say that the expressive aspects of sound as a physical process are intensified to the point that those processes are revealed to the listener, made noisy, in a way that they are often not – for good reason, no doubt, for during a live Merzbow concert one is sometimes made to attend to these physical properties of sound via pain or even nausea, as sub-frequencies act directly on the audience's internal organs in a far more literal staging of Roquentin's existential crisis, the inanimate (or, here, immaterial) being able not only to touch but to massage or pummel. This extremity of sound in such 'sonic dominance', to use Julian Henriques' term, intensifies the always already noisy operations of sound, the way that sound erases binary divisions. As Henriques suggests, 'As emphasized by sonic dominance, sound is everywhere, hardly even making the dualistic division between here and there'.[47]

From this first point, of course, one might be tempted to think that Merzbow's music contravenes the second point of our taxonomy, that there is no organisation or principle of structuration and that it is simply a uniform wall of something approaching pure white noise.[48] This, of course, for any who have listened to Merzbow, is blatantly not the case, and yet, at times, it is almost the case. In nearly every phase of Merzbow's career, much of his music has been based upon or circled around this kind of absolute sonic plenitude, a seemingly impossibly full sonic expression. Whenever this happens, though, the sound is never uniform. Whilst there are often more discrete sounds working on top of this foundational core, that core itself shifts and modulates, constantly transmogrifying and never remaining still.[49] It is in relation to these aspects of Merzbow's music, I would like to suggest, that we are able to attend to the organisational principle of music in such a way that it is that very organisational principle in itself that is made apparent to us and not an illusory sense of an internal and necessary transcendent order – as can be the case (as we have seen repeatedly) when the sounds are pitched and relate to each other in such a way as to form a line or melody. The organisational principle of music can have no such transcendent order and internal necessity, even though generic conventions and tradition at different times and in different cultures may lead us to believe that it can. Musical expression comes only through what is essentially an arbitrary infolding of a plane of noise, the sum total of all possible sonic frequencies, that seems to become less arbitrary through a secondary overcoding that takes place on top of music. By ignoring entirely any such kind of overcoding or 'musicality' and allowing his music always to remain at the very edge of the absolutely arbitrary, the plenitude of the plane of noise, Merzbow enables us to hear how music is nothing other than this contraction of sound into different forms via an operation taking place in relation to the absolute outside of music, or all-sound. This absolute outside, though (and this is what becomes apparent in listening to Merzbow), must never (indeed, cannot, even if many think it can) be able to pass over to the inside of music, to inhabit one of the discrete infoldings of the outside, imbuing that particular musical expression with an identity that will be mistaken for that of all music. For music can have no such identity, there can be no such ultimate piece of music, and if Merzbow is said here to be über-musical then this is only because what it reveals to us is not the discrete forms and lines of much music (indeed, there are no melodies in Merzbow), but simply the organisational principle that gives rise to music.

Something similar is suggested by Hegarty when he writes of Merzbow:

> this is a form that undoes itself, that acts as form, while in fact offering something else where form is supposed to be. Arguably it attains something of the essence of music, as, like repetition, it reveals that music is a structuring of time, and that this appears in or through the perception of the listener. The disruptiveness of this 'form' or formless, as Bataille would have it, through volume, unpredictability and relentless change, makes settling or dwelling difficult. This ecstatic non-music continually structures and destructures both the listening subject and music, or, in another theoretical register, it deterritorializes and reterritorializes them.[50]

At the end of this quotation, Hegarty is of course referencing Deleuze and Guatttari's ideas on the nature of music. For them, the operations of music are indeed similar to what I am suggesting here. Indeed, they write:

> Music is a creative, active operation that consists in deterritorializing the refrain. Whereas the refrain is essentially territorial, territorializing, or reterritorializing, music makes it a deterritorialized content for a deterritorializing form of expression.[51]

However, whilst I am absolutely in agreement with the operational aspect of music posited here, what I believe apprehending Merzbow as an eminently musical expression allows us to intuit, through its noise, is that Deleuze and Guattari's assumptions in regards to the *content* of music are erroneous or, rather, culturally conditioned.[52] For if in this quotation there is great emphasis placed on the notion of the refrain, this is because, for them, 'the *refrain* is properly musical content, the block of content proper to music'.[53] This, though, is a historically and

culturally situated definition of what the content of music is, as
Deleuze and Guattari actually allow when they qualify their own
assertion by saying,

> We are not saying that the refrain is the origin of music, or that
> music begins with it. It is not really known when music begins.
> The refrain is rather a means of preventing music, warding it off,
> or forgoing it.[54]

So whilst the operations of music consist of rendering musical
what is both properly musical content and at the same time the
antithesis of music, the refrain itself (the content upon which music
works) is a strangely closed entity, a fixed identity with a reassuring
internal necessity. It is this aspect of it, of course, that makes it into
a dwelling in which we can take refuge, a song that the child can
sing in the dark for comfort[55] – or even, perhaps, an earworm that
inhabits *us*. There is no reason to believe, though, that the *content*
of music need be this or even resemble this, if indeed we wish to
examine music in the absence of pre-formed notions of musicality.
And Merzbow provides the opportunity to do precisely this, for it
is resolutely not music that one can hum along to as Woodward
points out;[56] rather, it is like a kind of anti-refrain that 'makes
settling or dwelling difficult'.[57] As such, of course, it wards off the
bad faith of Roquentin, preventing the listener from imagining that
the transcendent unity of the work of art might be transferred onto
his own identity which would then become justified and necessary,
and thus favours the kind of post-identitarian politics espoused
by Deleuze and Guattari. As Woodward suggests, this is music
'designed to disorient the listener, break apart existing notions and
leave them in a state of suggestibility, more willing to accept and
respond to queer leanings'.[58] And it is for this very reason that we
must reject even Scruton's more subtle definition of the tonal base
of music, because there also a necessary order existing within the
musical object itself needs to be extrapolated by the listener for
sound to exist as music. He writes: 'When we hear music, we do not
hear sound only; we hear something in the sound, something which
moves with a force of its own. This intentional object of the musical
perception is what I refer to by the word "tone" '.[59]
     It is then precisely by *not* building its expression from anything
that could take on a stable identity that Merzbow's music is able

to intensify the incommensurability between form and content that many have insisted is the preserve of music. So whilst it is indeed the case, as Hegarty writes, that 'this is a form that undoes itself, that acts as a form, while in fact offering something else where form is supposed to be',[60] it is also the case that the content of Merzbow's music (for all of its sonic solidity) is such that it never petrifies into a block of content with definable contours, it is only ever a content that arises in expression, expression itself then coming to occupy the place where content should be.

Merzbow's music is then eminently expressive and, as such, absolutely irreducible and resolutely anti-representational. If, as we have seen, many have contended that this also is an essential quality of music, with Merzbow the point is made deafeningly obvious. For whilst scholars such as Ridley may contend that music can be considered representational in a similar way to other art forms, that, for instance, it can represent cathedral bells, it is impossible to imagine what referents in the real world might lie behind Merzbow's music if ever it could be imbued with an indexical function.[61] There are no objects that are represented here; if anything – and this itself is doubtful – this music refers only to events, to haecceities that have no identity as a thing or substance but only as a relation between different elements at conflict with each other yet somehow miraculated around an indeterminate centre in such a way as to appear as though a thing that might be apprehended as a unity: fog, war, apocalypse. Yet even this may venture too close to something resembling a representational mode, and it may be better to suggest simply that Merzbow's music is interested above all in a principle, the principle according to which anything comes to be. I wish, then, to modulate Hegarty's comment that 'Noise music is intervention to keep material material [...]. It is interested in material being stuff, not a source',[62] and suggest that noise music is intervention to keep material mobile, it is interested in matter being expression, and expression becoming material. Or, as Masami Akita himself puts it perhaps, 'Noise is the nomadic producer of differences'.[63]

And yet, even if music like this cannot be tied to objects in the real world via the mechanics of representation, it is nonetheless dependent on objects in the real world for its expression. For music must indeed, I would contend, be expressible in sonic form if its essence is sound. This, of course, brings us to the last point of my taxonomy, and once again Merzbow's music displays a very high coefficient of noise in revealing to us the extent to which music is necessarily conditioned by the technological and material assemblage through which it is expressed. Indeed, if I have already suggested something similar in relation to *musique concrète*'s ability to, for the first time, open music up to all possible sounds thanks to a technological advance, Merzbow shows that there is an entire sound world that was not available even to the early composers of *musique concrète*. This newly expanded sound world again becomes available only through new technological advances or, indeed, practices – a necessary qualification since Merzbow was creating noisescapes with analogue-based equipment not entirely dissimilar to the equipment used by Schaeffer *et al.* long before he expanded his palette even further via a move to laptop composition.[64] Just as the message in any communications channel is dependent on the technological and material specificities of that assemblage and is conditioned by it whilst expressing it in the carriage of its semantic (or other) content which is only transmitted via a resistant operation, so Merzbow takes this logic to its most logic-confounding extreme and consistently begs the question 'what is that noise?'. In saying this, I am not, of course, ventriloquising the imagined response of a Brahms-loving Merzbow virgin's first time with the woolly mammoth, but suggesting, rather, that Merzbow asks us this question in the way that it has been posed throughout this study. Which is to say, where does noise come from, what does it *do*, what *is* noise?

Notes

1 This is a remix of Brett Woodward's cover versions of Merzbow. Or, to put it another way, this text consists solely of excerpts of descriptions of the 50 compact disks in the Merzbow retrospective, *Merzbox*, written by Brett Woodward and published in the book that accompanied these CDs in the Merzbox, namely *Merzbook: The Pleasuredome of Noise*, ed. Roger Richards (Melbourne: Extreme, 1987), 82–132.

2 Henry Cowell, 'The Joys of Noise', in *Audio Culture: Readings in Modern Music*, ed. Christoph Cox and Daniel Warner (orig. 1929; New York and London: Continuum, 2004), 23. Cowell goes on

to suggest that even though it would be theoretically possible to produce a pure and noise-free tone in an acoustical laboratory, 'even there it is doubtful whether, by the time the tone has reached our ear, it has not been corrupted by resonances picked up on the way' (23). The impossibility of pure tones is commented on also by Russo and Warner. See Mary Russo and Daniel Warner, 'Rough Music, Futurism, and Postpunk Industrial Noise Bands', in *Audio Culture: Readings in Modern Music*, ed. Christoph Cox and Daniel Warner (New York and London: Continuum, 2004), 49.

3 Andy Hamilton, *Aesthetics and Music* (New York and London: Continuum, 2007), 41–2.

4 Hamilton, *Aesthetics and Music*, 45.

5 Hamilton, *Aesthetics and Music*, 45. Scruton's point is slightly different. For him, musical expression is necessarily tied to meaning and understanding and, as such, it is exclusively tonal or perceived as such even when a conscious decision has been made to avoid the tonal system. He writes: 'The possibility remains that tonal music is the only music that will ever really mean anything to us, and that, if atonal music sometimes gains a hearing, it is because we can elicit within it a latent tonal order' (Roger Scruton, *The Aesthetics of Music* (Oxford: Oxford University Press, 1999), 296).

6 Hamilton, *Aesthetics and Music*, 122. For an alternate take on such musical expressions and an attempt to consider them precisely from an aesthetic and musical perspective, see Joanna Demers, *Listening Through the Noise: The Aesthetics of Experimental Electronic Music* (Oxford: Oxford University Press, 2010); Robert Fink, *Repeating Ourselves: American Minimal Music as Cultural Practice* (Berkeley: University of California Press, 2005).

7 Aaron Ridley, *The Philosophy of Music: Theme and Variations* (Edinburgh: Edinburgh University Press, 2004), 11.

8 Roger Scruton, *The Aesthetics of Music*, 16.

9 Scruton, *The Aesthetics of Music*, 17.

10 See Scruton, *The Aesthetics of Music*, 17–18, 39. It should be noted that the linguistic analogy used by Scruton imbues music with a cultural specificity that the pretensions of his work would seem to reject, in spite of occasional statements that are tantamount to an admission that he is not talking about music but, rather, a culturally determined idea of music. He writes, for instance: 'Pitch, rhythm, melody, and harmony are not the only forms of musical organization; but they provide the core musical experience in our culture, and perhaps in any culture that is recognizably engaged in music-making' (20).

11 Scruton, *The Aesthetics of Music*, 79. Scruton rehearses similar arguments in his *Understanding Music: Philosophy and Interpretation* (New York and London: Continuum, 2009).

12 Ridley, *The Philosophy of Music*, 11.

13 Ridley, *The Philosophy of Music*, 8.

14 Ridley, *The Philosophy of Music*, 13.

15 Hamilton, *Aesthetics and Music*, 57. Note also that for Scruton too, music is a resolutely non-representational artform. See *The Aesthetics of Music*, 118–39.

16 Eduard Hanslick, *On the Musically Beautiful*, trans. G. Payzant (orig. German, 1854; Indianapolis, IN: Hackett, 1986), 80.

17 In order to clarify this point, it may be useful to think back to Flusser's distinction, in relation to photography or communication more broadly, between the dialogic and discursive phases in his conception of such informational objects.

18 Whilst it should hopefully be clear, it is worth stating nonetheless that all derivatives of the term 'express' used here are in line with the meaning given to this term throughout this book. This is to say, then, that 'expression' points to an ontological deployment and as such there is no reason to suppose, as does Scruton, that there is a necessary relation between 'expression' and 'feeling', 'emotion' or 'understanding'. See Scruton, *The Aesthetics of Music*, 140–70.

19 It is important to note that whilst attendant to the historical and technological conditions in which music comes into being, this typology has the particular advantage of being able to account for music across all musical traditions, be they defined in terms of a cultural distinction (East vs. West) or a generic one (song vs. symphony, scored music vs. improvisation).

20 Julian Dodd, *Works of Music: An Essay in Ontology* (Oxford: Oxford University Press, 2007), 1.

21 For an excellent brief discussion of some of the different arguments concerning musical ontology, see Ben Caplan and Carl Matheson, 'Ontology of Music', in *Aesthetics: A Reader in Philosophy of the Arts*, 3rd edn, ed. David Goldblatt and Lee Brown (Upper Saddle River, NJ: Prentice Hall, 2010).

22 See Chapter One for some examples.

23 It should be noted that Paul Hegarty suggests the very opposite to this, suggesting that 'Schaeffer is making the world musical, performing a noise reduction' (*Noise / Music: A History* (New York

and London: Continuum, 2007), 34). Whilst I agree with many points that Hegarty makes in regards to *musique concrète*, I disagree with this suggestion entirely because, of course, the definition of noise being used here is a very different one that does not allow noise to be recoded as it is in Hegarty's analysis in which 'in bringing noise into music, [noise] becomes musical, therefore losing noisiness' (34).

24 See the discussion of white noise in the introduction.

25 Hamilton, *Aesthetics and Music*, 125.

26 Hegarty, *Noise / Music*, 33.

27 Joel Chadabe gives many fascinating accounts of the specific ways that this has been so throughout the history of electronic music. See Joel Chadabe, *Electric Sound: The Past and Promise of Electronic Music* (Upper Saddle River, NJ: Prentice Hall, 1997). In relation to laptop music see also Rolf Grossman, 'The Tip of the Iceberg: Laptop Music and the Information-Technological Transformation of Music', *Organised Sound*, 13, no. 1 (2008).

28 Michel Chion, *La musique électroacoustique* (Paris: PUF, 1982), 33; my translation.

29 Hegarty, *Noise / Music*, 33.

30 The documentary possibilities of recordings are vehemently rejected by Francisco López who often makes field recordings and releases them with little or no further manipulation but insists that his only interest is with the sound in and of itself and not its source. For an excellent discussion of López's work, see Thomas Bey William Bailey, *Microbionic: Radical Electronic Music and Sound Art in the 21st Century* (Clerkenwell: Creation Books, 2009), 131–41.

31 For a discussion of this point in relation to Messiaen's use of birdsong, see Ronald Bogue, *Deleuze on Music, Painting and the Arts* (London: Routledge, 2003), 28–31. Bogue's discussion here renders very problematic the kinds of analyses proffered by Ridley in relation to musical representation, such as Debussy's attempts to reproduce cathedral bells, for instance. See Ridley, *The Philosophy of Music*, 52–6.

32 Hegarty, *Noise / Music*, 33.

33 Within the context of this study, the logic here is of course not in the slightest surprising, for noise here is claimed always to be a matter of ontology and to make more apparent the relational aspect of ontology as it comes to pass in expressive assemblages.

34 Achim Szepanski, 'A Mille Plateaux Manifesto', trans. Judith Funk, *Organised Sound*, 7, no. 1 (2002), 226. Having said this, it should

be noted that I believe this principle must be applied to ALL music and not only the clicks and cuts music that Szepanski releases on his label, that, this is to say, music has always been purely operative and that this does not only arise at a specific technologically-determined moment in recent history.

35 Hegarty, *Noise / Music*, 155.

36 Hegarty, *Noise / Music*, 155.

37 Brett Woodward, 'The Nomadic Producer of Differences', in *Merzbook: The Pleasuredome of Noise*, ed. Roger Richards (Melbourne: Extreme, 1987), 9.

38 Hegarty, *Noise / Music*, 156.

39 Hegarty, *Noise / Music*, 156.

40 Eugene Thacker, 'Bataille / Body / Noise: Notes Towards a Techno-Erotics', in *Merzbook: The Pleasuredome of Noise*, ed. Roger Richards (Melbourne: Extreme, 1987), 63.

41 Thacker, 'Bataille / Body / Noise', 64.

42 Hegarty, *Noise / Music*, 156.

43 Thacker, 'Bataille / Body / Noise', 64.

44 Thacker, 'Bataille / Body / Noise', 64.

45 Hegarty, *Noise / Music*, 155.

46 Paul Hegarty, 'Full With Noise: Theory and Japanese Noise Music', *ctheory*, a097 (2001), http://www.ctheory.net/articles.aspx?id=314 [accessed 15 May 2001]. Hegarty's position is more nuanced in a later paper where, working against Adorno, he suggests that with Merzbow, 'We are not left with a spurious empiricism of pure sound or noise, but with something like an absence signalling the absent presence of music: music is not here, not possible here, but can take its coming into being from this impossibility' (Paul Hegarty, 'Noise Threshold: Merzbow and the End of Natural Sound', *Organised Sound, 7*, no. 1 (2002), 198). In spite of this, this paper still ends up suggesting that, 'In the end, though, Merzbow is not the superseding of Adorno, but the noise, the exterior, the distortion, the excess, the death, the catastrophe of – [*sic*]' (200).

47 Julian Henriques, 'Sonic Dominance and the Reggae Sound System Session', in *The Auditory Culture Reader*, ed. Michael Bull and Les Back (Oxford and New York: Berg, 2003), 459. As his title indicates, Henriques is not talking about Merzbow but, rather, reggae sound systems in Jamaica; nonetheless, the same principles apply here.

48 It is necessary to say 'approaching' of course because, as we have seen, pure white noise can only ever be a mathematical abstraction.

49 Analysing Merzbow's *Venereology*, Paul Hegarty describes a specific example of this kind of operation, writing: 'There is emergence at play here, of the simplest kind, where some order is formed chaotically, but this forming is no sooner established than it unforms' (*Noise / Music*, 159).

50 Hegarty, *Noise / Music*, 139.

51 Gilles Deleuze and Félix Guattari, *A Thousand Plateaus: Capitalism and Schizophrenia 2*, trans. Brian Massumi (orig. French, 1980; Minneapolis: University of Minnesota Press, 1987), 300.

52 Whilst I will not draw on it here, readers may wish to refer to an alternative take on the relationship between Deleuze and Guattari and musical ontology, namely, Michael Szekely, 'Becoming-Still: Perspectives on Musical Ontology After Deleuze and Guattari', *Social Semiotics*, 13, no. 2 (2003).

53 Deleuze and Guattari, *A Thousand Plateaus*, 299.

54 Deleuze and Guattari, *A Thousand Plateaus*, 300.

55 Deleuze and Guattari, *A Thousand Plateaus*, 299.

56 Brett Woodward, 'SCUM Scissors for Cutting Merzbow VOL. 1', in *Merzbook: The Pleasuredome of Noise*, ed. Roger Richards (Melbourne: Extreme, 1987), 113.

57 Hegarty, *Noise / Music*, 139.

58 Woodward, 'SCUM', 113.

59 Scruton, *The Aesthetics of Music*, 19–20.

60 Hegarty, *Noise / Music*, 139.

61 Roger Scruton notes how sound is not in fact a secondary quality or property of objects in the world in the same way as a colour, for example, but, rather, something that is emitted by (and thereby separated from) objects in the world, a '"secondary object" heard as a pure event' (Scruton, *The Aesthetics of Music*, 2, 39).

62 Hegarty, *Noise / Music*, 140.

63 Masami Akita, 'NOISE*BEING*NOW', *Silver Star Club Magazine*, 7 July 1987.

64 Since the example of Merzbow has shown how dangerous it is to make absolutist claims about the possible range of possible sounds that can be expressed by various kinds of technological assemblages, I will not suggest that he now provides us with a new limit that will not be surpassed.

CONCLUSION

It is fitting that the last chapter of this book should have finished with a question, for even if I have attempted here to sketch an ontology of noise, I have, from the outset and as indicated by my title, always been aware that noise would remain out of reach in some way, that we would only ever be able to move towards it. Indeed, if the ontology of noise is relational, as has been suggested, then it can never be pinned down to one definitive thing, its points and coordinates will never remain fixed, able to be mapped, but will always only ever arise in different sites, with different characteristics according to the specificities of the expressive assemblage in which it is born again. Noise, then, requires us to keep asking questions of it and will never allow us to believe that we have definitively, once and for all, contained it. Nonetheless, I do not believe that this gives us an excuse, as critics, scholars or philosophers, to throw up our hands in surrender and not attempt to talk about noise in a consistent manner because the task seems so hard or even impossible. If we cannot talk about noise as though it is a thing with a core, definable essence, we can nonetheless talk about what it *does*, about its operations, and attempt to find in the multifarious sites, subjects, objects, texts, expressions and channels in which it arises some commonality or shared principles that allow us to talk about it in terms of an ontology. This book has been an attempt to do precisely this.

In talking about something so open, something that can perhaps only be talked of in terms of a set of operations that arise in an immanent situation, this book is, of course, necessarily incomplete; indeed, it could never be complete. If I have suggested in my introduction that the attitude adopted towards noise in the twentieth century has often been akin to that of a dog who, having discovered its tail, tries to run away from it, it seems only fair that I should subject myself to such treatment and admit that my endeavours in this book resemble rather the actions of the dog in the more common cliché who tries, unsuccessfully, to catch his own tail.[1] Thus, if I have proffered examples of the operations of noise in film, photography and music, suggesting how attending to noise in the way it has been figured here enables us to think differently about certain texts or modes of production/expression, I am fully aware that there are many other kinds of expression that could have helped me to formulate my argument just as well as those I have chosen, or perhaps even better. In all cases, of course, the choice as to what has been included here comes down to a matter of personal taste and experience, factors which are themselves, one might say, noisy elements insofar as they partially determine and are expressed in every work of this kind.

It should be noted also, however, that the potential work that remains to be done on this subject is far greater than this, and it should not be thought that this work would be complete were it to include, for example, chapters on literature, painting and new media art. Far from it. In saying this, I am not glibly suggesting that the potential objects of this study are almost infinite since, as I suggested in the introduction, when ontology is conceptualised relationally there can be no ultimate distinction drawn between animate and inanimate matter, between different kinds of objects in the world – as there necessarily must be for the tenets of most philosophies of music to be upheld.[2] In admitting the necessarily incomplete nature of this study, I wish also to point out that I have chosen to examine here only works in which noise is foregrounded or intensified in such a way that we are forced to, or at least invited to attend to it. I have done this though in the context of a theoretical assertion that *all* expression carries noise within it, and there is thus no reason to believe that we would not be able to carry out the kind of noise archaeology undertaken here on any text or form of cultural (or other) expression[3] – and this, of course, *contra* Kittler who contends that noise, considered as a Lacanian '[signature] of the real', only emerges in our media with the advent of photography and phonography, toppling the 'writing monopoly' of noise-reductive print technologies which were confined to the realm of the symbolic.[4] It is thus my hope that this book might serve as an invitation or, perhaps, provocation for others to continue this work and to attend to noise of this kind in other sites and expressions, to extend the 'idea of noise' proposed here which, in line with Douglas Kahn's view of all such ideas, is intended to be 'tetchy, abusive, transgressive, resistive, hyperbolic, scientistic, generative, and cosmological'.[5]

In saying this, I am fully aware that this may not be to everyone's taste and that the very different figuration of noise proposed here, as well as the very different analyses of specific texts proffered, may well be simply rejected by some. Let me stress, then, that I do not pretend to be offering, for instance, the definitive reading of Lynch that disproves any psychoanalytic analysis of his œuvre. What I want to suggest is that if we attend to the noise of a text as opposed to what would generally be considered its manifest semiotic content, we will necessarily arrive at very different conclusions that, hopefully, should entertain a more direct relation with the actual specific operations of that expression, its matter. This is not to say that other approaches are debunked, merely that they will necessarily, precisely because they insert texts into different kinds of assemblages, produce different results that express the noise that arises in the specific conjunction of that text with a specific critical apparatus. To return to the terminology used earlier, we might say that approaches such as these interrogate the discursive phase of their objects of study, whereas what I have attempted to do here is to remain within the dialogic phase.

Finally, just as I do not wish to pretend that noisy analysis necessarily yields a *better* result, merely a different kind of result, I hope that no reader will leave this book with the impression that I am advocating an abandonment of all common sense definitions of noise or suggesting that its meaning should be altered. Apart from the impossibility of such a task, to do so would also be undesirable. The common sense definitions of noise that are in common usage may be subject to massive subjective variation, contradiction and inconsistency, like any anthropological code they can nonetheless allow certain people in certain contexts talking about certain things access to a shared understanding. (And let it not be thought that I am unaware of the fact that I myself, at various points in this book, have had to waiver between a common sense usage of this term and the ontological definition proposed, oftentimes relying on the former as a possible point of entry into the latter.) With noise perhaps more than most other phenomena, however, the lack of consensus on what actually *does* constitute noise can also lead to massive misunderstanding and disagreement – not only amongst scholars, as we have seen, but also neighbours, engineers, musicians and so on. It is in part because of this that I believe an inquiry such as this one is not only justified but necessary. However, this book is born also and primarily out of a (not uncommon) deep conviction that the work of scholarship and philosophy must consist in large part of kicking against the assumptions, metaphysical certainties and unquestioned Truth of common sense perspectives on the world.[6] And whilst some might say that in going against the grain of common sense one can only end up producing nonsense, I would prefer to think that, in fact, this kind of critical approach introduces into our understanding of the world nothing other than noise.

Notes

1   Whilst it may seem ridiculous to extract from such an absurd image a serious point, I would like to point out that the figure of a dog chasing its tail does in fact come close to describing well the critical methodology adopted here which consists precisely of circling round an indeterminate centre in such a way as to draw a sphere of reference that is only partially defined since the circle can never be closed. (For this to work it is of course essential that the dog, unlike the Ourobouros, never actually catch its tail in its mouth.) There is a difference, however, for whilst the movement followed may resemble that of a dog chasing its tail, the object that I have been chasing is not in fact the tail itself, but rather that which lies at the centre of the path my investigations have traced.

2   See, for instance, Andrew Bowie who writes: 'It is the possession of intentional content of the kind that makes a noise a linguistic sign or a note that distinguishes both music and language. This means that they have to be understood in terms of their world-disclosive nature, *which is not the case for objects in general*, and this depends on how the elements of music and language are related to other linguistic and musical elements, and to contexts in the world' (Andrew Bowie, *Music, Philosophy and Modernity* (Cambridge: Cambridge University Press, 2007), 120; my italics).

3   Including, of course, all of those texts that I have suggested, in the opening chapters of this book, are not really all that noisy, for they have only been said to be so because the ways in which they are generally said to be noisy draw on common sense definitions of the

term 'noise', meaning that the kind of noise figured here and that necessarily exists in these texts also has not been probed.

4   Friedrich A. Kittler, *Gramophone, Film, Typewriter*, trans. Geoffrey Winthrop-Young and Michael Wutz (orig. German, 1986; Palo Alto, CA: Stanford University Press, 1999), 188, 16.

5   Douglas Kahn, *Noise, Water, Meat: A History of Sound in the Arts* (Cambridge, MA: MIT Press, 1999), 20. These are adjectives that some might apply to the work of Giorgio Agamben (and I mean that as a compliment) whose notion of the exception can, according to Crocker, be usefully elaborated through a consideration of mediality and noise and whose project may then already be an example of the kind of analysis proposed here. See Stephen Crocker, 'Noises and Exceptions: Pure Mediality in Serres and Agamben' *ctheory*, td053 (2007), http://www.ctheory.net/articles.aspx?id=574 [accessed 29 August 2007].

6   Or indeed, disciplinary norms. Something similar is suggested by Paulson, for instance, in relation to literary studies when he writes, 'If literature assumes its noise, and consequently its unreliability, as a constitutive factor of itself, then as readers and critics we are called to construct a kind of knowledge radically different from that of any discipline, one that may be described as the creation of meaning out of noise and disorder' (William R. Paulson, *The Noise of Culture: Literary Texts in a World of Information* (Ithaca, NY and London: Cornell University Press, 1988), 142). I would of course contend that it is important to do this whilst *not* bringing noise into the order of meaning and allowing noise to remain irrecuperable and operational, therefore.

BIBLIOGRAPHY

Akita, Masami, 'NOISE*BEING*NOW', Silver Star Club Magazine, 7 July 1987.

Altman, Rick, ed., *Sound Theory Sound Practice* (London: Routledge, 1992).

—'The Material Heterogeneity of Recorded Sound', in *Sound Theory Sound Practice* (London: Routledge, 1992), 15–31.

—'Introduction: Four and a Half Film Fallacies', in *Sound Theory Sound Practice* (London: Routledge, 1992), 35–45.

—'Sound Space', in *Sound Theory Sound Practice* (London: Routledge, 1992), 46–64.

Arnold, James, '*La Nausée* Revisited', *The French Review*, 39, no. 2 (1965): 199–213.

Attali, Jacques, *Noise: The Political Economy of Music*, trans. Brian Massumi (Minneapolis: University of Minnesota Press, 1985).

Bailey, Thomas Bey William, *Microbionic: Radical Electronic Music and Sound Art in the 21st Century* (Clerkenwell: Creation Books, 2009).

Banks, Joe, 'Rorschach Audio: Ghost Voices and Perceptual Creativity', *Leonardo Music Journal*, 11 (2001): 77–83.

Barad, Karen, 'Posthumanist Performativity: Toward an Understanding of How Matter Comes to Matter', in *Belief, Bodies, and Being: Feminist Reflections on Embodiment*, ed. Deborah Orr, Linda Lopez McAlister, Eileen Kahl and Kathleen Earle (Lanham, MD: Rowman and Littlefield, 2006), 11–36.

Barthes, Roland, *Camera Lucida: Reflections on Photography*, trans. Richard Howard (orig. French 1980; New York: Hill and Wang, 1981).

—'The Grain of the Voice', in *Image Music Text*, trans. Stephen Heath (orig. French 1972; New York: The Noonday Press, 1988), 179–89.

—'Introduction to the Structural Analysis of Narratives', in *Image Music Text*, trans. Stephen Heath (orig. French 1966; New York: The Noonday Press, 1988), 79–124.

Bates, Eliot, 'Glitches, Bugs, and Hisses: The Degeneration of Musical Recordings and the Contemporary Musical Work', in *Bad Music: The*

Music We Love to Hate, ed. C. J. Washburne and M. Derno (New York and London: Routledge, 2004), 275–93.

Baudrillard, Jean, *Simulacra and Simulation*, trans. Sheila Faria Glaser (orig. French 1981; Ann Arbor: University of Michigan Press, 1994).

Bazin, André, 'The Ontology of the Photographic Image', trans. Hugh Gray, *Film Quarterly*, 13, no. 4 (1960): 4–9.

Benjamin, Andrew, 'Porosity at the Edge: Working Through Walter Benjamin's "Naples" ', *Architectural Theory Review*, 10, no. 1 (2005): 33-43.

Benjamin, Walter, 'The Work of Art in the Age of Mechanical Reproduction', in *Illuminations*, trans. H. Zohn (orig. German, 1936; Fontana Press, London, 1992), 211–44.

Bergson, Henri, *Matter and Memory*, trans. N. M. Paul and W. S. Palmer (orig. French, 1896; New York: Zone Books, 1994).

Bijsterveld, Karin, 'The Diabolical Symphony of the Mechanical Age: Technology and Symbolism of Sound in European and North American Noise Abatement Campaigns, 1900–40', in *The Auditory Culture Reader*, ed. Michael Bull and Les Back (Oxford and New York: Berg, 2003), 165–89 [abridged from original published in *Social Studies of Science*, 31, no. 1: 37–70].

Blesser, Barry and Lind-Ruth Salter, *Spaces Speak, Are You Listening?* (Cambridge, MA: MIT Press, 2007).

Bogue, Ronald, *Deleuze on Music, Painting and the Arts* (London: Routledge, 2003).

Bois, Yve-Alain and Rosalind Krauss, *Formless: A User's Guide* (Cambridge, MA: MIT Press, 1997).

Bose® Pty Ltd, 'Acoustic Noise Cancelling® Headphone Technology', http://www.bose.com.au/site/index.aspx?path=products&CTRL=PTC H&pfid=10&tid=6 [accessed 28 March 2006].

Botte, Marie-Claire and René Chocholle, *Le Bruit*, 4th edn (Paris: PUF, 1984).

Bowie, Andrew, *Music, Philosophy and Modernity* (Cambridge: Cambridge University Press, 2007).

Brophy, Phil, 'Collapsing Image Into Noise Part 2: Noise, Noise, Noise', *The Wire: Adventures in Modern Music*, 165 (November 1997).

Bull, Michael and Les Back, eds, *The Auditory Culture Reader* (Oxford and New York: Berg, 2003).

—'Introduction: Into Sound', in *The Auditory Culture Reader*, ed. Michael Bull and Les Back (Oxford and New York: Berg, 2003), 1–18.

Burns, William, *Noise and Man* (London: John Murray, 1968).

Burt, Warren, 'Alvin Lucier (1931–)', in *Music of the Twentieth-Century Avant-Garde: A Biocritical Sourcebook*, ed. Larry Sitsky (Westport, CT: Greenwood Press, 2002), 269–74.

Caplan, Ben and Carl Matheson, 'Ontology of Music', in *Aesthetics: A Reader in Philosophy of the Arts*, 3rd edn, ed. David Goldblatt and Lee Brown (Upper Saddle River, NJ: Prentice Hall, 2010), 171–6.

Cascone, Kim, 'The Aesthetics of Failure: "Post-Digital" Tendencies in Contemporary Computer Music', *Computer Music Journal*, 24, no. 4 (2000): 12–18.

—'Ten Years of Not Being There', *Vague Terrain 15: .microsound* (2009), http://vagueterrain.net/journal15 [accessed 10 April 2012].

Cascone, Kim and Jeremy Turner, 'The Microsound Scene: An Interview with Kim Cascone', *ctheory*, A101 (2001), http://www.ctheory.net/text_file?pick=322 [accessed 23 January 2003].

Chadabe, Joel, *Electric Sound: The Past and Promise of Electronic Music* (Upper Saddle River, NJ: Prentice Hall, 1997).

Chanan, Michael, *Musica Practica: The Social Practice of Western Music From Gregorian Chant to Postmodernism* (London: Verso, 1994).

—*Repeated Takes: A Short History of Recording and its Effects on Music* (London: Verso, 1995).

Chion, Michel, *La musique électroacoustique* (Paris: PUF, 1982).

—*L'Art des sons fixés ou La Musique Concrètement* (Fontaine: Éditions Metamkine/Nota-Bene/Sono-Concept, 1991).

—*Musiques, médias et technologies* (Paris: Flammarion, 1994).

—*David Lynch*, trans. Robert Julian (orig. French, 2001; London: British Film Institute, 2006).

Christov-Bakargiev, Carolyn, 'Thomas Ruff at the End of the Photographic Dream', in *Thomas Ruff*, ed. Carolyn Christov-Bakargiev (Milan: Skira, 2009), 12–23.

Chua, Eu Jin, 'The Film-Work Recomposed into Nature: From Art to Noise in Four Minutes and Thirty-Three Seconds', *Moving Image Review & Art Journal*, 1, no. 1 (2012): 89–96.

Cobussen, Marcel, 'Noise as Undifferentiated Sound', http://deconstruction-in-music.com/proefschrift/300_john_cage/313_noise_undifferentiated/noise_undifferentiated.html [accessed 18 April 2012].

Cohen, Leon, 'The History of Noise (On the 100th Anniversary of its Birth)', *Signal Processing Magazine, IEEE*, 22, no. 6 (2005): 20–45.

Corbett, John, *Extended Play: Sounding Off from John Cage to Dr Funkenstein* (Durham, NC: Duke University Press, 1994).

Cowell, Henry, 'The Joys of Noise', in *Audio Culture: Readings in Modern Music*, ed. Christoph Cox and Daniel Warner (orig. 1929; New York and London: Continuum, 2004), 22–4.

Cox, Christoph and Daniel Warner, eds, *Audio Culture: Readings in Modern Music* (New York and London: Continuum, 2004).

—'Music and Its Others: Noise, Sound, Silence: Introduction', in *Audio Culture: Readings in Modern Music*, ed. Christoph Cox and Daniel Warner (New York and London: Continuum, 2004), 5–6.

Critchley, Simon, *Very Little … Almost Nothing: Death, Philosophy, Literature* (London and New York: Routledge, 1997).

Crocker, Stephen, 'Noises and Exceptions: Pure Mediality in Serres and Agamben' *ctheory*, td053 (2007), http://www.ctheory.net/articles. aspx?id=574 [accessed 29 August 2007].

Cubitt, Sean, Daniel Palmer and Les Walkling, 'Reflections on Medium Specificity Occasioned by the Symposium "Digital Light: Technique, Technology, Creation", Melbourne 2011', *Moving Image Review and Art Journal*, 1, no. 1 (2012): 37–49.

Damisch, Hubert, 'Five Notes for a Phenomenology of the Photographic Image', *October*, 5 (1978); reprinted in *The Photography Reader*, ed. L. Wells (London: Routledge, 2003), 87–9.

Dargis, Manohla, 'The Trippy Dream Factory of David Lynch', *New York Times*, 6 December 2006, http://movies.nytimes. com/2006/12/06/movies/06empi.html [accessed 15 October 2009].

Davison, Annette and Erica Sheen, eds, *The Cinema of David Lynch: American Dreams, Nightmare Visions* (London: Wallflower Press, 2004).

Dax, Max, 'An Interview with Thomas Ruff', in *Thomas Ruff*, ed. Carolyn Christov-Bakargiev (Milan: Skira, 2009), 70–5.

Deleuze, Gilles, *Expressionism in Philosophy: Spinoza*, trans. Martin Joughin (orig. French, 1968; New York: Zone Books, 1990).

—*The Logic of Sense*, trans. Mark Lester with Charles Stivale (orig. French, 1969; New York: Columbia University Press, 1990).

—*Difference and Repetition*, trans. Paul Patton (orig. French, 1968; London: The Athlone Press, 1994; New York: Columbia University Press, 1994).

Deleuze, Gilles and Félix Guattari, *A Thousand Plateaus: Capitalism and Schizophrenia 2*, trans. Brian Massumi (orig. French, 1980; Minneapolis: University of Minnesota Press, 1987).

Demers, Joanna, *Listening Through the Noise: The Aesthetics of Experimental Electronic Music* (Oxford: Oxford University Press, 2010).

Diederichsen, Diedrich, 'Clicks', trans. Judith Funk, in the liner notes to *Clicks and Cuts 2* (Mille Plateaux, 2001), 6–9.

Dodd, Julian, *Works of Music: An Essay in Ontology* (Oxford: Oxford University Press, 2007).

Dodson, Will, 'Review of *David Lynch in Theory*', *Screen*, 52, no. 3 (2011): 415–19.

Dufour, Eric, *David Lynch: Matière, temps, et image* (Paris: Vrin, 2008).

Dunsby, Jonathan, 'Roland Barthes and the Grain of Panzéra's Voice', *Journal of the Royal Musical Association*, 134, no. 1 (2009): 113–32.

Dyson, Frances, 'The Ear That Would Hear Sounds in Themselves: John Cage 1935–1965', in *Wireless Imagination: Sound, Radio, and the Avant-Garde*, ed. Douglas Kahn and Gregory Whitehead (Cambridge, MA: MIT Press, 1992), 373–407.

—*Sounding New Media: Immersion and Embodiment in the Arts and Culture* (Berkeley: University of California Press, 2009).

Eisenstein, Vsevolod Pudovkin and Grigori Alexandrov, 'Statement on Sound', in *The Eisenstein Reader*, ed. Richard Taylor, trans. Richard Taylor and William Powell (orig. Russian, 1928; London: BFI Publishing, 1998), 80–1.

El-Sheikh, Tammer, '*Zycles*', in Thomas Ruff, *Oberflächen, Tiefen/ Surfaces, Depths*, ed. Cathérine Hug (Vienna: Kunsthalle/Nuremberg: Verlag für moderne Kunst, 2009), 80.

—'*Stereo Photographs*', in Thomas Ruff, *Oberflächen, Tiefen/Surfaces, Depths*, ed. Cathérine Hug (Vienna: Kunsthalle/Nuremberg: Verlag für moderne Kunst, 2009), 144.

Emmerson, Simon, ed., *The Language of Electroacoustic Music* (New York: Harwood Academic Publishers, 1986).

Enns, Anthony, 'Voices of the Dead: Transmission/Translation/ Transgression', *Culture, Theory and Critique*, 46, no. 1 (2005): 11–27.

Evens, Aden, 'Sound Ideas', in *A Shock to Thought: Expression After Deleuze and Guattari*, ed. Brian Massumi (London: Routledge, 2002), 171–87.

—*Sound Ideas: Music Machines and Experience* (Minneapolis: University of Minnesota Press, 2005).

Fink, Robert, *Repeating Ourselves: American Minimal Music as Cultural Practice* (Berkeley: University of California Press, 2005).

Flint, R. W., ed., *Marinetti: Selected Writings*, trans. R. W. Flint and Arthur A. Coppotelli (London: Secker & Warburg, 1972).

Flusser, Vilém, *Towards a Philosophy of Photography*, trans. Anthony Matthews (orig. German, 1983; London: Reaktion Books, 2000).

Fogle, Douglas, 'Dark Matter', in Thomas Ruff, *Oberflächen, Tiefen/ Surfaces, Depths*, ed. Cathérine Hug (Vienna: Kunsthalle/Nuremberg: Verlag für moderne Kunst, 2009), 188–204.

Galster, I, ed., *La Naissance du phénomène Sartre, raisons d'un succès 1938–1945* (Paris: Seuil, 2001).

Gann, Kyle, *No Such Thing as Silence: John Cage's 4'33"* (New Haven, CT: Yale University Press, 2010).

Geymüller, Maximilian, 'Interieurs', in Thomas Ruff, *Oberflächen, Tiefen/ Surfaces, Depths*, ed. Cathérine Hug, trans. Nelson Wattie (Vienna: Kunsthalle/ Nuremberg: Verlag für moderne Kunst, 2009), 184.

Gleyzon, François-Xavier, ed., *David Lynch in Theory* (Prague: Litteraria Pragensia, 2010).

Goldblatt, David and Lee Brown, eds, *Aesthetics: A Reader in Philosophy of the Arts*, 3rd edn. (Upper Saddle River, NJ: Prentice Hall, 2010).

Goldsmith, Kenneth, 'It Was a Bug, Dave: The Dawn of Glitchwerks' (1999), http://www.wfmu.org/~kennyg/popular/articles/glitchwerks. html [accessed 28 March 2006].

Goodman, Steve, *Sonic Warfare: Sound, Affect, and the Ecology of Fear* (Cambridge, MA: MIT Press, 2010).

Goodwin, Andrew, 'Sample and Hold: Pop Music in the Digital Age of Reproduction', in *On Record: Rock, Pop, and the Written Word*, ed. Simon Frith and Andrew Goodwin (New York: Pantheon Books, 1990), 258–73 [reprinted from *Critical Quarterly*, 30, no. 3 (1998): 34–49].

Grathwohl-Scheffel, Christiane, 'Cosmos of Images', in Thomas Ruff, *Schwarzwald.Landschaft*, ed. Christiane Grathwohl-Scheffel and Jochen Ludwig (Freiburg: Museum für Neue Kunst, 2009), 23–31.

Grau, Oliver, *Virtual Art: From Illusion to Immersion* (Cambridge, MA: MIT Press/Leonardo Books, 2003).

Grossman, Rolf, 'The Tip of the Iceberg: Laptop Music and the Information-Technological Transformation of Music', *Organised Sound*, 13, no. 1 (2008): 5–11.

Gunning, Tom, 'The Cinema of Attractions: Early Film, its Spectator and the Avant-Garde', in *The Cinema of Attractions Reloaded*, ed. Wanda Strauven (Amsterdam: Amsterdam University Press, 2006), 56–62 [first published in *Wide Angle*, 8, nos. 3/4 (1986): 63–70].

Gutton, Jean-Pierre, *Bruits et sons dans notre histoire: essai sur la reconstitution du paysage sonore* (Paris: Presses Universitaires de France, 2000).

Hainge, Greg, 'Weird or Loopy? Specular Spaces, Feedback and Artifice in Lost Highway's Aesthetics of Sensation', in *The Cinema of David Lynch: American Dreams, Nightmare Visions*, ed. Annette Davison and Erica Sheen (London: Wallflower Press, 2004), 136–50.

—'Unfixing the Photographic Image: Photography, Indexicality, Fidelity and Normativity', *Continuum: Journal of Media & Cultural Studies*, 22, no. 5 (2008): 715–30.

—'Red Velvet: Lynch's Cinemat(ograph)ic Ontology', in *David Lynch in Theory*, ed. François-Xavier Gleyzon (Prague: Litteraria Pragensia: 2010), 24–39.

Hamilton, Andy, *Aesthetics and Music* (New York and London: Continuum, 2007).

Hanslick, Eduard, *On the Musically Beautiful*, trans. G. Payzant (orig. German, 1854; Indianapolis, IN: Hackett, 1986).

Happel, Reinhold, 'Thomas Ruff', in *Thomas Ruff* (Sindelfingen: Kunst + Projekte Sindelfingen, 1991), 61–5; reprinted in *Thomas Ruff*, ed. Carolyn Christov-Bakargiev (Milan: Skira, 2009), 198–202.

Haraway, Donna, *Simians, Cyborgs, and Women: The Reinvention of Nature* (London: Free Association Books, 1991).

Hegarty, Paul, 'Full With Noise: Theory and Japanese Noise Music', *ctheory*, a097 (2001), http://www.ctheory.net/articles.aspx?id=314 [accessed 15 May 2012].

—'Noise Threshold: Merzbow and the End of Natural Sound', *Organised Sound*, 7, no. 1 (2002): 193–200.

—*Noise/Music: A History* (New York and London: Continuum, 2007).

Henriques, Julian, 'Sonic Dominance and the Reggae Sound System Session', in *The Auditory Culture Reader*, ed. M. Bull and Les Back (Oxford: Berg, 2003), 451–80.

Higgins, Sean, 'A Deleuzian Noise/Excavating the Body of Abstract Sound', in *Sounding the Virtual: Gilles Deleuze and the Theory and Philosophy of Music*, ed. Brian Hulse and Nick Nesbitt (Farnham: Ashgate, 2010), 51–76.

Hinant, Guy Marc, liner notes to *Folds and Rhizomes for Gilles Deleuze* (sub rosa, 1995).

—liner notes to *An Anthology of Noise & Electronic Music/First a-chronology 1921–2001* (sub rosa, 2004).

Hollier, Denis, '*La Nausée*, en attendant', in *La Naissance du phénomène Sartre, raisons d'un succès 1938–1945*, ed. I Galster (Paris, Seuil, 2001), 86–100.

Holmes, Thom, *Electronic and Experimental Music: Pioneers in Technology and Composition* (New York and London: Routledge, 2002).

Huelsenbeck, Richard, 'En Avant Dada: A History of Dadaism', in *The Dada Painters and Poets: An Anthology*, ed. Robert Motherwell (orig. German, 1920; New York: Wittenborn, 1951; reprint, New York: G. K. Hall, 1981), 21–48.

Hug, Cathérine, 'Surfaces, Depths', in Thomas Ruff, *Oberflächen, Tiefen / Surfaces, Depths*, ed. Cathérine Hug, trans. Fiona Elliott (Vienna: Kunsthalle/Nuremberg: Verlag für moderne Kunst, 2009), 48–66.

Hulse, Brian and Nick Nesbitt, eds, *Sounding the Virtual: Gilles Deleuze and the Theory and Philosophy of Music* (Farnham: Ashgate, 2010).

Huxley, Aldous, *The Perennial Philosophy* (New York: Harper and Row Perennial Library, 1970).

Janus, Adrienne, 'Listening: Jean-Luc Nancy and the "Anti-Ocular" Turn in Continental Philosophy and Critical Theory', *Comparative Literature*, 63, no. 2 (2011): 182–202.

Jordan, Randolph, in the transcription of a roundtable discussion transcribed in *Offscreen*, 13, no. 9, http://www.offscreen.com/biblio/pages/essays/roundtable_inland_empire_pt2/ [accessed 19 October 2009].

Kahn, Douglas, 'Introduction', in *Wireless Imagination: Sound, Radio, and the Avant-Garde*, ed. Douglas Kahn and Gregory Whitehead (Cambridge, MA: MIT Press, 1992), 1–29.

—*Noise, Water, Meat: A History of Sound in the Arts* (Cambridge, MA: MIT Press, 1999).

Katz, Mark, *Capturing Sound: How Technology has Changed Music* (Berkeley: University of California Press, 2004).

Keane, David, 'At the Threshold of an Aesthetic', in *The Language of Electroacoustic Music*, ed. Simon Emmerson (New York: Harwood Academic Publishers, 1986), 97–118.

Keizer, Garret, *The Unwanted Sound of Everything We Want: A Book About Noise* (New York: Public Affairs, 2010).

Kelly, Caleb, *Cracked Media: The Sound of Malfunction* (Cambridge, MA: MIT Press, 2009).

Kenny, Glen, 'Inland Empire', *Premiere*, 6 December 2006, http://www.premiere.com/Review/Movies/INLAND-EMPIRE [accessed 19 October 2009].

Kim-Cohen, Seth, *In the Blink of an Ear: Toward a Non-Cochlear Sonic Art* (New York and London: Continuum, 2009).

Kittler, Friedrich A., *Gramophone, Film, Typewriter*, trans. Geoffrey Winthrop-Young and Michael Wutz (orig. German, 1986; Palo Alto, CA: Stanford University Press, 1999).

Kohl, Paul R., 'Reading Between the Lines: Music and Noise in Hegemony and Resistance', *Popular Music and Society*, 21, no. 3 (1997): 3–17.

Kojève, Alexandre, *Introduction to the Reading of Hegel: Lectures on the Phenomenology of Spirit*, ed. Allan Bloom, trans. James Nichols (orig. French, 1947; Ithaca, NY: Cornell University Press, 1980).

Kosko, Bart, *Noise* (London: Viking Penguin, 2006).

Krapp, Peter, *Noise Channels: Glitch and Error in Digital Culture* (Minneapolis: University of Minnesota Press, 2011).

Kristeva, Julia, Σημειωτική: *Recherches pour une sémanalyse* (Paris: Seuil, 1969).

—'Le texte et sa science', in Σημειωτική: *Recherches pour une sémanalyse* (Paris: Seuil, 1969), 7–26.

—*La Révolution du langage poétique: l'avant-garde à la fin du XIXe siècle. Lautréamont et Mallarmé* (Paris: Seuil, 1974), published in abridged form as *Revolution in Poetic Language*, trans. Margaret Waller (New York: Columbia University Press, 1984).

—*Powers of Horror: An Essay on Abjection*, trans. Leon S. Roudiez (orig. French, 1980; New York: Columbia University Press, 1982).

—'Semiotics: A Critical Science and/or a Critique of Science', in *The Kristeva Reader*, ed. Toril Moi, trans. Seán Hand (Oxford: Blackwell, 1986), 75–88.

LaBelle, Brandon, *Background Noise: Perspectives on Sound Art* (New York and London: Continuum, 2006).

—*Acoustic Territories: Sound Culture and Everyday Life* (New York and London: Continuum, 2010).

Licata, Thomas, ed., *Electroacoustic Music: Analytical Perspectives* (Westport, CT and London: Greenwood Press, 2002).

Lingis, Alphonso, 'Contact and Communication', in *The Obsessions of Georges Bataille: Community and Communication*, ed. Andrew J. Mitchell and Jason Kemp Winfree (New York: State University of New York Press, 2009), 119–32.

Link, Stan, 'The Work of Reproduction in the Mechanical Aging of an Art: Listening to Noise', *Computer Music Journal*, 25, no. 1 (2001): 34–47.

Lynch, David, *Catching the Big Fish: Meditation, Consciousness, and Creativity* (New York: Jeremy P. Tarcher/Penguin, 2006).

Macnab, Geoffrey, 'Inspired and Incomprehensible, a Russian Doll of a Film', *The Guardian*, 7 September 2006, http://www.guardian.co.uk/world/2006/sep/07/filmfestivals.film [accessed 11 May 2012].

Manovich, Lev, *The Language of New Media* (Cambridge, MA: MIT Press, 2001).

Marinetti, Filippo Tommaso, 'The Founding and Manifesto of Futurism', originally published in *Le Figaro*, 20 February 1909, reprinted in *Marinetti: Selected Writings*, ed. R. W. Flint, trans. R. W. Flint and Arthur A. Coppotelli (London: Secker & Warburg, 1972), 39–44.

—'The Birth of a Futurist Aesthetic', from *War, the World's Only Hygiene*, orig. 1915, reprinted in *Marinetti: Selected Writings*, 80–3.

—'Technical Manifesto of Futurist Literature', orig. 1912, reprinted in *Marinetti: Selected Writings*, 84–9.

—'Geometric and Mechanical Splendor and the Numerical Sensibility', orig. 1914, reprinted in *Marinetti: Selected Writings*, 97–103.

—'Tactilism', orig. 1924, reprinted in *Marinetti: Selected Writings*, 109–12.

—'Manifesto of the Futurist Dance', orig. 1917, reprinted in *Marinetti: Selected Writings*, 136–41.

Marshall, Lee, 'The Inland Empire', *Screen Daily*, 6 September 2006, http://www.screendaily.com/the-inland-empire/4028545.article [accessed 11 May 2012].

Massumi, Brian, *A User's Guide to Capitalism and Schizophrenia: Deviations from Deleuze and Guattari* (Cambridge, MA: MIT Press, 1992).

McGowan, Todd, *The Impossible David Lynch* (New York: Columbia University Press, 2007).

McLuhan, Marshall, *Understanding Media: The Extensions of Man*, 2nd ed. (New York: McGraw Hill, 1964; New York: New American Library, 1964).

McWeeny, Drew, 'Moriarty Visits David Lynch's *INLAND EMPIRE* and Lives to Tell About It!!', *Ain't It Cool News*, 29 October 2006, http://www.aintitcool.com/node/30544 [accessed 19 October 2009].

Mitchell, Andrew J. and Jason Kemp Winfree, eds, *The Obsessions of Georges Bataille: Community and Communication* (New York: State University of New York Press, 2009).

Moi, Toril, ed., *The Kristeva Reader*, trans. Seán Hand (Oxford: Blackwell, 1986).

—Introduction to Kristeva, 'Semiotics: A Critical Science and/or a Critique of Science', in *The Kristeva Reader*, ed. Toril Moi, trans. Seán Hand (Oxford: Blackwell, 1986), 75.

Moles, Abraham A., *Les Musiques expérimentales*, trans. Daniel Charles (Paris: Éditions du Cercle d'Art Contemporain, 1960).

Moliné, Keith, 'Review of Hegarty *Noise/Music: A History*', *The Wire: Adventures in Modern Music*, 285 (November 2007), 74.

Murray, Matt, '*Inland Empire*', http://www.cornponeflicks.com/inland.html [accessed 15 October 2009].

Nancy, Jean-Luc, *Listening*, trans. Charlotte Mandell (orig. French, 2002; Bronx, NY: Fordham University Press, 2007).

Nochimson, Martha, *The Passion of David Lynch: Wild at Heart in Hollywood* (Austin, TX: University of Texas Press, 1997).

—'*Inland Empire*', *Film Quarterly*, 60, no. 4 (2007): 10–14.

Paulson, William R., *The Noise of Culture: Literary Texts in a World of Information* (Ithaca, NY and London: Cornell University Press, 1988).

Pearson, Jesse, 'Interview with David Lynch', *Vice*, 7, no. 9 (2009): 78–81.

Pierce, J. R., *Symbols, Signals and Noise: The Nature and Process of Communication* (London: Hutchinson, 1962).

Pinedo, Isabel Cristina, 'Postmodern Elements of the Contemporary Horror Film', in *The Horror Film*, ed. Stephen Prince (Piscataway, NJ: Rutgers University Press, 2004), 85–117.

Prince, Stephen, ed., *The Horror Film* (Piscataway, NJ: Rutgers University Press, 2004).

Prochnik, George, *In Pursuit of Silence: Listening for Meaning in a World of Noise* (New York and London: Doubleday, 2010).

Reynolds, Simon, *Blissed Out* (London: Serpent's Tail, 1990).

Richards, Roger, ed., *Merzbook: The Pleasuredome of Noise* (Melbourne: Extreme, 1987).

Ridley, Aaron, *The Philosophy of Music: Theme and Variations* (Edinburgh: Edinburgh University Press, 2004).

Risset, Jean-Claude, 'Foreword', in *Electroacoustic Music: Analytical Perspectives*, ed. Thomas Licata (Westport, CT and London: Greenwood Press, 2002), xiii–xviii.

Rockwell, John, 'How the LP and CD Sounds Compare', *New York Times*, 31 March 1983, C13.

Ronell, Avital, *The Telephone Book: Technology, Schizophrenia, Electric Speech* (Lincoln: University of Nebraska Press, 1989).

Ross, Alex, *The Rest is Noise: Listening to the Twentieth Century* (London: Harper Perennial, 2009).

Rothkopf, Joshua, '*Inland Empire*', *Time Out*, http://newyork.timeout. com/articles/film/3423/inland-empire [accessed 19 October 2009].

Rouillé, André, *La Photographie* (Paris: Gallimard, 2005).

Ruff, Thomas, *Thomas Ruff: Photography 1979 to the Present*, ed. Matthias Winzen (New York: Distributed Art Publishers, 2003).

—*jpegs* (New York: Aperture, 2009).

—*Oberflächen, Tiefen/Surfaces, Depths*, ed. Cathérine Hug, trans. Fiona Elliott (Vienna: Kunsthalle/Nuremberg: Verlag für moderne Kunst, 2009).

—*Schwarzwald.Landschaft*, ed. Christiane Grathwohl-Scheffel and Jochen Ludwig (Freiburg: Museum für Neue Kunst, 2009).

—*Thomas Ruff*, ed. Carolyn Christov-Bakargiev (Milan: Skira, 2009).

Russo, Mary and Daniel Warner, 'Rough Music, Futurism, and Postpunk Industrial Noise Bands', in *Audio Culture: Readings in Modern Music*, ed. Christoph Cox and Daniel Warner (New York and London: Continuum, 2004), 47–54.

Russolo, Luigi, *The Art of Noises*, trans. Barclay Brown (orig. Italian, 1913; New York: Pendragon Press, 1986).

Sangild, Torben, *Støjens æstetik*, English summary published as: *The Aesthetics of Noise* ([np]: Datanom, 2002).

—'Glitch: The Beauty of Malfunction', in *Bad Music*, ed. C. Washburne and M. Derno (London: Routledge, 2004), 198–211.

Sartre, Jean-Paul, *Nausea*, trans. Robert Baldick (orig. French, 1938; London: Penguin Books, 1965).

—*Les Mots* (Paris: Gallimard, 1964).

—*The Imaginary: A Phenomenological Psychology of the Imagination*, trans. Jonathan Webber (orig. French, 1940; London and New York: Routledge, 2004).

Scarry, Elaine, *The Body in Pain: The Making and Unmaking of the World* (Oxford: Oxford University Press, 1985).

Schaeffer, Pierre, *À la recherche d'une musique concrète* (Paris: Éditions du Seuil, 1952).

Schafer, R. Murray, *The Soundscape: Our Sonic Environment and the Tuning of the World* (New York: Knopf, 1977; reprint, Rochester, VT: Destiny Books, 2009).

Schneider, Steven Jay, 'The Essential Evil in/of *Eraserhead* (or, Lynch to the Contrary)', in *The Cinema of David Lynch: American Dreams, Nightmare Visions*, ed. Erica Sheen and Annette Davison (London and New York: Wallflower Press, 2004), 5–18.

Schwartz, Hillel, *Making Noise: From Babel to the Big Bang and Beyond* (New York: Zone Books, 2011).

Scruton, Roger, *The Aesthetics of Music* (Oxford: Oxford University Press, 1999).

—*Understanding Music: Philosophy and Interpretation* (New York and London: Continuum, 2009).

Serres, Michel, *Genesis*, trans. Geneviève James and James Nielson (orig. French, 1982; Ann Arbor: University of Michigan Press, 1995).

—*The Parasite*, trans. Lawrence R. Schehr (orig. French, 1980; Minneapolis: University of Minnesota Press, 2007).

Shannon, Claude and Warren Weaver, *The Mathematical Theory of Communication* (Urbana: University of Illinois Press, 1949).

Sherburne, Philip, 'The Art of Noise', *Frieze,* 62 (October 2001): 48–9.

Simpson, Bennett, 'Ruins: Thomas Ruff's *jpegs*', in Thomas Ruff, *jpegs* (New York: Aperture, 2009).

Sinnerbrink, Robert, *New Philosophies of Film: Thinking Images* (New York and London: Continuum, 2011).

Sitsky, Larry, ed., *Music of the Twentieth-Century Avant-Garde: A Biocritical Sourcebook* (Westport, CT: Greenwood Press, 2002).

Sterne, Jonathan, *The Audible Past: Cultural Origins of Sound Reproduction* (Durham, NC: Duke University Press, 2003).

—'The MP3 as Cultural Artifact', *New Media & Society*, 8, no. 5 (2006): 825–42.

—*MP3: The Meaning of a Format* (Durham, NC: Duke University Press, 2012).

Straw, Will, 'In Memoriam: The Music CD and its Ends', *Design and Culture*, 1, no. 1 (2009): 79–92.

Stuart, Caleb, 'Damaged Sound: Glitching & Skipping Compact Discs in the Audio of Yasunao Tone, Nicolas Collins & Oval', *Leonardo Music Journal*, 14, no. 1 (2004): 47–52.

Szekely, Michael, 'Becoming-Still: Perspectives on Musical Ontology After Deleuze and Guattari', *Social Semiotics*, 13, no. 2 (2003): 113–28.

Szepanski, Achim, 'Music', trans. Judith Funk, in the liner notes to *Clicks and Cuts 2* (Mille Plateaux, 2001), 10–15.

—'A Mille Plateaux Manifesto', trans. Judith Funk, *Organised Sound*, 7, no. 1 (2002): 225–8.

Taylor, Richard, ed., *The Eisenstein Reader*, trans. Richard Taylor and William Powell (London: BFI Publishing, 1998).

Teruggi, Daniel, 'Technology and Musique Concrète: The Technical Developments of the Groupe de Recherches Musicales and their Implication in Musical Composition', *Organised Sound*, 12, no. 3 (2007): 213–31.

Thacker, Eugene, 'Bataille/Body/Noise: Notes Towards a Techno-Erotics', in *Merzbook: The Pleasuredome of Noise*, ed. Roger Richards (Melbourne: Extreme, 1987), 57–65.

Thompson, Emily, 'Machines, Music, and the Quest for Fidelity: Marketing the Edison Phonograph in America, 1877–1925', *The Musical Quarterly*, 79, no. 1 (1995): 131–71.

—*The Soundscape of Modernity: Architectural Acoustics and the Culture of Listening in America, 1900–1933* (Cambridge, MA: MIT Press, 2002).

Thorn, Benjamin, 'Luigi Russolo (1885–1947)', in *Music of the Twentieth-Century Avant-Garde: A Biocritical Sourcebook*, ed. Larry Sitsky (Westport, CT: Greenwood Press, 2002), 415–19.

Tone, Yasunao and Christian Marclay, 'Record, CD, Analog, Digital', in *Audio Culture: Readings in Modern Music*, ed. Christoph Cox and Daniel Warner (New York and London: Continuum, 2004), 341–7.

Van Leeuwen, Theo, *Speech, Music, Sound* (London: Macmillan, 1999).

Van Nort, Doug, 'Noise/Music and Representation Systems', *Organised Sound*, 11, no. 2 (2006): 173–8.

Voegelin, Salomé, *Listening to Noise and Silence: Towards a Philosophy of Sound Art* (New York and London: Continuum, 2010).

Warde, Beatrice/Paul Grandjean, 'The Crystal Goblet, or Printing Should be Invisible', http://gmunch.home.pipeline.com/typo-L/misc/ward.htm [accessed 14 July 2004]. Also available in Beatrice Warde, *The Crystal Goblet: Sixteen Essays on Typography* (Cleveland, OH: World Pub. Co., 1956); and in *Graphic Design and Reading: Explorations of an Uneasy Relationship*, ed. Gunnar Swanson (New York: Allworth Press, 2000), 91–6.

Warner, Marina, 'Voodoo Road: Lost Highway by David Lynch', *Sight and Sound*, 7, no. 8 (August 1997): 6–10.

Washburne, C. and M. Derno, eds, *Bad Music* (London: Routledge, 2004).

Weaver, Warren, 'Recent Contributions to the Mathematical Theory of Communication', in Claude Shannon and Warren Weaver, *The Mathematical Theory of Communication* (Urbana: University of Illinois Press, 1949), 95–117.

Weissberg, Jay, '*Inland Empire*', *Variety*, 6 September 2006, http://www.variety.com/review/VE1117931480/ [accessed 11 May 2012].

Wells, L., ed., *The Photography Reader* (London: Routledge, 2003).
Whitelaw, Mitchell, 'Inframedia Audio: Glitches & Tape Hiss', *Artlink*, 21, no. 3 (September 2001): 49–52.
Winzen, Matthias, 'A Credible Invention of Reality: Thomas Ruff's Precise Reproductions of our Fantasies of Reality', in *Thomas Ruff: Photography 1979 to the Present*, ed. Matthias Winzen (New York: Distributed Art Publishers, 2003), 131–59.
Wolfe, Cary, 'Introduction to the New Edition', in Michel Serres, *The Parasite*, trans. Lawrence R. Schehr (orig. French, 1980; Minneapolis: University of Minnesota Press, 2007), xi–xxviii.
Woodward, Brett, 'The Nomadic Producer of Differences', in *Merzbook: The Pleasuredome of Noise*, ed. Roger Richards (Melbourne: Extreme, 1987), 1.
—CD descriptions, in *Merzbook: The Pleasuredome of Noise*, ed. Roger Richards (Melbourne: Extreme, 1987), 82–132.
—'SCUM Scissors for Cutting Merzbow VOL. 1', in *Merzbook: The Pleasuredome of Noise*, ed. Roger Richards (Melbourne: Extreme, 1987), 113.
Woods, G., ' "Sounds, Smells, Degrees of Light": Art and Illumination in *Nausea*', in *Sartre's Nausea: Text, Context, Intertext*, ed. Alistair Rolls and Elizabeth Rechniewski (Amsterdam and New York: Rodopi, 2006),
Worby, Robert, 'Cacophony', in *Music, Electronic Media and Culture*, ed. Simon Emmerson (Aldershot: Ashgate, 2000), 138–65.
Yochim, Emily Chivers and Megan Biddinger, ' "It Kind of Gives You That Vintage Feel": Vinyl Records and the Trope of Death', *Media Culture & Society*, 30, no. 2 (2008): 183–95.
Young, Rob, 'Undercurrents #12: Worship the Glitch', *The Wire: Adventures in Modern Music*, 190/191 (December 1999/January 2000), 52–6.

INDEX